Celebrating the Spirit of Christmas

Much Love -
to the Hamiltons

Dude B

Celebrating the Spirit of Christmas

Twelve Stories

Andy Smith

TKR Publishing Co
Nashville

Contents

Dedication

To the makers of
Vanilla Ice Cream
A very good ice cream
That goes with anything.
BUT
My book is all about
Diversity
So I had to throw you under the bus
Sorry

Introduction

2020 was a crazy year for those of us who pretend to be human. We had this virus thing called COVID19 that literally took over the world, leaving us hiding in our homes for a year with visions of Hollywood coming out with a number of Godzilla vs COVID19 movies once we are allowed to come out, come out, wherever we are.

It wasn't a big deal for me, to be honest. I was retired anyway. I had my SSI and pension to pay my bills and enough savings to buy better hot dogs to go with my beans. No worries for this guy, right?

By Christmas 2020, I was becoming a bit dismayed at how my impressive nest egg savings account wasn't so impressive any more. I mean really, $100.00 a week for groceries isn't that bad when you're trying to keep up with the Jones's and they're spending at least that much every week on toilet paper!

I figured it might be a good time to dust off some of my stories to see if I might be able to make some money to invest in toilet paper stocks to supplement my retirement income. I had a few great stories featuring the Christmas spirit and I knew there was a channel on TV that had Christmas movies 24/7. Surely they would need some good material, right?

Wrong! I spent some time watching said channel and was

dumbfounded. Every movie was the same plot. Boy meets girl in rural America where they spend 90% of their yearly budget on Christmas decorations – plot twist#1 – plot twist#2 – mushy kiss in front of the big Christmas tree in the town square and everyone lives happily ever after.

I was appalled. How can you take the spirit of Christmas and make it one dimensional 24/7, when we all know for fact that the Christmas spirit comes in many different ways. These people would open an ice cream shop and sell nothing but vanilla ice cream. They would argue that it's the best vanilla ice cream anywhere, but.... REALLY? You're really going to go with one flavor?

Being the rebellious type, I decided to take my two Christmas stories and raise them ten more. I'll show them that there are many different ways to create the Christmas spirit. Sure, I'll give you the mushy, kissie-kissie vanilla story, but I'll also show you how Santa can find a new home for a little girl during the depression. I'll show you how the animals put on a great festival for the Reindeer's greatest night. I'll show you how the snow bird works with God to capture the unselfish requests from children and turn them into magical moments.

You want the Christmas spirit, pal, I'll give you a lot more than vanilla!

Don't piss off a creative writer, my friend!

It was a pandemic, after all. It wasn't like I was giving up a lot of social moments of meeting up with friends to have a good time. Isolation is the perfect time to dust off those creative juices and crank out story after story of the many ways to celebrate the spirit of Christmas.

By the time they created a vaccine, I had created twelve wonderful stories that should lift any heart that longs for more than kisses in front of a Christmas tree. There is surely something for everyone. They cover many different eras as well as many different storylines.

My ice cream shop has enough flavors for everyone.

Enjoy!

Author

Disclaimer

I'm fully vaccinated. People are slowly coming out of their COVID19 Hibernation. Summer is slowly coming of age, and I'm feeling pretty good. My book of stories celebrating the spirit of Christmas is pretty much done. I have my artist busily creating the perfect cover. I've downloaded the stories into my publishing program and I have at least three months before it goes to market, so there is plenty of time to tweak it and make sure I provide a good product for the five or so people who will actually read it.

Life is good as I head into my kitchen to fix me a drink to celebrate.

I notice there is no Chris in my recliner, which makes me pause. The deal is that if my guardian angel is NOT in the recliner, that means that I need to write a disclaimer stating that God would prefer I publish this book as non-fiction. If my guardian angel IS in my recliner, that means that he is there to make sure I publish my book as fiction, because God does not want people thinking that I have any special knowledge of reality and I just make this stuff up.

If Chris is NOT in my recliner, it means God wants me to publish these stories as non-fiction?

I'm a bit hesitant, as Chris has always made a good case about *7Days in Heaven, Johnny's Story, Hannah's Huggers* and *Carpe Diem*

Plan being published as non-fiction, even though they were published as fiction for obvious reasons in my world.

But this book has twelve separate stories in it. Different settings, different eras in history. There simply is no way anyone – even my annoying guardian angel – could justify this book as non-fiction!

I want to say my guardian angel is an idiot again and has forgotten the deal we made about publishing my books, but I have a sinking feeling because every time I do, Chris has a nasty way of dishing out the humble pie, so I might want to show a great deal of restraint here.

Sure enough, as I head back to my room – with my drink I anticipated correctly needed to be a double – I find Chris laying on my bed casually reading a magazine.

"Oh come on, Chris. There is no way you can be here to tell me God wants this book to be non-fiction. There's twelve different stories, for crying out loud, and most of them even Hollywood would have trouble selling as real. You forgot the deal, right?"

"Andy boy, you once again forget that I am from the spirit world. Remember how impressed you were in *My First 7Days in Heaven* how you could remember every member of your family tree? The spirit world retains everything. You earthlings are the ones that forget things because of the distractions you create. And yes – I wasn't in the recliner because God does want you to publish this book as non-fiction."

"You're nuts! There are twelve stories, with twelve different plots and several different eras in time. You're crazy if you think this book can be published as non-fiction!"

Chris looks up from his magazine with an expression of sheer boredom, "What's the title of your book?"

I look cautiously at Chris as I hate it when he starts to pull me in a direction I wasn't planning to go.

"Celebrating the Spirit of Christmas."

Chris smiles that annoying smile, "BINGO!"

"Don't bingo me, pal. Non-fiction means these stories are all true. How can anyone read these stories and think they are true?" I say with a strong dose of frustration, knowing full well that he is likely going to deliver a perfectly logical response.

"Your book is about celebrating the spirit of Christmas. You have done a wonderful job in reflecting that spirit in a very real, diverse manner that clearly establishes to the readers that the spirit of Christmas truly does come in many forms. Just like your ice cream shop you referred to that has a variety of flavors, each one is absolutely and truly real ice cream. Your stories have many different settings and flavors, but they represent the true and real spirit of Christmas – which is absolutely what the book is all about. The spirit of Christmas – as you have perfectly illustrated in this book – is non-fiction no matter what flavor you put it in."

You'd think that I would have learned by now that I should approach every story I write with the understanding that God wants me to publish them as non-fiction, regardless of what I think – so here it is:

NOTE TO READER

This book is published as fiction, but the theme of the book is celebrating the SPIRIT of Christmas which is absolutely real, or non-fiction. May you all embrace the real spirit of Christmas throughout the year – with a scoop of ice cream … whatever flavor you choose.

I think I'll have another drink.

One True Love Again

Jane Rutledge is a single mom who works in New York City as a Human Resource Director for a mid range corporation. Her husband, a very successful corporate lawyer at the same company, passed away three years ago in a boating accident that killed three other friends when they were on a fishing trip.

Jane, and her seven year-old daughter, Lucy, live very comfortably as they have adjusted to their world without the man they both loved so much. It's been a rough road, but with each day, they are learning that you never get over a loss like that. You can survive if you open your heart to the memories and talk to one another about the day-to-day ups and downs of dealing with the loss.

After three years, Jane and Lucy have become more comfortable in their new world alone and are able to laugh a little more and find joy in the simple things in their daily routines.

With the holidays approaching, Jane feels this would be a good time to have a real Christmas holiday by spending a few weeks with her parents in McAdenville, North Carolina, a small town outside of Charlotte that is named Christmas Town USA for the way they go all out for the holiday season.

As Jane and Lucy arrive in McAdenville and settle into their accommodations at the grandparents home, Jane is feeling very excited that this is going to be a great Christmas for her family.

Her parents, Betty and Bill Bartlett, are very involved in their community. Betty owns a small bakery with a big reputation for her rolls, breads, muffins and cookies. Her booth at the Christmas festival is always the busiest, as Betty doesn't hold back with her selections of holiday cookies and treats.

Bill is retired from his career as writer, editor, publisher, accountant and janitor for the local newspaper after selling it to a younger couple that was able to transition the paper into the new online digital world of information. Bill now spends much of the time helping Betty at the bakery by working with the customers so she can spend her time baking.

While exploring the town shops and sites, Jane, not paying attention to where she is going, slams into a man and knocks him off his stool as he is helping to string holiday lights in the town. As he gathers himself and gets up from the train wreck, he finds the young attractive woman who was the source of his interruption. After a series of apologies and small talk, the attraction was becoming as obvious as the resistance of either one to acknowledge it.

"I'm so sorry. I wasn't paying attention. Are you hurt?" says Jane.

"It's okay. I'm pretty sure I'll live. Are you visiting?"

"My daughter and I came here for the holidays from New York City. My parents live here."

"What's their name?"

"Bartlett – Betty and Bill"

"Oh yes: the Bs – Betty and Bill Bartlett's Bakery with the best bread in town"

He is humored while Jane is less so as Lucy giggles.

"Yes. We'll be here for Christmas."

"Well you couldn't find a better place for the holidays than McAdenville, North Carolina, that's for sure," he says, as he gathers his stool and gets back to his work.

Lucy chimes in: "Are you going to decorate all the lamp posts?"

"Well, if I don't get killed, I should be able to get most of it done today." He looks at Jane and smiles, then back at Lucy. "What's your name, young lady?"

"Lucy."

"I'm Carl. You come back at night by this weekend and see how magical this town lights up, okay?"

"I promise. Do you have to put them all up yourself?"

"Oh no. I'd have to start in August if it was all up to me. We have lots of volunteers helping out." He pauses as he looks at Jane. "So, pay attention as you walk around."

They smile at each other.

"I said I was sorry," Jane says with a guarded, flirtatious grin.

"Well you ladies enjoy the holiday and be sure to take advantage of all the holiday events we have."

As they part ways, Carl is in no hurry to stop watching Jane walk away, until she turns and looks at him, which causes him to nearly fall off his stool again as he scrambles to get back to his work, and Jane nearly runs into another lamp post.

******

That night as they are finishing up their dinner, Betty, a true American mother, can't resist in delving into her daughter's private life.

"So are you seeing anyone yet?"

"Mom."

"Well it's been three years and I know Frank was a very special man, but there are other men out there that might be a good fit for you and Lucy. That's all I'm saying."

Lucy perks up. "We met a man today when we were shopping."

Grandma raises her eyebrows. "Oh really?"

Jane quickly moves to put a halt to the direction of this conversation. "Lucy, why don't you go get ready for bed while Grandpa makes the popcorn and hot chocolate and Grandma and I clean up? Then, we'll sit by the fire and watch a good holiday movie."

Grandpa gets up with his plate, "Sounds like a splendid idea! Come on, kiddo, grab your plate and let's get this party going."

Lucy doesn't need to be told twice as she gathers her plate and heads off to drop it in the kitchen sink before heading off for her room.

As Jane and Betty are cleaning up in the kitchen, Betty has no intention of letting go of the conversation that her daughter so cleverly aborted.

"So who was the man you ran into in town?"

"Oh Mother, really. His name was Carl, I think. He was putting up Christmas lights and I literally ran into him. It was clearly the least romantic meeting you can have."

"Honey" Betty pauses in thought. "Oh, Carl – tall, handsome, about your age?"

"Yes, that sounds about right. But seriously, Mom, I literally just ran into him. He seemed like a nice man, but certainly not the kind of situation that just screams romance at you."

"Don't kid yourself, deary. You watch enough romance movies or read some of those romance books you'll find a lot of stories start out just like that. Carl Franklin is a really good man that a lot of women would love to run into. I'm just saying."

"Well I didn't come here to look for romance. I came to enjoy a wonderful holiday with my family."

Betty turns off the water and as she dries her hands, says, "I know Jane, and your father and I are so happy to have you and Lucy with us this year. Carl's a good man and I am not pushing him on you. I'm just saying that you're a wonderful woman with a lot to offer someone. I just want you to keep your heart open to the possibilities of love again, that's all."

Jane hugs her mom. "I will Mom, but you have to understand that what Frank and I had was very special. My one true love and we both knew it. A lot of people never find that kind of love. I'm pretty sure it doesn't happen twice. Any man I meet will never have what Frank and I had. I'm okay with that, Mom. I don't want to bring a bunch of men in and out of Lucy's life trying to capture a love like Frank and I had. It just doesn't happen twice."

Betty looks at her daughter compassionately. "Frank was a special man, for sure. But there are no rules in love that say you can only have that kind of love once. Just keep your heart open. The good news is that you and Lucy don't need to find a man. If nothing ever comes, you both will be fine. But you never know."

******

For the next few days, while her parents are busy at the bakery, Jane and Lucy keep busy taking in all the activities that give this town the title of Christmas Town USA. Ice skating, shopping, visiting Santa and all the other events certainly keep them busy.

Jane sees Carl almost every day as he seems busy helping everyone out with their Christmas booths and decorating. It's never anything that evolves into another meeting and conversation, but it's enough to get her attention and keep that little spark of interest from going out. He sees her a few times, as well, and waves from a distance, but is always too busy to go beyond that. It's just enough to draw attention to that little spark of interest stirring inside as he watches her and Lucy enjoying their time together.

One day, Jane and Lucy decide to stop by the bakery after a day of fun to see Grandma and Grandpa. As they walk in, they find Carl behind the counter drying his hands.

"Carl, please don't tell me that my parents have put you to work in their bakery."

Carl laughs, "They could probably use the help, but not from me. I love to cook, but I'm no good at baking. I was just fixing some shelves that were giving them problems."

Lucy perks up. "Maybe we could help them, Mommy. I would love to learn how to make cookies."

"We can ask them. That would be fun, Lucy."

As Jane hangs up their coats, Bill comes out from the back.

"Hey kiddos. Did we have a fun day in Christmas Town today?"

Lucy runs to give her grandpa a hug and explodes into a play by play run down of her day as Carl gathers his tools and prepares to leave and Betty comes out from the back as well.

"Thank you so much, Carl. That shelf is really needed this time of year, so it's a big help to us. What do I owe you?"

"Whatever you want, Betty. Happy to help you out."

Betty takes some money out of her drawer and hands it to Carl, who puts it in his pocket without even looking at it. He says goodbye to everyone, then turns to Jane. "Good to see you again, Jane. Hope to see you again soon."

"Well at least I didn't knock you over this time." She smiles.

"I do appreciate that. I'm pretty busy this time of year, but I'd make time if you and Lucy want to do anything," he says a bit awkwardly, and a bit shocked that he even said anything at all.

Jane hesitates, but has no excuses. "Sure. That'd be great."

Carl reaches into his shirt pocket and pulls out his business card and hands it to her. "Here's my number. If you want to do anything, just call or text, and I'll make the time for you."

They look at each other for an awkward, uncomfortable moment, both trying to figure out if this was asking for a date or just being friendly.

Carl quickly says goodbye to every one and bolts out the door as Jane looks down at his business card.

"Carl Franklin 704-555-6242 – That's it? Impressive." As she goes over to her mom.

"Hey Mom. Lucy and I wanted to see if you need any help. Lucy helps me at home and loves to cook. It'd be fun for us to help you and Dad out."

"Oh honey, you're on vacation. You didn't come here to work at a bakery."

"I wouldn't want to put in twelve hour shifts until Christmas Eve, but I know Lucy would love to make some Christmas cookies and I can help out, as well."

"Well I do have a couple of aprons in the back that aren't being used. And we were going to tell you that you are on your own for dinner because we have to get these cookies going. And I suppose it would be nice if you two stayed and helped and we ordered some pizza or something here. And..."

"Mom stop! I'll get the aprons. Let's do this."

That night finds them cranking up the Christmas music, snacking on pizzas and sharing memories while the cookies for the festival are quickly filling up box after box and ready to go.

The next morning, Lucy runs into the guest room where Jane is going through her computer with the normal routine of checking emails and social media sites before she gets ready for the day.

"Mommy, can I go with Grandpa to the bakery and help out today?"

Jane looks at her daughter, "Did they ask you to?"

"Yeah. Grandpa said it would be a great day to spend with his granddaughter, and since I'm the only granddaughter, I figured he was talking about me."

Jane's face has a noticeable flood of compassion as she gets up, grabs her robe and heads downstairs where she finds her dad finishing a cup of coffee and a newspaper at the table.

"Did you want to take Lucy to the bakery today?"

Her dad looks up, "Absolutely. Your mom and I haven't spent a lot of time with Lucy, but when we have, it has always been a great time. She had so much fun last night. We thought it would be great to spend the whole day with her at the bakery. She can help grandma cook, or she can help me out front. It would be great for me and your mom and I and it would give you the day to shop on your own and do whatever you want."

Jane looks down at Lucy who is an expert with her pleading smiles, then back at her dad, "Well I do have shopping to do that would be a lot easier if she wasn't hanging around me so much, so if you're okay with it, I'd be happy to take you up on the offer."

"Great," says Bill as he gets up and heads to the kitchen, "Grab your coat, kiddo." Then he looks at Jane, "And you relax and have fun today. You're on vacation, you know."

"Thanks Dad. I'll make the bakery my last stop."

"Okay. We close late today, so we don't want to see you anytime before five. Got it?"

"Yes sir!" she says in a very formal tone as she heads up the stairs to shower and get ready for her day of exploring McAdenville alone, while Grandpa and Lucy head out the door for their day of hanging out with the grandparents.

******

Jane looks at her watch with a hint of frustration. It's just past eleven and she's pretty much done shopping. Jane has always been the kind of shopper that doesn't spend a lot of time debating a gift. When she sees what she likes, she buys it. With McAdenville having such a wonderful selection of shops and booths, she appreciates her style of "see it, like it, buy it." She never worries about her decisions and has always considered herself a good gift giver.

But today, that approach in shopping has left her with a lot of free time to kill, and she is not sure what to do.

She is getting a bit hungry, so she puts her attention on possibly finding a nice place to sit down, relax, have a nice lunch and maybe even a glass of wine. She's got the time, so that seems like a good starting point.

As she strolls down Main Street, considering her options, she thinks of Carl and how it might be nice to have some company. But, she doesn't want to appear too aggressive. She doesn't want to give Carl the wrong impression. After all, she goes out to lunch with friends all the time back home, so this certainly shouldn't be seen as a lunch "date," right?

She pulls his card out and texts him.

"Free for lunch – want to join me?" She pauses before sending to make sure she wants to do this.

Send.

Before she can get her phone back into her pocket, she gets a reply.

"Where are you?"

"Walking on Main Street near Terra Mia"

"Don't go in. I'll pick you up in five minutes. I have a small dark blue truck"

"Okay"

Sure enough, within a few minutes, the blue truck pulls up as Carl opens the passenger window. "Throw your bags in the back and get in."

Jane gets in as Carl drives off.

"Is Terra Mia not a good place?" Jane asks.

"It's a great place if you like Italian food. But you don't want to eat lunch there. The food is so good, you'll be in a food coma for the rest of the day."

"Good to know. So where are we going?"

"The Spruced Goose Station. They have good sandwiches and good service."

Jane pauses. "Spruced Goose Station?"

"Yeah. It's run by the Holy Angels, so you get good food and support a good cause. It's a win-win lunch."

Jane has no idea what Carl is talking about' "Holy Angels?"

"Oh, sorry. I forgot you're from the big city. Holy Angels is a program here in North Carolina that serves the intellectually and physically challenged population. They have a handful of cafes that hire high end clients so they can learn to live more independently. The sandwiches are great and you're helping a good cause, so I like to have lunch there when I can."

"Oh. Great," says Jane, who thinks the crisp green salad and glass of Pinot Grigio she was feeling won't be on the menu.

As they settle into their seats and pick up their menus, Jane looks around. It's a very simple environment but very clean looking and most of the tables are full.

As Jane looks over the menu, Carl gives her the rundown.

"Do you have any restrictions as far as food goes?"

"No, not really."

"Good. Their sandwiches are all good. Their chicken salad is excellent – as a wrap or on a croissant. The flat breads are okay and the salads are fresh and crisp and have dressings they make fresh every day. Almost everything is locally supplied, so you're not just helping charity, you're eating good food, so you can't go wrong."

"Okay. Since I don't want to have a food coma the rest of the day, I think I'll go with the Point Garden salad. And, water is fine with me."

"Good choice."

As the server comes over to take their order, Jane sees that she is friendly and very careful to give the best service.

"My name is Sherry. What can I get for you ma'am?"

"I'll have the Point Garden Salad and glass of water please."

"Yes, ma'am. What kind of dressing would you like?"

"What do you recommend?" Jane asks with a smile.

"Well the ranch is made fresh every day and I could drink it by the cup, but you're a pretty lady with a nice figure, so I think you'd probably like the lemon vinaigrette. It's made fresh too and has less calories."

Jane is delighted with the server. "Then I'll go with the vinaigrette, please."

"And you, sir?" She notices that it's Carl, "Hi, Mr. Carl. Is this your girlfriend?"

"No, no. This is a good friend visiting from New York City."

"Oh, the Big Apple. Go, Yankees."

Jane laughs. "Well if you ever come to New York, Sherry, let me know and I'd be happy to show you around."

The server has a panicked expression "Oh no! I can't go there. Too many people. I get really nervous around too many people."

"No problem. New York has a lot of people, for sure. You're much better off staying here in McAdenville."

"Thank you," she says, as she turns and looks at Carl, ready for his order.

"I'll have the Cherubs Classic Wrap, Sherry."

"Yes, sir. And just water, as usual?"

"That would be great."

"Anything else?"

"No – that should do it for us. Thanks, Sherry."

"Okay, I'll get your water, but I don't cook, so you'll have to wait for them back there to get your lunch made, okay?"

"No problem. Thanks."

As Sherry heads off to place their order, Jane is really impressed. Totally not what she was thinking about for lunch, but delighted that she is here.

"So what do you do in the Big Apple?" asks Carl.

"I am a Human Resource Director for a corporation in Manhattan," she says.

"Sounds impressive."

"It's a good job at a good company and pays well. I'm not complaining."

"Always good to have a job you enjoy." He pauses before his next question, "And I assume there is no husband?"

Jane smiles, "If I had a husband, I'm pretty sure he wouldn't approve of me having lunch with you."

"Yes, that was my assumption."

"My husband died three years ago in a boating accident. It was pretty rough for Lucy and me, but we're getting around to having fun again. That's what this Christmas is all about. I buried myself in my work after Frank died, but I realized that I wasn't helping Lucy, so I took the rest of the year off so Lucy and I could have a real Christmas with her grandparents."

"I'm sorry about your husband. I can't imagine having to deal with that. But you're doing a great job. Lucy seems like a really good kid. I wouldn't have guessed that she was living without a dad."

Sherry brings the food out and as they settle into their lunch, Jane picks up the conversation.

"So what about you? Do you do anything else besides being a

handy man around town?" She immediately feels bad about the question.

"I love what I do. I help a lot of people, and get to do different things every day. I'm not a suit and tie kind of guy, anyway. As long as the bills are paid and I have food to eat, I'm perfectly content with my life."

Jane just looks at him. She doesn't think she's ever met a man with such simple expectations. She's not sure if she's impressed or disappointed with his style.

"But don't you have any goals? Ambitions to make more money so you can travel and have nice things?"

Carl shakes his head. "I learned a long time ago not to let money control my life. I am glad to get up every day knowing that I am going to be helping my neighbors and being kind. I traveled a lot when I was younger and I've seen enough to know this is a great world we live in. We all just need to find our own slice of life in this world and simply embrace it. What's wrong with that?"

Jane is baffled. It sounds ideal, yet very unrealistic in today's world.

"Nothing, I guess. I've just never met a man before that has no ambition to better himself, that's all."

Carl is getting frustrated, "So making people happy and being kind is not ambitious enough for you? Tell me, are you happy being an HR Director in a tall building in Manhattan? I mean, when you were a little girl and people asked you what you wanted to be when you grew up, is that what you told them?"

Jane snaps. "I worked hard to get to my position and I've done a lot of really good work. I certainly don't need a handy man with no ambition criticizing my life choices."

She continues, "You know, I'm going to go back and shop some more. I'm not going to let you or anyone else ruin my Christmas."

She pulls out some money and drops a twenty on the table as she storms out the door as Carl is left shaking his head.

Sherry comes over as he gets up to leave.

"Did you make your girlfriend mad, Mr Carl?"

Carl smiles at Sherry. "Well she's not my girlfriend, Sherry, but she is a prime example of why I live alone. Men don't understand women and women don't understand men."

"Oh Mr. Carl, it's not that hard. You just have to love them."

Carl smiles at Sherry as she cleans off the table and pulls out another ten for the table.

"Well Sherry, that's the best tip I've had all day. I hope this is the best tip for you."

"Thanks, Mr. Carl," she says excitedly as Carl makes his way out the door.

The rest of the day found Jane doing a lot of thinking. She had a feeling that she may have blown any potential relationship with Carl and the more she thought about what he said, the more she knew he wasn't entirely wrong. He seems like a very happy man who is content with his life, which she didn't see much of in the big city. And she knows he hit a sensitive nerve when he questioned her job. But the truth was that she only had that job because she and Frank worked together in the corporation. Everybody loved Jane and Frank and it worked out to be a perfect arrangement for them, especially when Lucy was born.

After Frank died, Jane seriously thought about leaving the company and getting a fresh start somewhere else. Her degree was in journalism with a dream of moving back to McAdenville and helping her dad with the newspaper. When he sold the business, she was already falling in love with Frank, so the dream of being a writer was quietly put on the back shelf of her heart.

As the afternoon sun slowly made its way over the mountains in the western sky, Jane quietly made her way back to the bakery.

She found her mom, dad and Lucy having a great time. From the look of Lucy, Jane wondered if her mom would run out of flour or icing.

"Gee Mom, do I need to buy more flour and icing?" She looks at Lucy, "You're supposed to bake with it, not wear it, you know."

"Oh Lucy, don't listen to your mom," says Betty, who is drying off her hands, "Lucy was a great helper today. We really got a lot of things done."

Bill agrees, "We had a great time and we really are in pretty good shape for the festival. Did you get your shopping done?"

"I did. All I have to do is wrap them up, so I'm good," says Jane.

As she puts her packages down and hangs her coat, Jane offers to jump in and help.

"There's another apron in the back if you want to help out," her dad says.

"We're almost done, really," says Betty, "But if you get started cleaning up, we can all head out for dinner, if you want."

"Sure – that would be great," Jane says as she works her way to the back to get started.

******

The next day, the family is busy working their booth at the festival. The crowd is large and business is brisk. This is the last weekend before Christmas, so people from all over like to come and take in all that McAdenville has to offer.

After a busy morning, Jane, Betty and Lucy take a break from the booth to mingle as a voice is heard from behind them.

"Jane Bartlett!"

Jane turns around and sees her old friend, Sally, from her high school days running up and nearly jumping into Jane's arms.

"Girl, I didn't know you were home for the holidays. It's so good to see you!"

"I decided to have a real old-fashioned Christmas this year and let Lucy spend some time with her grandparents."

"Is this Lucy? My goodness. Your mommy and I were best friends in high school. The last time I saw you was…" she pauses. Then she looks at Jane.

"Frank's funeral – three years ago," Jane says with assurance and without emotion to her friend who seems hesitant.

Sally looks at Betty. "Mrs. Bartlett, you must be in heaven. I thought your cookies had a pinch of sunshine in them."

"We certainly love having Jane and Lucy with us, for sure."

"How long are you in town, Jane?"

"'Til the end of the year."

"Great! We just have to get together and catch up."

"Why don't you two go now? Bill and I can watch Lucy."

Jane looks at Sally. "I'm game, if you are."

"Are you sure, Mrs. Bartlett? I don't want to take Jane away from you."

"Oh it's fine. We're actually enjoying our time with Lucy, and I think she's having a good time, too. Right?" she says, looking at Lucy who is all smiles, "You two go get a glass of wine and catch up. Just don't close down the bar, okay? We'll still have a week after Christmas, you know."

With that, Jane and Sally head off to a local bar on Main Street while Grandma and Lucy continue on.

As they settle into a quiet table in the back of the bar, Sally seems anxious to catch up.

"So how are you and Lucy doing?"

"We're doing good. It's been rough, of course, but Lucy and I have a deal not to hold in our feelings, so every night when I tuck her in, we tell stories about Frank. I think it really helps to talk about him in a realistic way – just tell her memories I have about her dad. Sometimes we have a good cry, but other times we have a good laugh. Either way, it's much better than trying to bury it and pretend everything is okay."

"I can't imagine. Well keep doing whatever you're doing, because you and Lucy seem to have adjusted so well. You seem happy."

"I think coming home really helped."

"How's your job doing?"

Jane pauses. "After Frank died, I really buried myself into my work. It felt like everyone was watching me. Frank worked in the legal department and one of the other people on the boat worked there, as well, so everyone in the corporation felt the sadness of loss. Coming here this week has really made me think. I loved working there because Frank worked there. We went to work together. We ate lunch together every day. We were the only ones that never complained when the company Christmas party was employees only." Jane takes a sip of her wine as she continues, "But Frank isn't there any more and stepping away from it this week has made me really think that maybe Lucy and I need a new start. Maybe it's time to look for a job somewhere that doesn't remind me constantly of Frank. I feel like everyone is staring at me because they know."

"Are you thinking about coming home?" asks Sally, with a hopeful smile.

Jane pauses and looks around, then back at Sally, "I don't know

Sally. I know I could help out at the bakery until I figure out what I want to do, so I'm warming to the idea."

"You always talked about being a writer and even though I don't know anything about it, I'm pretty sure a good writer can write from anywhere." Sally pauses and smiles at Jane. "Besides, word has it that you and Carl have been sending out a lot of sparks of late."

"No, no. There's nothing to it. He's a nice guy, but there really is nothing going on." Jane seems to trip over every word.

"I don't know, Jane. I work at the bank, you know, and it sure sounds like the mutual attraction is obvious to everyone. And even though he may not be another Frank, you could sure do a lot worse than Carl Franklin."

"Sally, I know he's a nice guy and all, but we went to lunch the other day and he just seems so content being a handy man with no goals for the future. Why would any woman want to get involved with a man like that?"

Sally stares at Jane for a moment with a confused expression.

"Did he talk about his past at all?"

Jane thinks, "No. He said something that really upset me, so I walked out on him."

"What did he say?"

"He asked me if I told people that I wanted to be an HR Director for a big corporation in New York City when I was a little girl."

"No, you did not," says Sally

"That's not the point, Sally. I've worked hard to get where I am and I've done a lot of good things. I am not going to listen to some handy man with no ambition criticize the choices I've made in my life, that's for sure."

Sally just stares at Jane with her mouth open as if completely dumbfounded.

Their server comes and breaks the stare down and asks if they want another round.

Sally quickly gets out some cash and lays it on the table. "No, we're leaving. This should be enough."

The server takes the money and whispers to herself, "Nice tip." She walks away and Sally looks to Jane, "Let's go. I have something to show you."

Sally rushes out the door dragging Jane for about three doors down, where she stops and opens the door, "Come on. I want you to see something."

They go in as Sally explains, "The couple that owns this shop only handles items made by locals." She leads Jane back to a corner of the store that has a lot of wood work: Rocking chairs, furniture items, nic-nacs and some toys. They are all very well crafted.

"You like these?" Sally asks Jane who is a bit confused, but is impressed with the quality of work.

"Sure. It's beautiful work, so?" she says, looking at Sally.

"These are made by Carl. Just about everyone in McAdenville has something in their home that Carl has made."

"Well I'm sure he does nice work."

Sally takes a deep breath with her continued dumbfounded look on her face.

"Okay, let me show you something else," she says, as she grabs Jane's arm and leads her out the door and down the sidewalk.

Jane doesn't know what Sally is up to, but she's known her long enough to warrant a subtle sinking feeling in her stomach. Part of Sally's charm is how brutally honest she can be, and Jane has a bad feeling that this is not going to be a feel-good moment.

They get into Sally's car when Jane asks, "Where are we going?"

Sally holds her hand up. "Be quiet and pay attention."

As Sally drives with an intense posture, Jane looks out the window. They seem to be leaving town and getting more into a rural setting when Sally suddenly pulls into a lookout spot that overlooks the South Fork River below. Across the way are beautiful mountains and valleys. Obviously a great place for taking pictures.

Sally turns her car facing away from the scenery and turns off the engine.

"See that house?"

Jane looks at the beautiful home across the street. It was big, but not huge. It had a long wrap-around porch. It sat on the hill and obviously had a killer view. The landscaping was perfectly manicured, with a big red barn set back on the property.

"Nice," Jane says.

"Nice?" Sally takes Jane's hand as Jane looks at her and has a feeling she needs to brace herself.

"That's Carl's home and it's way more than nice. It's beautiful inside and out. Carl did all the work."

She pauses as Jane looks back at the house.

"Remember Jane, I work at the bank. Carl has two accounts and I manage both of them. In one account, he keeps all the money he gets from the furniture, toys and handy work he does around town. He uses that money to help people out. He got baseball equipment for the high school, computers for the elementary school and every time I hear of a family in crises, I know I'll be hearing from Carl telling me to help them out. He does everything anonymously because he doesn't want the recognition."

"The other account is where he paid for that house and fixing it up. It comes from his past that you never asked about, because you were too busy walking out on a man you thought to be a handy man with no ambition."

Jane looks back at her friend with an expression of fear of what Sally may say next.

"Jane, when Carl was twenty-one, he signed one of the biggest baseball contracts at the time. He pitched for the San Francisco Giants for only five years because an injury to his arm brought his career to a halt. But in that five year span, he was one of the best pitchers in the game. He made more money from baseball, endorsements and book deals than he could ever imagine spending. Even all these years later, I still post handsome paychecks every quarter into his account."

Jane looks painfully at Sally as tears begin to run down her cheeks and she begins to realize what a big mistake she has made.

Sally shakes her head compassionately, "Girlfriend, Carl is one of the most decent men you could ever hope to find, and don't think for a minute that I – and pretty much every other married woman in town – don't hesitate to remind my husband when he gets out of line."

Sally pauses before she puts a bow on it. "Jane, I love you. There is not a single woman in town that isn't jealous of you. They see the way Carl looks at you and swallow a big sigh. I wouldn't be a good friend if I didn't say it, Jane. That was a really bad move walking out on Carl like that."

Jane melts into Sally's arms and weeps, "I didn't know. I totally blew it. How can I ever face him again?"

Sally holds Jane's head up, "It won't be easy Jane, but it will certainly be worth the try. You simply can't let someone like that get away."

As they look at each other, a blue truck pulls into the driveway across the way. Carl gets out and slowly heads for the front door, stopping to take a moment to watch the sun falling behind the mountains across the way. He goes in and turns on his lights which of course include a pretty nice display of festive decorations as Sally starts her car.

"I am so sorry, Jane. I didn't mean to ruin your vacation. But you still have time while you're here to regroup and make this a memorable Christmas."

******

The next day, Jane was clearly subdued. It was snowing which made for a festive setting. Betty and Bill knew that something was bothering Jane, and though they didn't know what was going on, they felt the best thing they could do right now is take Lucy out to enjoy the winter wonderland of the day.

"You sure you don't want to join us?" her mother asks as they put on their coats.

"I might catch up with you later, but I have a few things to take care first." says Jane who is desperately trying to keep a positive face that her parents can see right through.

"We'll be in town skating, building a snowman or having a snowball fight. I'm sure you can find us," says her dad, as they all head out the door and Jane heads up the stairs.

Jane sits at her computer and takes a sip from her coffee, then a deep breath and says to herself, "Okay, let's do this."

Paul;

It is with a heavy heart – and yet an excited heart – to inform you that I will be leaving the company at the end of January.

I have appreciated the many opportunities your company has given me and I will do all that I can to make the transition a smooth one for the company.

As you know, Frank was a beloved part of my life and your company.

After his passing I could not ask for a more supportive and caring group to help me deal with the loss than your company and the people I have had the honor to work with. I will always be indebted to you and my co-workers for helping me through such a dark time.

But the truth is, Paul, that it has been extremely difficult to come to work every day without hearing Frank's voice at a meeting, or see him and I eating lunch every time I walk by the break room. I feel it's in the best interest of both myself and Lucy if we break away and get a new start in our journey moving forward.

Please let me know if there is anything I can do to help before I leave.

I am deeply appreciative,

Jane Rutledge

After Jane reads her email a few times, she sends it, feeling a sense of relief and confidence with her decision. She knows it's the right decision, but she knows it also comes with a lot of risk.

As she goes downstairs to warm up her coffee, she looks out the kitchen window at the gentle snowflakes fluttering about when her phone rings.

"Jane, this is Paul," says her CEO, who's always been good at responding to emails, but this response is quicker than usual.

"Paul, you got my email, I presume?"

"I did. And I'm going to deny your request to resign."

"Excuse me?"

"Yes. I've deleted it and I'm asking you to delete your copy, as well. It never happened."

"I don't understand."

"Jane, you and Frank have always been a vital part of this company. If you just quit now, you'll walk away with nothing. If you trust me to take care of it, I can help you leave the right way."

"How do you mean 'the right way,' Paul?"

"I've been working all week with board members and finance directors. You've heard the rumors, I'm sure. I have to make cuts in every department. Not big cuts, but any cut is too much in my view. In order for the company to remain healthy going into next year, we have to downsize and adjust our overhead. I've been going over the list of employees from every department to cut staff and you just made my job easier."

"How so?"

"If I put you on the list for the HR department with your salary, it will save two jobs. It would be great for me because I will be saving two jobs and losing one, which as your email that never happened indicated, I would have lost anyway. It will be great for you, because instead of just walking away, you'll be getting a nice severance package that anyone with over ten years with the company will get that should help you and Lucy out as you consider your future options."

"Oh, okay. That's very nice of you, Paul. What do I need to do then?"

"Enjoy Christmas with your family and relax. You have plenty of vacation days. If your plan is to move back home to McAdenville, don't even think about coming back. I know you'll have to take care of your personal business, so let me know when you do and let's plan for you to come back here to say goodbye the right way. Maybe mid-January."

"Wow! Thank you, Paul. I wasn't expecting all that."

"Jane, I'll take my CEO hat off now and speak to you as a friend. When I was going over the list of names in each department, I was giving serious thought to putting you on the HR list before you sent the email, and for the same reasons. When Frank died, I figured you would probably leave the company within a year. There are many memories of you and Frank in this company. And here you are three years later still working for us. I was seriously thinking that maybe you needed a little push out the door. Jane, you have a lot to offer in the business world and in your private world. I love having you on my team, but you'll never obtain the happiness you deserve in our company. I think you're absolutely making the right move."

"Thanks Paul. It's a risk, but I really do feel it's best for Lucy and me."

"Absolutely. I see it all the time, Jane. People stay at the same job for years, not because they love it, but because it's safe and it beats taking a risk to step away and follow their passions. That's why I thought you'd be gone within a year. You're not the kind of person who would compromise with your heart. You certainly didn't with Frank, and you shouldn't moving forward."

"Thanks Paul. I'll let you know when I'm coming back to take care of things."

"That would be great. I'll make sure to hold a spot in the garage so you don't have to drive around. And Jane, when you come, take whatever you need from your apartment, but part of your severance package will be to have a moving company pack up your apartment and take it wherever you need it to go."

"That would be a big help, Paul. Thank you."

"My pleasure. I know you have some Christmas tasks to get to and even though I've got the HR department settled, I still have to figure out the finance department, so I'll let you go."

"Thanks again, Paul. And when you go over finance, you better keep Karen. I know she's fairly new to the company, but she's a sharp woman. She can help the company for many years."

"Thanks for the advice. Maybe I could email you the lists of names I'm wrestling with and you can tell me who stays and who goes."

"No thanks, I'm on vacation."

Paul laughs. "Take care, Jane, and thank you for all you've done for the company. I'll talk to you again soon."

"Take care, Paul."

With that, Jane looks out the window at the snow with a smile, knowing she has made the right decision for herself and Lucy. She feels like she's on a roll and the sooner she deals with her mess-up with Carl, the better.

She reaches for her phone and texts Carl.

"Can I buy you a glass of wine? I owe you at least that and want to talk to you."

"Tell me where and what time and I'll be there."

"Terra Mia Bar, 2pm?"

"See you then."

Jane heads back upstairs to wrap some presents before cleaning up and heading to the bar.

After going over her apology over and over again, she's feeling nervous yet confident as she walks into the bar. Carl is not there yet, so she gets a table off to the side that she thinks would be better for a conversation.

As she takes her coat off and sits down, Carl comes in, which makes Jane relax as she hates waiting alone for people to show up.

"Hi Carl. I appreciate you coming. I know you're busy."

"No problem. I said I would make time for you and I'm a man of my word."

The server comes by to take their order.

"I'll have a glass of Pinot Grigio, please."

The server looks to Carl who is thinking.

"That sounds good for me as well, please."

As the server leaves to get their drinks, Jane wants to move quickly before she loses her nerve.

"Carl, I am so sorry I walked out on you the other day. I could give you excuses, but it doesn't really matter. I was wrong. I said some hurtful things without really knowing you and that was wrong. A friend told me about your baseball past and it all made sense then. I was totally wrong to criticize the work you do around here. You really are a special man and I should have taken more time to get to know you, past and present, before I judged you. I'm really sorry."

"So now that you know I have a big bank account and famous past of being a baseball player, being a handy man with no ambition is okay?"

"Carl, it's not that, please."

"Listen Jane, I played in the majors for five years. I learned a lot. Most people get baseball players totally wrong. They think we are rich, spoiled athletes who spend all their time whining for more money. Some of them do, but those are the players I almost always threw my fastball right at their fanny. 'Stop whining about the money, you idiot. It's a privilege to play this game.' But for the most part every player I played with would probably play for ten bucks an hour. It's not about the fame and fortune. You'll never make it to the big show if you're focused on fame and fortune. You have to have a passion for the game. People see nine players standing around and call it a boring game. But every ballplayer out there has a mind that is going 100 miles an hour. I'm watching that batter stepping into the batter's box. He's watching me. I got him out in the third with my slider, but maybe I should start him off with my curve. My curve has been awesome tonight. But he's also been yelling at my players a lot from the dugout. He's always been a cocky player. Maybe I should start him off with a nice fastball just under his chin to cool him down a bit. It's a chess game on grass and you're always trying to guess what the other guy is going to do. And when you play at that level, you better be guessing right or I'm going to make you look really bad.

"I was really sad when I had to leave it. I never missed all the other stuff, though. Traveling a lot and staying in the best hotels sounds glamorous, but it's not. You walk down the steps to the lobby and there are faces all around. People who want a piece of you. Everyone knows what you're worth. Beautiful women who would love to flatter you and make you fall in love with them. The gold-diggers. I don't miss any of that." He takes a sip of his wine, "I miss the game. I miss walking onto a field in February and the smell of fresh cut grass beneath my feet. I have the best lawn in McAdenville because I could mow my lawn twice a day just for the smell of fresh cut grass." He pauses and leans in. "You know, sometimes I wear my glove when I'm mowing. The smell of leather and freshly cut grass is just heaven to me."

Carl gets up to put on his coat as Jane gets a panicked look.

"Jane, you are a fine woman. I don't deny the attraction I feel for you. But you have your life in New York City and I wish you and Lucy nothing but the best. I don't mind you finding out about my past. I loved being a baseball player. Ever since I was a small kid, I wanted to be a baseball player. And I made it. Not many people can say they lived out their dream like I did. I'm very grateful. But now, I'm just that handy man with no ambition but to help people out. I'm okay with that. I really do wish you well, Jane. You seem like a really good lady."

With that, Carl drops a twenty dollar bill on the table and walks out.

Jane sits quietly stunned with tears in her eyes. This was not what she was hoping for today. She can't formulate any thoughts or words.

She feels heavy and unable to breath. She is numb and overwhelmed with hopelessness.

The server comes to her table, "Can I get you anything else?"

Jane crashes back to reality and scrambles for composure.

"No. No, I'm fine, thank you." As she gets up, she drops another twenty on the table and rushes out the door praying that she doesn't see a blue truck as she heads for her parents' home.

That evening was a very quiet night at the Bartletts home. While Betty, Bill and Lucy watched holiday movies with popcorn and hot chocolate, Jane requested to be left alone in her room.

Her parents didn't know the reason for her solitude, but every now and then they could hear the sobbing and sniffling coming from upstairs and they knew their daughter was really hurting. Everyone was really sad without knowing what they were sad about. They only knew that upstairs was a mother and daughter they loved very much, having an emotional melt down.

Without a word spoken, it was understood. It must have been Carl.

******

The next day, Betty, Bill and Lucy are busy working at the bakery when Carl comes in.

"Hey Bill. Did you need something fixed?"

"Ah yes, Carl. It's out in the back," he says, as he tells Lucy to watch the front and takes Carl back to the back storage room.

When they are alone, Bill – never one to beat around the bush – gets right to the point.

"You know, Carl, I've known you long enough to know you are one of the most decent, caring men around. I'm also biased, but I know my daughter enough to know that she too, is one of the most caring people around. Now I don't know what's going on between you two, and I know it's none of my business. But I know the sparks of love when I see you looking at my daughter. And I know my daughter enough to know when she has fallen in love."

"But something is broke right now. I'm not an expert, Carl, but I'm an old man who's been around the block a few times. Whatever it is going on between you two is going on between you two. But I can guarantee you that whatever it is, it almost always has to do with a misunderstanding in communication. You said something that touched a nerve with her, or she said something that touched a nerve with you. Or maybe it was both. But I know for fact that neither you nor my daughter would ever hurt each other on purpose. I'm not telling you what to do, Carl. I'm just asking you to think about it."

"Bill, there's a lot of truth in what you're saying. It's been really hard for me to let women into my life, I know. When I played ball, I grew to really be guarded with all the plastic, pretty gold diggers whom I knew wouldn't give me the time of day if I wasn't connected to fame and fortune. It's always been hard for me to think of women any other way, which I know isn't fair."

"I get it, Carl. I don't have any answers for you. I just know that you both are special people and deserve to find the happiness of life in love. She'll be here another week, so just think about it."

"I will, Bill." As Carl heads back to leave, Bill stops him with a final point.

"And Carl." Carl stops and turns to Bill who glares at him and speaks in a much more fatherly tone. "My daughter is not a gold-digger."

With his eyes moistening, Carl nods in agreement. "I know, Bill. I never questioned that."

As Carl gets out to the front, Lucy stops him, "Do you want a cookie, Mr. Carl?"

"That would be awesome, Lucy."

As she's getting a cookie, she continues, "Are you and Mommy fighting?"

"No, Lucy. Your mom is a wonderful lady."

"Oh. She seems really sad right now. And she seems really happy when she's around you, so maybe you should be around her more."

Carl smiles. "That's not a bad idea, Lucy. How much do I owe you for the cookie?"

Lucy shrugs her shoulders. "Grandpa keeps telling me to watch the front but hasn't taught me how to use the register, so I guess you can just have it."

Carl smiles as he gets out a dollar bill and slaps it on the counter.

"Well if he ever shows you, this can go towards the cookie sales. If he doesn't show you, then keep it and buy yourself a treat."

"Thanks, Mr Carl. Have a nice day," says Lucy, as Carl heads out the door.

Mary comes in to the bakery. She is an old friend of the family who always comes by during the holidays to help Betty out when she can, so Bill decides to take advantage of the extra help and tells Betty he needs to go run a few errands.

He heads home and as he enters, he finds a quiet house. He makes his way upstairs and knocks on Jane's door. He hears nothing and slowly opens the door, only to find Jane laying on her bed, still in her jammies staring off to nowhere. He walks in and gently sits at the end of her bed.

"It's been a pretty exciting holiday, don't you think?"

Jane looks at her dad. She looks like a wreck, not surprisingly.

"I don't want to talk about it."

"Well that's a problem, Jane, because I'm your dad and I don't care if you want to talk about it or not. I'd be happy to do all the talking and you can just stay there and sulk."

Jane takes a deep breath as she knows a daddy daughter moment like this never has a way out.

"I'm not sure what's going on between you and Carl. It's probably none of my business. But I've never seen you so happy as I have this past week. I know getting away from the city is a big step for you. And I'm sure spending time with your mother and I has certainly been great for you and Lucy. But I think meeting Carl has a lot to do with it, as well. Love doesn't hide, Jane. You light up like a Christmas tree when you are around Carl. And I know Carl and it's clear to me that it's a two-way street. Whatever gummed things up between you two is between you and Carl, but I'm guessing it probably had something to do with a miscommunication. You said something that hurt him, or he said something to hurt you. Or maybe it was both. I'm sure neither one of you meant to do it. It happens. Someone says something without looking at the big picture and everything comes crashing down."

"I'm not going to tell you what to do, Jane. But I will tell you that Carl is worth trying to fix this problem for. And I'll further tell you as your dad, I'm not going to let you hide in this room sulking through the holidays. Your mom, Lucy and I are waiting to have a wonderful Christmas with you, so do something."

At that, Jane melts into tears as she sits up and hugs her dad.

"Dad, I blew it so much with Carl. I'll never have a chance with him now. It's too late to fix it."

Bill holds his daughter up and looks at her, "Honey, love doesn't wear a watch. It's never too late for love."

She looks at him with such a sad face, trying to believe what her dad is saying as he continues.

"Tell me Jane. When did you feel that first spark of love with Carl?"

Jane looks at her dad thoughtfully, then cracks a very slight glimmer of a smile. "When I knocked him off his stool and nearly killed him," she says with a pained look.

Her dad smiles. "Yes Jane. There are much better ways to meet a man, but I suppose that was affective.

"Okay. And what was the next time you felt those sparks?"

Jane looks at him in thought before smiling. "It was when Lucy and I were walking around town and saw Carl helping people out. He just seemed like a good guy."

"Yes and he does that all year long. Okay, the next time?"

Jane smiles. "At the bakery when he handed me his card and it just had his name and number. It goes against every rule in business, but seemed so perfect for Carl."

"Yes indeed. He seldom gets to pass out his card because everyone around here already has his number. I'm sure he was a bit excited to hand you such a professional business card."

"And the next time?"

"When he took me to the Spruced Goose Station for lunch. How he interacts with the people is so genuine." She pauses. "At least until I walked out on him because he was so content being a handy man with no ambition." She shakes her head in shame.

"Yes, and that would be a prime example of miscommunication and saying something stupid without understanding the big picture." He smiles at Jane who continues to shake her head.

"And the next time?"

"When he was talking about his baseball career. I've never seen a person talk with so much passion and love for a game before." She hesitates, "And that would be just before he got up and walked out on me."

"Okay. Now if we set aside that last one, and look at the other moments of sparks, did you have any idea during those times of Carl's baseball past?"

"No Dad. That's the problem."

Bill holds up his finger to stops her, "No Jane. That is the answer."

Jane looks at her dad very confused.

"Jane, you fell in love with Carl the handyman with no ambition. When you found out about his past, it didn't change that love. It just helped to make more sense of why you were falling in love with him."

Jane considers what he's saying with tears falling down her cheeks again, as her dad continues.

"Jane, you are not a gold digger. Carl knows that. But he has a hard time letting a woman into his heart because so many women in his past were. It's up to you to tell him what you have just told me. It's time for you to fight for the love you both deserve."

Jane crashes into her dad's arms again, and he is in no hurry to move on.

"I love you, Dad."

******

Carl hears a knock on his door and gets up to answer it. He opens the door to find Jane who looks seriously determined and not waiting for an invitation to come in, as she bolts past him. He closes the door and turns to her.

Jane jams a finger into Carl's chest and continues to do so as she talks.

"I am NOT a gold-digger! I fell in love with you when I knocked you over... I fell in love with you when I watched you helping people out around town... I fell in love with you when you gave me your card with just your name and number on it... I fell in love with you when you took me to that Spruced Goose and watched how you were so kind to people... And I fell in love with you when I watched you talk about baseball! I am not a gold-digger, mister, and if you think for a minute that I am, you are dead wrong... I fell in love with YOU, not your bank account!"

Jane takes a break and remains standing there, panting and glaring at Carl who is thankful she has stopped poking him in the chest and is staring back at her with a pained look, yet his eyes are clearly full of compassion.

"Are you done?"

Jane gets more intense in her glare at him, but slowly backs off as her eyes dance around in thought as she regains her composure, she is looking down and softly says, "My parents want to know if you want join us for Christmas tomorrow."

She slowly lifts her eyes to Carl's as a smile slowly grows on his face. He puts his hands on either side of Jane's face and draws her into a passionate kiss that releases the tension and is replaced by the warm comfort of true love found again.

******

The next morning, as the Bartlett home comes to life with the excitement of Christmas morn, the door bell rings, as Jane quickly hurries to answer it. She embraces Carl as he comes in and removes his coat and Bill brings him a cup of coffee.

As everyone settles into their seats around the Christmas tree, Jane remains standing and gets everyone's attention.

"Before we get started, I have something to say. I meant to tell you all a few days ago, but I've been kind of busy fixing some messes I created." She looks to Carl and smiles.

"A few days ago, I sent an email to Paul – the CEO of the company – to inform him that I was leaving the company at the end of January."

Everyone starts cheering, but Jane is quick to cut them off.

"No, no, no, please, I'm not done. Paul called me five minutes later and denied my resignation."

Everyone mumbles and looks of confusion fill the room before Jane continues.

"He said that he has been spending his holiday going over the list of employees in every department because he has to make some cuts at the first of the year. He said if he put my name on the list for the HR department, it would give me a very generous severance package for Lucy and me to start fresh with and help him out because he'll be losing one position that he would have lost anyway, and save two positions of employees who don't want to leave. He said I have plenty of unused vacation time and if the plan is to move back here, he told me to just stay here. I'll have to go take care of personal issues like my bank account and apartment, and he says at that time, I could go by the company and say goodbye properly. He also said that he would pay for a moving company to pack up our apartment and bring it here whenever I close out my accounts."

She takes a deep breath. "So I know I didn't ask anyone, but if it's okay, Lucy and I can stay here in McAdenville and I could help out at the bakery. I'll have plenty of money to hold us until I figure out my next step. But only if it's okay with you all."

They all jump up and attack Jane with a big family hug as Carl looks on with a smile that clearly embraces the moment.

As they all get back to the Christmas celebration and begin to pass out presents, Carl asks Jane to come with him. They go out to his truck where he pulls out a package and hands it to her with a smile.

She opens it and pulls out a wooden statue of a Western man leaning with a shovel in his hands, a mound painted gold, and in the head of the shovel is a perfectly shaped red heart. Jane looks up at Carl.

"I will never accuse you of being a gold-digger. But I may have to say you are a heart digger. You got my heart. But I'd like you to keep it."

Jane wraps her arms around Carl as they kiss, and for the first time, Jane realizes that there really are no rules with true love.

You can absolutely find … *one true love again.*

2

North Forest Christmas Festival

"Thanks for coming everyone," says Harry, the bald eagle, who once again will be leading the Christmas Festival this year. "When I call your name, please come forward and take your place. The rest of you are welcome to stay, but since we have a limited time, we ask once again that you simply observe the meetings and not participate. If you have any ideas, you are to take that up privately with the committee member that represents you."

"Morgan, the moose."

Morgan represents all the deers, bears and moose of the forest and is highly respected for being a gentle giant who always looks out for the animals.

"Sam, the ram and Eunice, the ewe."

This couple of bighorn sheep have been representing the cliff-hangers for many years and have a reputation for always having creative ideas for decorating the forest.

"Larry, the lynx"

As Larry approaches, there is a spattering of boos and hisses from many of the animals who represent a lynx meal during the rest of the year. Larry has been on the festival committee for many years, as he is the only lynx that is capable of attending these meetings without getting hungry.

"Earl, the flying squirrel"

Earl represents all the rodents of the forest who, although small compared to most of the others, are one of the reasons the forest has a strong reputation for its Christmas spirit. Absolutely no one in the animal kingdom decorates the trees better than the flying squirrels.

"Harriet, the snowshoe hare"

Harriet represents all the rabbits who, with their big back feet, are excellent at packing the snow and helping out with building the many snow sculptures for the festival.

"Willie, the wolf"

Willie, like Larry, represents many of the carnivorous animals and is used to the boos and hisses from the others. He, like Larry, is one of the few wolves able to set aside his appetite in the interest of the festival.

"Okay, we have everyone here. This year is going to be another great year for our Christmas festival. I've talked with Santa, and he is once again excited to make our forest the first and last stop on Christmas Eve and Christmas morning.

The animals all burst into a chorus of cheering celebration.

"I trust those who represent the animals that are currently in hibernation have spoken to them for ideas. I don't have any pending issues to discuss myself, so unless there are any questions or issues from the committee, we can go ahead with the planning."

Larry raises his paw.

"Larry?"

"Once again, could you remind the squirrels decorating the trees to be more careful? There are many of us below who keep getting hit by debris, and there is enough to suggest it is not entirely accidental."

"Hey, Larry! Guess what I got you for Christmas? Some lead boots! YOU WON'T CATCH NOTH'N!" says a squirrel in the crowd as the other squirrels roll in laughter while many of the other species on the lynx menu scramble to control their giggles.

"Please everyone, please settle down" says Harry, trying to get control of the meeting. "We must be reminded of our commitment to the spirit of Christmas. This is not the time for sharing our grievances."

"Sure it is, Harry," yells the squirrel. "It's the only time we can share our grievances without becoming his snack!"

The others break out into another round of laughing and high-fiving.

"Might I remind you that Larry and Willie have come here every year in good faith and been a great help in making our festivals the best?" says Harry. "I might also remind you that they both have very good memory, and although you can make those remarks without consequences right now, you may be endangering your kind come springtime. We have always encouraged the non-carnivores to work with the carnivores in harmony during the festival in order to keep the balance of nature just that in the spring, and not become an environment of pay-back time."

With that, many of the animals outside of the committee turn and head back to their separate worlds, giggling and making small talk, while the committee focuses on the meeting, which goes on without any further interruptions.

"Okay, I think we can move forward now," says Harry, as the committee settles in without anyone else around.

Earl raises his paw.

"Yes, Earl?"

"I would like to apologize to Larry and Willie for the squirrels' behavior. He's a teenager, and I assure you, he will be encouraged to fill his mouth with nuts, not words, if he plans to become an adult."

"Willie?" Harry calls out to the raised paw.

"I can't speak for Larry, but I think he'd agree that we feel our participation in the planning of this festival truly is important to the balance of nature, as Harry suggests. Carnivores working with non-carnivores during the festival helps us to encourage our kind to only hunt for survival and never for sport or revenge."

Larry chimes in. "I totally agree with Willie." Then, he smiles as he looks to Earl. "But maybe we could get that kid's name after the meeting so we can just give him a little scare later on to think about?"

Everyone laughs.

"Okay, okay," says Harry. "We're here to plan the festival, not a teenager's demise."

The committee moves on, planning this year's festival.

Earl, again, takes charge of the tree decorations, and as always, promises to make this year the best ever.

Sam and Eunice share some great new ideas about the ice and snow sculptures they want to include this year.

Morgan and Willie, again, take ownership of the fire pit, as Morgan gives his powerful talk about safety and the need to pay attention to their surroundings so as not to have any mishaps.

They all agree to gather nuts, berries and other foliage for the reindeer to help them during their busy night with Santa.

"Well we seem to have everything in place. Remember, Santa will once again be choosing a helper to go with him on the sleigh, so start thinking about whether you want to put someone's name in the hat for the drawing, but do make sure it's someone who truly wants to go. We'll meet here once a week until the festival, so please try to be on time and bring your concerns and ideas at that time. Thanks, everybody!"

******

As the fall quickly slips into winter, the animals keep busy organizing, gathering and preparing for the Christmas festival. Most of the work early on is just getting everything gathered and organized. They typically wait until the day before the festival to actually decorate as decorating too soon could quickly be swept up in a blizzard and they'd have to start all over.

Sam and Eunice have been going over the plans for the many ice and snow sculptures they hope to have with many of the snowshoe rabbits and other volunteers who love to help create their masterpieces, which always features big sculptures of each of Santa's reindeer.

Earl has a group of volunteers busily gathering up decorations for the trees, as well as nuts and berries for the reindeer. Earl also has his annual meeting with Cy, the firefly spokesman, to make sure they are again available for lighting the trees. Fireflies go into hibernation in September – so the humans think, anyway – but in truth, they are always happy to come up to the North Forest to help light up all the trees on Christmas Eve for Santa.

Morgan and Willie have recruited many beavers to volunteer with cutting logs and branches for the fire pit, as well as some male deer and caribou with big antlers that are always good helping out with moving logs. It's considered an honor to be chosen for the log moving chores.

The forest is a happy place this time of year. Santa is the only human that the animals trust. He's been visiting these animals every year and has always been nothing but kind and loving to the animal kingdom. Every Christmas Eve is their opportunity to celebrate their world with Santa. They appreciate how quick Santa is to put anyone who is not kind to animals on his Naughty List, too.

It's a fun time in the North Forest.

******

Christmas Eve's Eve, the forest begins to get busy. There has been a lot of snow recently that makes the forest look even more magical, and the animals can tell that there should be no weather-related issues for the next few days. Snow is welcomed; blizzards are not.

Everyone is busy and in great moods as the anticipation for the festival draws nearer. Everybody knows their assignments and are busily scurrying about.

The schedule is pretty much what you would expect for a group that has been doing this festival for many years. There is no sense of urgency as everyone knows the plan and understands that everything will come together nicely if each one stays on schedule.

During the day, it's all about getting the layout of the festival set up.

Mounds of snow and ice are positioned where the sculptures are to be created, with Harriet working with several volunteer hares to pack the snow into general shapes that will make it easier later on for the sculptures to be created.

Morgan and Willie are working with their volunteers in the middle of the field, digging out the pit for the fire, with some deer and caribou busy stacking firewood off to the side.

Many birds and smaller animals are busy creating the various food stations with sticks and leaves that are carefully woven together to make place mats for the mounds of seeds, nuts, fruit and foliage to come later.

Everything is meticulously situated in the exact position called for. The atmosphere is bright with birds chirping their Christmas songs, and all the animals seem to be in a very festive mood as they prepare for the big day tomorrow.

As the sun grows dimmer, there is a call for all paws and beaks on deck to help out as they can with the sculptures. It's always a good idea to get the sculptures done before nightfall so they have a full night of freezing temperatures to make them solid. In the morning, the birds with sharp beaks can go back and do the detail work, but they like to have as much of the sculptures done by the evening.

Meanwhile, Morgan is working with some fireflies in doing a test run on the fire pit. You need five fireflies to connect their behinds together to create a beam of light pointed at the brush to start a fire, so Morgan needs to see how many groups of five fireflies are needed to create the best fire. Typically four groups spaced around the pit are enough, but if the brush has a lot of moisture, it could require more groups, and Morgan likes to know in advance so he can better prepare.

As night falls, the animals gather around the test fire to make sure nothing has been forgotten and to embrace the results of all their hard work that day. There is a great sense of appreciation for one another as the animals look around the festival field, understanding that everyone did their part to make this festival a great time of celebration.

******

"Do we have everyone?" says Harry as he takes a head count. "Morgan, Sam, Eunice, Larry, Earl, Harriet and Willie. Good. Thanks for coming."

The final committee meeting is always on Christmas Eve morning to tie up any loose ends and go over final preparations before Santa arrives just before dusk.

While they gather near the fire pit, there is still plenty of last minute activity around the festival field. Nothing major; it's mostly setting out the food and touching up the snow sculptures, and general business that avoids having nothing to do but wait for Santa.

"It looks like we had another great year, so I thank you all for doing a great job. Are there any issues we need to consider before the festival gets started?"

The moose raises his hoof.

"Morgan?"

"Earl, I got the fire started last night with four groups of fireflies, but I checked the foliage this morning and it seems a little moist. If you could have Cy send me six or even eight groups today before they decorate the trees, I'd appreciate it."

Earl nods in agreement, "That would be no problem, Morgan."

Harry asks for a report from each committee person for review.

"Morgan – the fire pit looks great. Do we have enough logs to burn? It's going to be a long night."

"We have plenty. I kept telling the beavers to leave some of the forest in tact, but they assured me that any unused logs will be used for their dens, so there won't be any waste."

"Glad to see they left many trees standing, but I do agree with the beavers. Better to have too many tonight that can be utilized tomorrow by the beavers, than not enough."

"Sam and Eunice? The sculptures look exceptional this year."

"Thanks, Harry," says Eunice. "I think everyone did a fabulous job this year and we were able to create some extra pieces that I think everyone will enjoy. We think having each of Santa's reindeer featured in a sculpture turned out really special and should be a great tribute to their hard work"

"Great. Larry?"

"Thanks, Harry. Our group did an excellent job again this year. The birds and porcupines really stepped up to create some wonderful ornaments, and there are plenty of fireflies to light the place up nicely, so it's been another great year for our group."

"Yes, those ornaments are superior, to be sure. Thanks."

"Harriet?"

"We had a great time this year, Harry. The snow was perfect for packing, which really helped get the sculptures in good form, as well as packing Santa's landing strip. We really had a lot of fun."

"Excellent. Willie?"

"We had a good year as well, Harry. We helped dig out the pit for the fire and did some gathering of branches and foliage with the beavers. There were a few moments of annoyance from the younger rodent population taking advantage of the peaceful work environment, but I thought my volunteers handled it well as there were no issues of conflict."

"Good to hear. There always seems to be a few younger animals who take advantage of the peace time working environment, and as a carnivore myself, I do appreciate your volunteers showing such restraint in these situations."

"I went by Santa's workshop this morning before coming here and I'm happy to say that everything in the North Pole is on schedule and Santa and his reindeer are excited to come. Santa tells me we should expect him just before dusk, but he said that if everything continues to run smoothly, he may come a little earlier and have more time to enjoy the festival before heading out for the Christmas blitz. I have the normal lookout stations covered, so we should have ample time to get into position when the time comes."

"Okay, well it's shaping up to be another great festival, so I'll end this meeting and let you all get ready. Thanks for all the hard work. Now, it's time to have fun and enjoy our efforts."

With that, the animals break up and head for their various stations for last minute preparations and to enjoy the festive wonderland they have created.

******

As the morning gives way to the afternoon and slowly crawls towards sunset, everything in the North Forest is ready to go. The mood is festive and there is no sense of urgency anywhere. The animals have been doing this every year, and unlike their human counterparts, the animals are exceptional at staying focused and seeing every task to its finish.

Morgan has a nice fire going in the pit with a couple volunteers stationed by the stacks of logs to make sure the fire remains beneficial.

All the fireflies are in position on the branches surrounding the festival field, mostly relaxing and catching a few more winks of sleep while they wait for the signal.

Down on the field, rabbits and squirrels are playing, some snowball fights and others just chasing one another as they wait for the signal.

Suddenly, off in the distance, the faint sound of a horn blowing gets the attention of many.

Then another horn; this time, even closer.

Then, the announcement from nearby: "They are on their way!"

Activity breaks out as every animal scurries to take their place, creating two lines on either side of the landing runway, while all the fireflies crank up their tails to create a sparkling wonderland to greet Santa.

As the sound of sleigh bells announce his arrival, Santa circles the North Forest field, waving and taking in the sights of the festive surroundings, before turning towards the runway for a gentle landing to the chorus of cheers from all the animals.

As the sleigh comes to a stop, Santa releases the reindeer so they can gather with their animal friends. This is their time as the reindeer are truly rock stars of the North Forest Christmas Festival. Each reindeer has a large ice sculpture, and at the base of each sculpture are mounds of food the reindeer loves to eat.

Santa takes a seat on a log near the fire and puts his hat on a stump for the animals to put their nominations for shotgun that night. He loves starting his Christmas Eve night here at the North Forest because it's all about the reindeer. They work so hard to make the night possible to bring so much joy to so many children, so Santa thinks it's only fitting that he starts and ends the night here for them. Santa is more than happy to sit back and let his trusted reindeer have the spotlight.

As darkness settles in, Harry works to gather all the animals around the fire pit for the drawing of the animal for shotgun, as well as some parting words from Santa before he heads out.

As in every year, there aren't many names in the hat. The bigger animals don't want to go and slow the sleigh down. The carnivores don't like the humans and they taste terrible, so they want nothing to do with helping Santa out. The birds don't have the need to fly in the sleigh since they have wings already. So, it pretty much goes to one of the smaller animals like the squirrels, rabbits and others.

"If I may have your attention, it's time for Santa to say a few words and draw his shotgun host for this year," says Harry, as he nods to Santa.

"Thanks, Harry," says Santa as he stands before his adoring animals. "Once again, you have created the best stop for me and my reindeer. That's why the North Forest is the only place I stop at two times on Christmas Eve night."

The animals break into cheers of celebration before Santa can continue.

"I truly love starting my night, and ending it with all my animals friends of the North Forest."

Another chorus of cheers, which Santa is in no hurry to stop.

"As you know, my reindeer are very special to me. There simply is no way I could get all the presents to all the children without the loyal and dedicated work of my reindeer. It pleases me so much to have this send off every Christmas Eve and the truly warm welcome we receive after the hard night of creating the Christmas magic for all the children of the world. I can not thank you all enough for your participation."

More cheers.

"So without further delay, I'm going to reach into my hat and see who gets to help me tonight."

As Santa reaches and grabs a name, the animals look on with great anticipation. As Santa looks at the name, a big smile comes over him as he looks to the animals.

"Pete, the snowshoe hare."

The animals break into a loud, enthusiastic celebration.

Pete is the oldest member of the rabbit family of the North Forest. He has never been chosen to assist Santa, so everyone is extremely happy for him. Everyone loves Pete. Even the carnivores , no matter how hungry they may be, always pass on Pete out of respect.

Pete makes his way to Santa, who lifts him up and places him in his seat in the sleigh as everyone cheers. Pete is humbled, yet thrilled to have been given this opportunity at his age.

Santa removes the sleigh bells as he doesn't want to disturb the children sleeping during the night. He always leaves them with his animal friends of the North Forest while he quietly makes his way around the world on Christmas Eve.

As Santa and Pete take their place on the sleigh, and the reindeer take their positions on the reigns, he waves and declares:

"Let the Christmas night of celebration begin!"

With a crack of his whip, the reindeer take off to a thunderous roar from the North Forest animal kingdom, as Christmas begins.

******

It takes Santa a little bit before he gets into the groove of the evening. He spends a lot of time at his first couple of stops explaining everything to Pete. But, Pete is a quick learner, and as he gets into the routine, they both settle in and the pace gets better.

"Do I have to slide down the chimney" asks Pete at the first stop.

"And ruin that beautiful white coat of yours? No way. I'm the spirit of Christmas, Pete. I don't need doors or chimneys to get inside. I can just appear. So when we get to a stop, you get into my bag and we'll both appear inside the home. You get whatever the children leave for the reindeer as I put the presents under the tree, then you climb back in my bag and we're off to the next one."

"What if the children don't leave anything for the reindeer?" asks Pete.

"I leave a little message about how hard my reindeer work on Christmas Eve and it sure would help if the children left a little nourishment for them. They don't want to be on the Naughty List, after all. They're pretty good about leaving me cookies – which you can see I don't need – but it takes a little more effort for me to get the children to leave carrots or veggies for my reindeer – which they do need."

Pete is so curious. "Are the cookies they leave you any good?"

"Some of them are. I can tell the ones that were made by the children. They're the best. But there are some that I know were made by Aunt Gertrude that nobody likes, so they tell the children that Aunt Gertrude has a special recipe for cookies that are perfect for Santa. The children think they're getting extra credit by leaving these special cookies, which in truth, they're just getting rid of Aunt Gertrude's lousy cookies."

Pete laughs. "What do you do with them?"

"I'll take them back to the North Forest. The raccoons will eat pretty much anything. But let me tell you, I never fault the children at those locations. The parents have a pretty tough time of it getting off my Naughty List though, that's for sure."

They both laugh.

With each stop, Pete and Santa move quickly to drop off the magical presents for the children based on the kindness in their hearts. Pete is really enjoying this evening and is becoming more and more helpful in knowing what to look for when they enter each house. He even has learned that if there are no treats for the reindeer left out, he can look in the refrigerator and usually find some veggies and knows he can justify it by claiming they must have been busy and just forgot.

Pete is also blown away at how quickly Santa and the reindeer work. Santa explains to Pete that he has complete support from God and that if he ever gets behind, he has the power to stop time so he can catch up – but only on Christmas Eve. In some of the more populated areas where there are many children in a neighborhood, Santa can push a pause button on his sleigh that stops time so he can get to every home without changing his schedule.

Pete thinks this is very cool.

Santa also explains that he doesn't take all the toys with him in the sleigh; that would require a rather large sleigh and be way too heavy for his reindeer. He takes the notes from the children and when he gets to their home, the note turns into the gift according to the heart of the child.

Pete thinks this is double cool.

Pete, who has never ventured out much from his North Forest home, is certainly amazed at the variety of styles and shapes of the many countries they travel through. He notices many different animals than he's used to seeing in the North Forest, but Santa is an expert at explaining it all to him.

"God made many different animals for all the different environments. The animals down here love the hot, dry weather and are important for this area in keeping the environment balanced correctly. They would hate living in the North Forest area like you, but that's because they were built for this area, just like you were built for the northern forests."

"Do they have a big Christmas festival for you, too?"

Santa laughs, as do some of the reindeer. "Well if they do, they have to invite someone else. Me and the reindeer are more suited for the cold snow of the north. That's why we always make up a lot of time when we get to the southern hemisphere. We get Australia done in no time at all. We waste no time down here because we can't wait to get back to the colder climates."

It's a magical night for Pete helping Santa, and as they head into the final leg of their journey, Pete has a keen sense of appreciation for being given this night with Santa. He's learned so much about this world and has come to appreciate the delicate balance of nature that is so important to making this planet what it is.

There is also a bit of sadness that it is almost over. He's come to appreciate what Santa does for the children of the world and understands why he does it every year. It certainly is a fun way to celebrate Christmas – giving, not receiving. He hopes that the lessons he learned tonight will help him back in his world in the North Forest.

But mostly, he has learned why the North Forest Christmas Festival is so important. He saw first hand why Santa's reindeer are so special and he knows that he will be sure to pass along all he has learned on this evening to the younger generations of snowshoe rabbits.

As the sleigh heads back towards the North Forest, and there are no more gifts to be delivered, Pete and Santa sit back and relax in a more casual ride that takes in the final moments of a wonderful, magical night.

As they approach the North Forest landing spot, Pete looks down at all his neighbors and friends that will once again provide Santa and his reindeer a great celebration to end the night.

When they land to all the cheering animals of the North Forest, Santa releases the reindeer again and then takes his big bag of goodies over by the fire pit.

"It's been another great year for the children of the world. I want to thank my reindeer, Pete, and all of you for making this one year that we will all remember."

The animals cheer.

"And it looks like Pete did pretty well gathering up all these treats for you," says Santa, as he dumps out his bag full of carrots, vegetables, nuts and treats for all the animals to share.

As the party gets into high gear, Santa, Pete, and the committee members sit around the fire and relax and share stories. The dawn is slowly breaking, but Santa is in no hurry to head back to the North Pole.

"Hey, Pete, what was the craziest stop of the night?" asks Earl.

"Well, I suppose the one where I was in the kitchen and a little human walked in on me. We stared at each other for a moment, but then she asked me if I was the Easter Bunny!"

The animals start laughing.

"What did you tell her?" asks Harriet.

"Well I tried to pretend I couldn't hear her, but she took a few steps closer and bent down to get a closer look at me. So I leaned forward to look closer at her. Then I just said 'BOO.' That girl scattered and ran up the stairs, so I grabbed some celery and told Santa we needed to get out of there."

They all laugh, almost in tears.

"They may be at the top of the food chain, but those humans sure are confused a lot." says Sam.

Larry speaks up, "They are at the top of the food chain only because there is not an animal on this planet that wants to eat them. They taste terrible."

Everyone laughs again until Pete gets a bit of a confused look on his face.

"What's an Easter Bunny?" he asks

The animals look at one another, then at Pete, before Willie, who is practically out of control in laughter, blurts out, "It's the wrong holiday!"

Everyone breaks into uncontrollable laughter, including Santa, as the North Forest Christmas Festival wraps up another successful year.

3

Rosemary's Gift

Most people know the story about the three wise men who journeyed from afar to bring the baby Jesus gifts in Bethlehem, but only a few have heard the story about a little girl they met along the way.

After traveling for many weeks, the three wise men knew that they were getting close to where the baby would be found. They had been following a bright star they believed would lead them to this special baby. They were tired and wanted to find a place to rest for the evening before they made their final journey into Bethlehem.

They were far from any towns, so they thought they would have to put up their tents in the open desert, when one of them saw a small light shining in the distance. They went towards the light and found that it was a small cottage. Inside, they found a widow and her little daughter named Rosemary.

Rosemary and her mother lived a quiet life and were not used to people dropping in at their small home far removed from the rest of the world. Rosemary's father had died when she was a baby, so her mother was the only person she had known through her early years. Her mother was a very religious woman who spent every evening telling Rosemary all the many wonderful stories about God that she had learned when she was a child.

With no other children around to play with, Rosemary spent most of her days helping her mother with the daily chores of tending to their small number of goats and chickens, making cheese from the goat milk, and working the simple garden. Her free time was spent playing with her simple toy figures made of small sticks and thread. Being that she knew no other life, Rosemary was a happy child who seemed quite content with the world she was living in.

When the three wise men told them about their journey, Rosemary's mother was more than happy to take them in for the evening. She, too, had heard about a special baby being born in Bethlehem and was hopeful that this truly might be the Messiah that they were looking for.

As the wise men settled in for the evening, one of them seemed to hit it off with little Rosemary. His name was Saul and he was a very wealthy and powerful man. He loved children and seemed very comfortable spending his free time playing and talking with Rosemary. Not used to having visitors around to talk to, Rosemary, of course, was very anxious to find out all that Saul knew about life outside of her little cottage. She wanted to hear about the places that he had been and all the stories that he had to offer her. But, she especially wanted to hear more about this special baby they were looking for. Saul was more than happy to accommodate young Rosemary as he held her in his lap to tell her the story.

"We had very good information about this special baby that was to be born. A baby unlike any other baby. A baby so special that all the kings of all the lands would have no power over him. A baby with so much love for everyone. We learned that if we followed the bright shining star in the sky, we would find this baby, so we have been watching the sky as we travel, and the bright star has brought us this far. We are very excited, because we know that in just a few more hours, we will find this baby."

"But what will you do when you find this baby?" asked Rosemary.

"Oh my little one, we have brought some wonderful gifts to give the child," said the wise man with great enthusiasm.

"But why do you give him gifts?" asked Rosemary. Living alone, she did not have any experience in sharing gifts with others.

Saul smiles, "A man's wealth means nothing if he cannot share it with others. When someone touches your heart with love and kindness, it's good to give them something special to show how much they mean to you."

Rosemary was still confused. "But you don't know this baby. How can he be so special to you when you have never met him before?"

Saul holds her close and tries to explain.

"There are many things that we do not understand, but we still believe to be true. We have been watching the stars at night and listening to all they say. They tell us of great miracles and wonderful changes in the people who will meet this child. Yes, we have never met him, but we have listened to the stars enough to understand that this is a baby we will want to meet. We are excited about being one of the first ones to greet him. We are anxious to bring him gifts and let him know that we want to be his friend."

Rosemary thinks about what Saul has said, but still a bit confused, asks, "Can only kings and wealthy people go see him?"

Saul laughs out loud as he hugs her. "No, no, my child. That's what's so good about this baby. If he is the baby that we think he is, even the poorest of the poor will be able to see him. He has come to bring hope to all people, not just the wealthy."

At that, Rosemary seems to accept the idea as her mother interrupts them by telling her it is time to go to sleep. Reluctantly, Rosemary says good night to the three wise men and heads off to her bed in the other room.

The next morning found the three wise men up early and eager to get started on the final leg of their journey.

Rosemary was a bit subdued. She really enjoyed their company and wished that they could stay longer. Better yet, she wished that she could go with them so that she could also meet this special baby.

When Saul was ready to leave, Rosemary ran to him and gave him a big hug. Then she showed him one of her stick figures that she had made.

"This is one of the people that I play with. Do you think that the baby would like to have it as a gift from me?" she asked Saul.

Saul gave her a big hug. He knew that this was the first gift that she had ever given anyone. He also knew that the little figures made of sticks were very important to Rosemary and that giving one to the baby was a big sacrifice for her.

"I'm sure that this will be the greatest gift the baby receives," he said with a big smile. With a final goodbye, the three headed out in their search to find the baby.

******

Time went by and Rosemary became a grown woman. Her life however, remained pretty much the same. She and her mother lived a quiet life in their small cottage out of touch with the rest of the world. It had become a rough life for Rosemary, as her mother, who had become quite old, was unable to do many of the chores. Though they lived in isolation, they had heard many wonderful stories about a man named Jesus from those occasional travelers who would pass through.

As her mother's health became worse, Rosemary didn't know what to do. She felt that if she could get to this man named Jesus, he could help her mother get well again. So she decided to leave her mother while she was still healthy enough to be left alone, and try to find the man everyone had been speaking about.

She asked people she came to where she could find Jesus, and after a few days, finally caught up with the man they were calling "Master."

At first, she thought she would just stay close and see if this man was truly as good as everyone was saying. What she saw was a gentle man full of compassion and love reaching out to all those who were in need. A man who spoke with more hope, wisdom and compassion than she had ever heard before. She knew that with only a few words, he could make her mother well again.

The next day, she decided to approach Jesus as he went off by himself.

"Master," she said nervously, "I was hoping that you could say a few words for my mother who is at home very ill. We live too far away for you to go see her, but I thought if you just said a few words, she might be well again."

Jesus looks at her with his loving eyes and began to speak to her when he notices the little stick figure hanging around her neck. He seems a bit shaken by it and stops speaking.

"Woman, where did you get that?" he asks of the figure.

Rosemary looks down at the figure and then to Jesus, a bit confused.

"When I was a little girl, I would make these figures to play with. I wear one to remind me of a man I met back then."

Jesus smiles at her as if to know something that she didn't.

"Do you remember who this man was?" he asks her.

"No, Master. He was with two other men. They stopped at my mother's home to rest. They were looking for a very special baby that was born in the area," she replies.

Jesus seems more certain as he continues, "Did they ever find this special baby?"

Rosemary looks at Jesus somewhat confused. She wanted him to help her mother, but he seemed more interested in her old stick figure.

"We never saw them again after they left." she said, "But they were very wise men and I'm sure they found the baby."

Jesus smiles as he reaches for his chest and pulls out a small stick figure from around his neck that looks very much like hers. Rosemary looks at the figure in disbelief. She knows that it is the figure that she had given to Saul those many years before.

Jesus takes Rosemary's hand, as she seems very frightened.

"My mother told me of the three men who had come to greet me when I was born. She told me how they brought wonderful gifts of wealth, but that one of them had brought this small figure from a little girl who lived alone with her mother far away. My mother told me to remember this gift as I grow old, as it was the greatest gift of them all because it came from the heart of a child. So I wear it close to my heart to always remind me that love shared should never be measured by wealth."

Rosemary falls to her knees with tears of disbelief. Jesus kneels beside her and puts his arm around her.

"You are that special little girl, aren't you?"

Rosemary nods as Jesus hugs her, then holds her head and looks into her eyes.

"Go and be with your mother, for soon she must go to my Father's house. When she does, I want you to make more of these and go out and give them to every child you meet. Tell them that the greatest gift is love that is shared by a child. Know that my Father will be with you always and will bless every child who holds this figure close to their heart as I do."

Jesus helps Rosemary to her feet and gives her a big hug, then sends her on her way.

It wasn't long after she returned that her mother passed away quietly in her sleep. It was then that Rosemary followed what Jesus had told her. She made many of her little stick figures and left her home to find children to give them to.

And so it was.

Rosemary spent the rest of her life going from village to village talking to the children about Jesus and how important it was for them to learn how to share with one another.

Rosemary never saw Jesus again. As she grew old, she continued to go to villages to talk to children. As she told them about the birth of Jesus, she would say that of all the fine gifts he had received, it was the simple little stick figure, given to him by that poor little girl, that he wore close to his heart even when he was a grown man.

4

Rhianna's Road Home

Rhianna Williams was an eight year old girl in 1932. Her parents, Ezra and Jaylen Williams were sharecroppers in southern Alabama. They did okay as sharecroppers go, but lived in poverty for the most part.

When the great depression hit, Ezra and Jaylen lost everything. Jaylen decided to take his family and head north in hopes of getting a factory job.

As they were traveling by foot through Tennessee, Jaylen got into a dispute with some other migrants that resulted in an ambush that killed the father, leaving Ezra and Rhianna scrambling to escape for safety.

For the next several weeks, Ezra and Rhianna continued their migration north. Ezra was hopeful of finding work in Detroit which was the hotbed of the new automobile manufacturing industry. She was a strong, hard working and determined woman who felt she could do any type of work available. She knew that she worked just as hard on their land as her husband, and was not afraid to take on any type of work.

It was a hard life for Rhianna. Too young to do much but follow her mother, Ezra spent most of her time sharing stories with her daughter about the world they lived in. She constantly reminded Rhianna that being black and being a female made for a challenging life ahead. She taught her that the key to survival was for her to be strong, be confident and never let anyone tell her she can't do something.

Rhianna loved her mother and felt very secure with her. It was a tough road, but Rhianna felt if anyone could overcome this world's hardships, it was her mother. She taught her many lessons about survival and how to avoid trouble. She taught her that God's commandments say 'do not steal' as it should, but she also taught her that when you are so poor and starving, God will understand if you take food to survive.

"God judges us by our hearts, Rhianna, so it's important to ask forgiveness before you take and only take enough to sustain you for a little bit. And never, ever take from someone else who is struggling" she would tell Rhianna many times.

It was a tough life, but all things considered, Rhianna was a happy girl. Her mother would tell her all the bible stories she could as they huddled together in the cold nights to rest. Her mother taught her all the good lessons about God and that his love would always be enough.

Rhianna had no idea what month it was, she only knew what season it was. She didn't know what day it was, she only knew it was morning, afternoon or night. And she never knew where they were, except for that one occasion when they passed a sign saying, 'Welcome to Indiana.'

Ezra showed Rhianna how to get a chicken from a farm, or vegetables without getting caught. She reminded her daughter to be quick and only take enough for now. She also taught her how to start a fire and where the best location to cook her food was so she didn't get caught.

"If you come to an apple tree, God will understand you taking one. If you take two or more, then you are stealing and God will hold you responsible for taking from others."

As they were getting close to Detroit, Rhianna could sense that her mother was excited about starting over. She knew her mother was anxious to find a home for them, and how she longed for the day when the two of them could relax, Rhianna could go to school and they both could finally enjoy a better life.

It was clearly winter time as the snow, wind and cold temperatures were extremely difficult for the two females coming from the Gulf of Alabama with very little to keep them warm.

Ezra was very good about knowing where to look for help. She was able to get them coats, blankets and good walking boots in Fort Wayne, Indiana. She also was able to get some food and temporary shelter from a charity in Toledo before making their last leg of their journey into Detroit.

When they reached a sign that read, 'Detroit City Limits', the two decided to find a place to spend the night and get a fresh start in the morning. Ezra was an expert at scouting out a good site and found a nice shelter under a street bridge that would protect them from the cold.

They didn't have much to eat, but Ezra didn't want to make a fire anyway, as to draw any attention to them. So they ate what they had and bundled up as much as they could and snuggled nice and cozy to keep each other warm.

Rhianna had been traveling for so long, she was very much accustomed to sleeping out on the streets. After a day of walking and very little food, she had no trouble falling asleep after the sun went down.

When she woke up the next morning, she found her mother laying still. She shook her to wake her up, but her body was cold and stiff. She knew instinctively that her mother wasn't going to wake up.

Rhianna didn't know what to do. She spent the better part of the morning sitting next to her lifeless mother crying and looking around. She was afraid to go for help as she thought that the people would take her away and put her in some horrible situation. Her mother had warned her to be careful who you ask for help, because often times, people would only want to take advantage of you instead of helping you.

She was too young to work, she thought, so if she was going to be on her own now, she thought she would head west and away from the cold.

She built a small fire as her mother taught her, thinking that the smoke would draw attention and someone would find her mother and know what to do. Then she gathered what she could and headed down the road leading west.

******

For the next several weeks, Rhianna created a routine of survival as she headed west. She first went south to get away from the bitter cold. It was Spring when she reached Nashville, Tennessee and started heading west from there.

She got to the Mississippi River and decided to spend a little time by the river. There were plenty of farms south of Memphis and her father had taught her how to fish, so she knew she would have enough to keep her going She decided to rest a bit before continuing on.

She found a nice place to set up camp according to what she had learned from her mother. She could see enough around her so as not to be surprised by anyone approaching, and yet there was a small crevice where she could build a small fire to cook the chicken she caught without sending too much awareness of her location. Being that Spring was quickly giving way to Summer, she only needed the fire to cook her chicken and once it was done, she quickly put out the fire.

She stayed there only a couple of days, but while she was there, she noticed in late afternoon, there was always a train going by heading west in a very slow speed in order to go over the Mississippi river ahead. She made plans to be ready the next day to get on the train and was hopeful she could hide on it for as long as she could heading west.

The next day, Rhianna had a refreshing swim in the river before gathering all she had and making her way towards the railroad tracks. When the train approached, Rhianna was careful to study the train and try to decide the best car to jump on.

When she chose her car, she jumped and grabbed the handles of the ladder and started to climb, always looking in both directions to make sure she wasn't being watched. When she got to the top, she looked over the edge – it was a box car with no roof – and saw that it was full of pigs. Not the best choice, she thought. But when she looked to the car behind it, she saw three men, and one noticed her, so she quickly decided the pigs were a perfect choice and climbed down to meet her new friends.

The pigs for the most part ignored Rhianna, which made her relax. She would pet them and speak softly to them as she constantly looked to see if those men were going to come after her. They never did, and she learned later that she was not the only one catching a ride with the trains during this troubling time. There were many people hopping on and off trains and there seemed to be an understanding that nobody bothered anyone else as nobody wanted to draw any attention. Get on, get off. Leave others alone and they will leave you alone. That was the code of the migrant train hoppers.

For the next several days, Rhianna got into a routine of getting on and off the trains. She always found a place to be left alone, and was happy when she was able to get into a car full of livestock. She loved animals and they seemed to know it, as she never had a bad experience when she stayed with any animals.
She'd always get off the train at sunset because she didn't feel safe sleeping on a moving train. As dusk came, she would always watch the landscape in search of a good place to stay for the night.

It was hot and she was amazed at how big the country was. Oklahoma seemed like a big dirt lot that never stopped and she was concerned that she might not be able to find a good place to get off. She needed a place with farms and landscape that suggested she would be able to eat and sleep without disturbance. But every day, she found a small town or big spread out farm.

She was able to avoid any contact with people because her mother had taught her so well how to survive on her own. She didn't need anybody, she felt.

In Oklahoma City, there was a man that she thought looked creepy. He kept looking at her and every time she turned around, he was nearby. She ran off and lost him, but even though she found a very good, quiet place to hide, she didn't sleep well that night.

The next day, after sleeping with one eye open looking out for the creepy man, Rhianna was pleasantly surprised when she jumped on a train and found herself in a car full of Lambs.

They were a bit noisy, but very friendly. She really enjoyed talking to them and hugging each one. In the afternoon, a young man jumped into the car which startled Rhianna. The Lambs gathered tightly around Rhianna and made it clear that the man was not welcome in this car. He got the message and moved on to another car.

As the afternoon quickly moved towards evening, Rhianna decided she would spend the night with the Lambs. She felt a strong connection to them and mostly, she felt safe with them.

As she slowly drifted off to sleep, she agreed with her heart that this was the very best day she has had in a long, long time.

With the dawn slowly pushing aside the darkness, Rhianna started to surface and found herself surrounded by lambs staring at her. She felt that this was probably the best way any person could wake up. She greeted her friends and spent some time hugging each lamb and talking with them.

She couldn't imagine any better way to start the day.

She looked over the car siding and had no idea where they were. At least the landscape was getting more interesting with trees and some buildings scattered about.

She noticed that the train was slowing down as it approached a real town with paved roads and a lot more people than she had seen in the past few days.

She thought it would be best for her to get off here, even though she really wanted to stay with her lambs as long as she could. But she couldn't take the risk, so she said goodbye to each lamb and carefully got off the train and found a good place to hide out until she was comfortable to get out and explore.

She felt that the place she found was such a good place for her according to what her mother had taught her, she decided to hide the few items she had and go into the town and spend some time walking about.

She found out that she was in a place named Albuquerque. It wasn't as big as Detroit or Memphis, but it was a nice place and the people seemed very friendly. She also found out that it was early October, which explained why it was cooler than when she was on the train leaving Memphis. She had survived the Summer which made her feel good about herself, as she looked ahead to Fall weather, which was okay by her – even though she wasn't sure what Fall and Winter were like in a place like Albuquerque. She did know that she had traveled quite a bit south, so she was thinking that winter in these parts wouldn't be anything like it was in Detroit.

She enjoyed her time in Albuquerque, but she felt the pull to move on. She wasn't sure where so was going and didn't really have much of a plan, which was starting to bother her. But she did think that wherever she ended up had to have water. Like a river in Memphis, or a gulf like in Alabama. She just knew if she was near a body of water, she would be able to survive.

So she decided to move on by foot. Even though she loved the lambs and pigs, traveling by train was a bit more difficult because you had no control. You could only go where the train took you. She thought it was good that she got to take a train through most of the hot summer, but with the temperatures more comfortable, she felt staying on foot gave her more options for her survival.

******

As days became weeks, Rhianna wasn't making as much progress as she would have thought. Of course, she understood that when she left Detroit, she was scared , it was cold, and she had seen her mother frozen to death. Obviously she moved much quicker then. But she also knew that she was slowing down because it was starting to sink in that she had no idea where she was going or what she was going to do.

She was still only nine years old now, and too young to work. And even though her mother did such a good job in teaching her how to survive, she knew in her heart that surviving alone out on the street was not a long term plan. But she had no family that she knew of. She didn't know anyone whom she could trust to help her out.

The further west she went, the slower her pace became. She knew she was approaching the time when she would have to stop running and decide what she was going to do.

As Rhianna found herself in the middle of nowhere again, she started looking around for railroad tracks. There didn't seem to be lights in any direction, nor could she see any suitable places for her to rest. It was just a big, flat desert. Thankfully, it seemed to be winter as the nights were pretty cool, but the days were not hot. But she had been a couple of days without food. She was hungry, tired and had become more uncertain of what her future would bring.

As she was sitting by the side of a road that lead nowhere, Rhianna heard a noise in the distance. It seemed to be coming from the sky. As it drew closer, it appeared to be bells.

Suddenly, she could see what appeared to be Santa in a sleigh being pulled by reindeer. She had heard the story about Santa Clause but had no reason to believe it was true. She had been poor all her life and always believed holidays like Christmas was for everyone but the poor.

Santa made a perfect, soft landing about ten feet from Rhianna.

"Young lady, what are you doing out here in the desert by yourself?" he asks.

"Are you Santa Clause?"

Santa smiles at her, "You better hope so, because if I'm not Santa, you are in a lot more trouble than you think."

"Is it Christmas time?" Rhianna asks, a bit confused.

"Indeed… the busiest night of the year for me, Christmas Eve."

"What are you doing out here then?"

Santa chuckles, "Ah young lady, that was my question for you, remember? Your guardian angel told me where to find you."

"I have a guardian angel?" Rhianna says a bit confused.

"Of course. Where do you think those lambs came from?"

"I don't understand."

"You must be hungry Rhianna. Come over here." Santa opens a bag, "I have plenty of carrots and apples, if you'd like."

Rhianna walks over, very excited at getting something to eat, as Santa continues.

"You can check all the records you want and you will not find any train that night, on that track, that had any lambs on it. That was your guardian angel's doing. She knew you had a tough night before, getting away from that creepy man and she also knew that there was danger in Amarillo, so she filled the car with lambs to comfort you and keep you on the train until Albuquerque."

Rhianna takes a break from all her chewing, "Really?"

"Really." says Santa as he looks at her compassionately, "You've had a rough go of it, haven't you Rhianna? You saw your daddy die, then your mother. You've been wandering all over for the better part of the year all by yourself." Santa looks at this young girl chewing away at her apples and carrots that she can't devour fast enough, with her eyes moist with the pain of what Santa is saying, "But you know what, Rhianna. You have been through all that and not once have you done anything to fall off my Nice list."

Rhianna stops chewing and raises her eyebrows a bit taken back.

"Would you like to ride with me tonight and help me deliver all these presents?"

Rhianna mumbles through her mouth packed with food, "Really?"

"Really. I'd love to have the company and I know you're a good helper, and I could use some help. And maybe when we get done passing out all these gifts, I can help you figure out where this road for you leads to."

Rhianna doesn't know what to say, as Santa scoots over, "There's plenty of room for you Rhianna. Come on, let's have some fun."

Rhianna climbs into the sleigh astonished at the thought that not only does Santa Clause exist, but she gets to go with him on Christmas Eve and help pass out the gifts for all the children of the world.

This, she thought, was going to be a very good night.

******

For the first time in a very long time, Rhianna found herself laughing and giggling so much her sides hurt. Riding with Santa has got to be the best thing anyone can do. He tells a lot of funny stories and he's always laughing. She thinks he must be the most fun adult ever.

Rhianna loves going with Santa into a home. He instructs her to get whatever the kids leave out for him and his reindeer, and what to do if she sees any kids sneaking around.

Santa is very careful to protect Rhianna. He explains that people in the house would be able to see her, but not Santa, so he tells her, much like her mother warned her, that being a young black girl standing in the living room taking cookies and carrots wasn't an ideal situation to have to deal with. So he would go ahead of her every time to make sure everyone was sound asleep.

"How come you don't bring present to the poor children like me?" Rhianna asks Santa.

"Because God doesn't want to make the parents feel any worse than they already do. So many adults are struggling right now. So many out of work. If I dropped off a nice toy for their children, when they are unable to do anything for them, it would not have a positive outcome. God makes it very clear to me that I am not allowed to give children more than their parents do. I have complete access to all the guardian angels, and we are always looking for ways to give hope to those families, not presents." He pauses and looks at Rhianna, "I would have loved to bring you toys every year, Rhianna, but your parents were really good parents, doing everything they could for you. How do you think they would feel if you woke up every Christmas with a new toy from Santa, but nothing from your parents? It confuses the children and makes the parents feel bad. That is unacceptable in God's eyes."

Rhianna thinks about it, "I guess it makes sense. I think you make a pretty good Santa." she says with confidence.

Santa laughs, "Well I think you make a great Rhianna!"

They both laugh as they land for their next drop off.

It was like this all night long. Santa would be busy dropping off presents and Rhianna would stay behind, for the most part, and visit with the reindeer and give them as much apples and carrots as they wanted. Then off they flew to the next neighborhood, telling stories and laughing a lot.

"How did you get to be a Santa?" Rhianna asks Santa.

"I went to school. There's a lot you have to learn to become a Santa, ya know."

"Where's the school at?" Rhianna says in a very curios state.

Santa laughs, "Oh Rhianna, I'm just messin' with you. There is no school. It's all about the spirit of Christmas and how people see it. That's why you and I don't have to go all over the world tonight. The spirit of Christmas is celebrated in so many different ways all over the world. The thing to remember is that it's a spirit – you can't see a spirit. Here in America, they give the spirit a rather large man in a red suit flying around with reindeer giving gifts to children. The spirit of Christmas is many other forms and shapes and traditions in other countries."

Rhianna thinks about it, "But where do the gifts come from?"

Santa looks at Rhianna and smiles, "Your heart. Everybody has a spirit and the spirit is in your heart. So when I – being a spirit as well-go into a child's home, I connect to their spirit and know just what to leave them"

"Wow. I guess it makes sense." says Rhianna

******

For the rest of the night, Santa and Rhianna pass out the presents to all the boys and girls. They have a lot of fun, Santa telling Rhianna so many great stories that inspire her to make her life the best she can make it. Every time they stop at a home, Santa takes a moment to tell her about the child inside and what makes them so special.

Rhianna is eating up every story.

But eventually, they run out of gifts and Rhianna once again feels the reality that it's time for her to get back to her life, whatever it may be.

"One more stop." announces Santa.

"But we have no more presents." states a confused little girl.

"Don't underestimate the magic of Santa Clause, young lady." says Santa as he looks to her with a smile and winks.

As they land on a rooftop, Santa looks to Rhianna.

"I want you to come with me on this one, okay?"

"Okay." she says as they appear in the living room.

It's a nice home. Not rich, but not poor either. Comfortable, she would say.

Santa whispers to Rhianna, "Be very quiet and stay here."

She shakes her head as Santa walks over to the door to the kitchen that has a light on. He looks back at Rhianna, smiles and winks. Then turns his attention to the kitchen again.

"Ida Williams?"

Rhianna shoots her hands up to her ears as a woman lets out a scream to wake up the dead.

"Who are you and what do you want?" says the frightened woman who now holds a frying pan with her hands ready to wallop him.

"I'm Santa Clause, and I brought you a present … it's Christmas Eve after all."

"Santa gives presents to children. I don't have any children here." she says as she studies this man who certainly fits the description of a Santa, but she thinks she should keep the frying pan held high, just in case.

Santa points to the oven that has a steaming pitcher and three mugs next to it, "Why don't you grab the hot chocolate and mugs and come out here." He says as he turns and goes stands by Rhianna, who's eyebrows are nearly on top of her head and her eyes are big as silver dollars.

"I didn't make any hot chocolate." says Ida as she smells the hot chocolate, then looks at the doorway.

Santa and Rhianna can hear Ida putting the frying pan back in the sink, then the clanging of the metal mugs.

Ida slowly sticks her head out from the kitchen and sees Santa standing by Rhianna, who has a smile dripping of confusion.

Ida slowly steps out from the kitchen and studies Rhianna. She looks terrible, of course. Her jacket is worn as are the boots that her mother got her in Fort Wayne. She's dirty, skinny and Ida doesn't think she's ever seen anything so precious.

"Who is this?" She asks Santa.

"This is your great niece, I believe. Rhianna is her name."

Rhianna looks at Santa confused. This is the first she's ever heard she had any relatives.

Ida looks at Rhianna as she also had no idea she had any relatives.

"My great niece?"

"Yes. Your brother had a son named Jaylen right?"

Ida thinks for a moment, "I believe so."

"Well there you go. This is his daughter, which I believe makes her your great niece."

Ida puts the chocolate and mugs down and sits in her chair. "Where did you find her?"

"Her guardian angel told me where she was. I found her on the edge of the desert in Arizona. She's had a pretty rough year, so I let her come and help me drop off all the presents to the children, and thought I'd make this the last stop." he says with a smile.

"And her parents?"

"Well that's the rough year I was talking about. Jaylen and Ezra – his wife- were sharecroppers in southern Alabama, but when the market crashed, they lost everything. They wanted to go north and try to get a job in the automobile factories. Jaylen died in Tennessee, so Ezra and Rhianna continued on until Ezra died of the cold under a bridge in Detroit. Rhianna took everything her mother taught her about surviving and headed west. Her journey took her to the Mississippi River. She hopped trains from Memphis in to Albuquerque. Then she walked from there until I found her in the desert."

Ida has tears in her eyes as she looks at Rhianna, "Is this all true, girl?"

"Yes mam." says Rhianna.

"I brought her to you Ida because I know your heart and it has always been a sore spot with you that you were unable to have children." Ida looks at Santa as the tears are unwilling to stay in her eyes, "Now I'd be happy to take Rhianna with me to the North Pole. She's a great worker, and I could use the help. But she doesn't have any family but you. And you don't have any family but her. You both have great hearts, so I think you'd both do well to have each other."

Ida looks at Rhianna. "Come here, child" she says as Rhianna steps over to Ida, who puts her hands on Rhianna's shoulders.

"I would be honored to be your auntie and take care of you if you want."

Rhianna smiles and shakes her head in agreement.

They embrace in a very wet hug as the tears flow from both.

When they finally gain a little composure, they look at Santa who smiles, "I'll take that as a yes?"

Ida looks to Santa, "How can I ever thank you"

Santa smiles "Well I promise you this Ida. I will be making this my final stop every Christmas to check on my girl Rhianna. It better be a good report, or I'll put you on the naughty list."

Ida laughs, "That ain't never gonna happen Santa."

Santa reaches into his bag and pulls out one more present and looks at Rhianna.

"This is for you young lady. For helping me out tonight."

She opens it up and finds a brand new outfit and beautiful new pair of shoes. She runs over to give Santa a big hug, "Thank you Santa."

Santa looks at her, "I want you to throw these raggedie old clothes out, but I want you to save those boots. I want you to keep those boots close by and every time you start to feel like you can't do something, I want you to look at those boots, you promise?"

Rhianna nods her head.

"Well I better be off. The reindeer are probably worried that I got stuck in the chimney"

They all laugh as Ida says, "I don't have no fireplace, Santa."

"They're reindeer, Ida …. flying reindeer …. I'll be back next year to visit you both." he looks at Rhianna, "And remember, if this lady turns out not to be much fun, you always have a job waiting for you at the North Pole."

"Okay Santa. Thanks for everything." says the young girl who thinks this might have been the best Christmas EVER!

And so it was. Every Christmas Eve, Santa would make the rounds passing out the gifts to all the children. And when they were gone, he always headed for Gulfport, Mississippi, where he sat with Ida and Rhianna with hot chocolate and wonderful conversations.

And before he headed back to the North Pole, he always made sure Rhianna had those boots out to remind her of her journey those many years ago.

5

The Legend of Amity's Farm

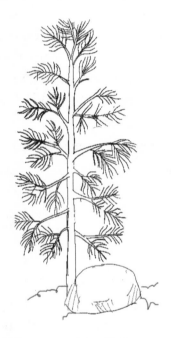

Bob Jacobs owns a small farm near North Conway, New Hampshire, just before Lower Bartlett area. Not a big farm, maybe twenty acres or so. He grows Pumpkins for the Fall, almost 2 acres of Christmas trees he sells after Thanksgiving, a few milk cows, pigs, goats and poultry and has a variety of vegetables and berries in the Spring that keeps his roadside stand busy with customers. He also has a grove of apple trees that he uses to make his very special apple cider every year.

He never advertises his apple cider because he knows the locals will buy him out as soon as he lets them know it's ready.

Bob lives alone on the farm. He's lived there all his life. He loves working on his various growing projects and has never had any desire to do anything else but wake up each day and work on his farm. He puts a lot of love into his farm, that's for sure.

Jacobs Farm has a reputation in the area of not only having great produce, but there was something about Bob's farm that was different. Nobody around town knew exactly what it was, but they all knew there was something special going on at the farm.

Every Christmas, something happened to a family that locals could only describe as a miracle. One family would have a magical Christmas that no one could explain, and the only common thread each year was that they bought their Christmas tree from Bob's lot.

Bob didn't have a lot of Christmas trees, so you could only get a tree by appointment each year. Bob always designated the trees that were available to cut down and when he sold them, he was done for the season.

Everyone wanted to be on Bob's Christmas tree list. How the magic happened was nothing more than speculation as even Bob had no answer for the magic that happened each year – at least he wasn't saying anything about it. But they were the best trees you could find. Full branches, perfectly shaped and with just the right amount of fragrance.

But every year, it happened.

It was always a family in need at the time, which wasn't surprising as Bob was always helping out those who were less fortunate. Every week he took produce to some of the older folks who couldn't get out very often. Teachers would often give him names of children whose families were going through a rough spot that he would get produce for.

The Jacobs farm had been in the same family going back to colonial times. The names changed often, as the family was populated heavily with females in every generation which made genealogy searches a challenge. Bob's mother, Elizabeth Jacob, was the one who inherited the farm when her mother, Harriet Smith died. Harriet inherited the farm from her mother, Charity Wilson, when she died….. Well you can see the problem of having so many daughters in your family tree. But if you follow the females, it will always lead you directly to the Pitman family, who came from Europe to settle in the new country.

It's a rich history of females with generous hearts that has made Jacobs Farm one of the most beloved in the region.

As Bob got older, he began to feel concern about the family farm. He was the youngest boy of Elizabeth and William Jacobs. His older brother Calvin went away to college and worked in Boston. Cal was married and they had three children, a daughter named Gayle, and two sons, Walter and Harry. They all lived in the Boston area, but Gayle was the only one who loved to visit her uncle and spend some time on the farm.

Bob never married, because he never fell in love. He loved working the farm and though he had many female friends growing up, he never thought about doing anything but working the farm. His dad died when he was a teen, so he quit school to help his mom on the farm. She died when he was in his twenties, and he has been working the farm on his own ever since. He got along fine with Calvin, but Cal seemed to really embrace the city life and had no interest in the farm life that his younger brother had. Being almost ten years separating the two brothers, there were no conflicts between them as they both simply went in different directions in life.

He was a generous man who carried on the many family traditions. Living alone, he didn't need much and was always happy to help others. The farm had three small cabins on the property that were used for the family and workers when the farm was much larger. Bob turned them into rentals that would bring in a little money to help with the few expenditures around the farm. He had no contracts or rules for his cabins as he would agree to a price based on how long they planned to be there.

******

I met Bob when I stayed at one of his cabins. I had just published my first novel, which was getting great reviews and I needed a quiet place to work on my next book. My publisher knew Cal from his college days and he told me to contact his brother for the cabin. It turned out to be perfect for me, too. Bob said I could stay as long as I wanted and he charged me well below market value – not so much because my publisher was a friend of his brother, but because he knew what he needed to charge to cover his expenses and he didn't want any more than that.

It was the perfect set up for a writer like me. I never start writing until after lunch as I love my mornings free. Of course, I could find Bob out working every morning and was always happy to visit with him and help out when I could. Being a city boy, I knew nothing about running a farm, and being a journalist major, I always had questions for Bob. He seemed to enjoy the company and was an excellent teacher in explaining to me the various chores of running a farm.

It was a good routine for me, as my writing always benefitted from my active mornings of helping Bob around the farm. Bob never asked for help, and in fact would always joke that if I did too much, he'd have to pay me instead of charge me for the cabin. But I loved the exercise – much better than jogging as was my normal morning routine back in the city – and learning about the farming world was a treat for me, so I didn't mind.

I got pretty good with some chores, and pretty awful with others. Bob showed me how to work the tractor, which I became pretty proficient with, although with such a small farm with a lot of space taken by apple orchards and Christmas trees, a tractor wasn't the work horse you would think. Mostly just getting around the farm and providing a little muscle when needed, like removing the tree trunks from the Christmas tree lot after the holidays and making room for the new trees Bob always had in a small green house.

I made Bob laugh a lot when I tried my hand at milking the cows. He only had four dairy cows, as well as a handful of goats, but it was enough to keep a good supply of milk and cheeses for the area. This was one city boy that would not have much dairy products if it was dependent on my skills for milking the cows, that's for sure. To my credit, I kept trying, but I think it was more because of the entertainment value for Bob. He was always so tickled at my lack of abilities under the cows. He'd get a good laugh then quickly relieve me before his cows turned against me, which I truly appreciated.

With every day, I was learning new skills in the farming world. Not enough to make me want to quit my writing, but enough to make me appreciate the work farmers do to provide food for us.

I also learned a lot from Bob that I knew would not be the norm on any other farm.

He built his own chipper machine that he used for the Christmas tree trunks as well as all the other remains from his vegetables each season. Everything was recycled and Bob had no chemicals anywhere on his farm. It was all natural and done the way it was suppose to be done from generation to generation. Bob was extremely proud that his farm had remained in the family since the first settlers in the area.

I was always fascinated at the history of Bobs family and how every generation would pass along the secret formulas, care and traditions that made the farm such a special part of the community. Bob was careful not to give me too much information when I asked him questions, but it was enough for me to know that there was a lot more to the history than he gave me. I could see it in his eyes when he'd stop, smile and tell me he'd better leave it there or the spirits may come back to haunt him.

Every day there would be plenty of chores, even with winter still hanging on. The livestock, of course, always needed tending to as well as the orchards of trees. Bob would spend hours pruning every tree on the farm.

Sometimes, I would hear Bob talking to himself when he was working the Christmas trees. I was never close enough to hear what he was saying, but it didn't really bother me much. I figured the guy has lived alone for all these years, and if he had each Christmas tree named, I wouldn't be surprised.

He was very meticulous when he was working in the apple orchard. Every tree was maintained at a specific height and every branch had a specific length with a specific number of offshoot branches per branch to ensure just the right amount of quality apples. I later learned that when the fruit blossoms sprouted, Bob would go branch by branch to remove many of the blossoms leaving an exact number of apples per branch. He used the removed blossoms to mix into a mulch specifically made for the apple trees.

Nothing was wasted on Bob's farm. Every task was purposeful and well worth the effort and time spent, as far as Bob was concerned.

There was a reason why his farm had the best reputation in the area, and I was quickly seeing first hand the reason it did.

******

One morning in early Spring, I went outside to find Bob. It was a busy time at the farm with a sense of urgency to get the ground ready for the seeds that would create this years crops.

I didn't see Bob out and about as I normally did, and when I looked up at the main house, I saw an ambulance, so I bolted to see what was going on.

When I got inside, I found Bob being placed on a stretcher.

"Bob, what happened? Are you okay?" I said.

"I'm sure I'll live. Just fell off the stool and took a pretty good hit. Probably just broke a rib or two."

I looked at the EMTs and they both smiled as one of them spoke.

"He took a bad spill. Was knocked unconscious. Apparently, it happened last night and he only called this morning because he couldn't get his shirt on."

"Bob, why didn't you call me?"

"Oh it wasn't that much. Probably just a rib or two and there's nothing the hospital can do for a broken rib. But when I tried to get up, my head was all spinning and acting funny, so I thought I'd better get these folks out here."

"We'll be taking him up to Memorial Hospital to check him out. I could have the doctor call you with any information." says the EMT

I get one of my business cards and hand it to him. "This is my cell# and I'll have it with me at all times. Thank you."

" Bob, what do you want me to do while you're gone?" I ask Bob.

"Don't milk the cows," he says with a chuckle that creates a cough that is obviously painful, "Just take the tractor and turn the soil where we are going to plant our vegetables. Make some nice straight rows. I'll probably be back in a couple hours."

I look at the EMTs who have a 'not-so-sure' expression that I understand.

For the better part of the morning, I was turning the soil with the tractor as Bob asked, waiting for a call from the hospital.

It finally came in the early afternoon.

Bob did have three broken ribs and a broken collar bone as well as a pretty good concussion. They wanted to keep him for the night for observation, but should be able to come home tomorrow.

"Do I need to come pick him up?"

"No. One of the EMTs here lives close to Bob and buys produce and cheese all the time. He volunteered to take him home and help out."

So at that, I settled into a routine of turning the soil and preparing the rest of the day without Bob.

I went up to his house to make sure everything was okay. I wasn't sure if I should lock all the doors. Being a city boy, I always lock up everything, but I've noticed here at Bob's farm, he leaves everything unlocked. He even leaves the key to the tractor in the ignition. And since I didn't know where the keys to the doors were kept anyway and didn't want to go through his drawers looking for them, I figured I'd lock the front door, but leave the side door in the kitchen unlocked in case I needed to get in.

That evening found me staring at a blank screen on my computer. My novel would have to take the night off as I found myself jumping at every noise I heard outside and was constantly getting up to look out the window to make sure everything was okay.

For a city boy that was use to sirens and noises all around my condo building, I was a complete basket case in the peaceful calm of this twenty acre farm this evening. It was clear that a good night's sleep was not happening tonight.

The next morning, I got a call from the EMT – Rick was his name – to tell me he would be bringing Bob home around noon. He said that it would be extremely difficult to keep Bob from working, but necessary to let his broken bones heal. He assured me that he had a lot of friends in the area and was already lining up time slots for people to spend at the farm watching Bob and working the fields, so I shouldn't worry about anything.

No kidding. I knew from the look on the EMTs faces yesterday that Bob was going to need some time to heal. I also knew that it was becoming a very busy time of year and Bob was not a person who was going to sit back and let his bones heal. It was a nice comfort to hear Rick tell me about the locals signing up to help out. After all, I was a city boy renting a cabin to write a novel. Helping Bob every morning was fun, but definitely not part of the deal for me being there.

I decided to start my morning giving the milking chore another try. I was determined to show the cows that I was a good guy and they could donate as much milk as they wanted with me under them.

I've always believed the notion that animals are all very good at picking up the vibes of humans, so I thought it would be best to take my time and just be around them for a bit before I start yanking on their bellies. I think it paid off, too. After a little time of hanging with them and brushing them, I asked if any of them wanted to get rid of some milk, and one of them started heading for the barn right away.

Of course, they hadn't been milked in a bit, so I'm guessing they weren't being so kind to me as they were just anxious to get rid of their milk. But I'll take victories any way they come.

I tried to be very gentle and take my time, but was pleasantly surprised when I found just the right method that opened up the milk flow and before long, I was gathering a lot of milk. I was glad that I paid so much attention to Bob and knew where to put the milk I was gathering, and hoped that Bob would be able to instruct me further when he got home.

It was a great way to start my day and I was excited that I would be able to let Bob know that the cows and I were finally getting along. I was certain that the cows were happy too.

With the cows back in their field and well relieved, I got the tractor out and went back to working the field to prepare for the crops.

It was close to noon when I saw a car pulling into the driveway that lead to the main house. That had to be Rick, so I maneuvered the tractor towards the main house to greet them.

"Welcome home, Bob! How are you feeling?" I say as I approach the car.

As Rick helps Bob out of the car, I can tell that he is pretty sore and slow.

"Well they didn't measure me for a casket, so I'm guessing I'll be around a bit longer." says Bob as he winces out of his seat. Rick hands him the cane that will likely be his support for a bit.

As Rick and I help Bob into the house and get him settled into his recliner, the three of us go over the plan moving forward.

I am blown away at how many people Rick already has signed up to help Bob out on the farm. He has several women booked to come over and cook and make sure he obeys the doctors orders, and several local men and women volunteering to come over and help get the crops in.

"Good grief, you seemed to get everyone booked in just one day. That's amazing." I say to Rick, who laughs.

"Are you kidding, they're all volunteering because they're hoping his medication gets him talking and telling us his secrets for growing his crops. Heck, I had three women sign up with a clear message that they plan to find out the recipe for that apple cider alone."

While Rick and I share a laugh, Bob makes it clear that this will never happen.

"I'll be in that casket long before anyone has that recipe, I promise you that."

After going over the schedule once more, I'm thinking I need to go back and wrap up my chores before I get to my writing.

"Oh, and Bob, you'll be happy to know that your cows and I had a nice visit this morning and they agreed to give me about five gallons of milk. I put it where I've seen you put it before, but I'm not sure what to do next."

"Hell, they weren't being nice to you, they were probably ready to burst." says Bob with a laugh as he looks to Rick, "I'll make a farmer out of this city boy yet."

Rick turns to me, "I have someone coming over every morning – Dave Locklear – he has a big dairy farm out towards Plymouth who said he will take care of the cows and goats for Bob."

"Well I'm a bit disappointed. Me and the cows were just connecting too." I say with a smile.

"Ray, before you go, can I ask you to do one favor for me?" asks Bob.

"Sure Bob."

"Over there by my telephone is my address book. I need you to call my niece, Gayle Jacobs, and make up whatever story you want, but I need her to come visit me okay?"

As I walk over to the phone and grab the address book, I look her up to make sure and there she is.

"Gayle Jacobs – she's out near the Boston area. Your brothers daughter I assume?"

"Yes. She's a great kid and if she hesitates tell her whatever you want, but make sure she gets here yesterday. Got it?"

"I'll give her a shout before I start writing."

"You're a good man, Raymond. It's not a long drive, so I expect her here tomorrow afternoon, hear?"

******

"Hello, Gayle?"

"Yes, this is Gayle. Who are you?"

"My name is Raymond Wise and I'm calling on behalf of your uncle Bob."

Gayle laughs, "That's funny. I just read a book by some guy named Raymond Wise. Small world, right?"

"Um, yes. The Joyce Brown Murder Mystery? Did you like it?" I ask, getting off track.

"I thought it was gross. If you wrote it, why did you have the guy cut off her head after he already shot her?"

"Well it's all part of ….. listen Gayle, I'm sorry, we can talk about the book when you get her."

Gayle jumps in, "I'm not going to uncle Bobs. And how do you know uncle Bob?"

"I'm staying in one of his cabins working on my next book. My publisher went to college with your dad apparently."

"Really, how cool is that? So what's this book gonna be about? Are you going to behead the girl in that one too?"

"Listen Gayle, I'm calling because your uncle had an accident and he wants to talk to you."

"What happened? It was that tractor wasn't it? I've told him a million times he drives that thing like a maniac."

"Gayle …. Gayle, no … it was nothing like that. He fell off a stool the other night in the kitchen and broke three ribs, his collar bone and has a concussion."

Gayle laughs, "Are you kidding me? Every time I'm up there I'm yelling at him to take it easy and now you're telling me he broke three ribs, his collar bone and has a concussion by falling off the stepping stool in his kitchen? Oh, the irony!"

I am trying desperately not to laugh, as she does make a good point. Bob does take a fair amount of risks when he's working his farm, that's for sure.

"Listen, Gayle, Bob wanted me to call you and tell you that he needs to talk with you. He sounded pretty serious about it too."

"Okay. He probably just wants me to cook for him."

"No, I don't think that's it. A guy named Rick has scheduled a lot of volunteers to come cook for him and help out in the fields. I think that's all going to be taken care of. I got the impression that he needs to talk to you about something else."

"Really? That's awesome. Uncle Bob gives so much to the people up there, it's nice to hear that in his time of need, the people are stepping up to help. That's so cool."

"Yes. I was amazed at how quickly Rick was able to get people signed up. So, does that mean you are going to be here tomorrow, then?" I ask persuasively.

Gayle pauses, "I guess I could come out, but only if you promise to talk to me about writing such a gruesome story. I really thought this Raymond Wise guy must be a creepy guy to come up with stuff like that – no offense, of course."

"No offense taken. I'll try not to be too creepy, I promise."

"Okay. Since Spring is coming and I'm sure even with all the help, Bob probably wants me to make sure I have them do things the Jacobs way. Are the other two cabins rented?"

"No, no, they're empty."

"Good. I'll pack enough clothes to stay awhile and take one of the cabins – unless it's not safe being next to your cabin?"

Gayle laughs as I am less humored, "I'll try to control my creepiness."

******

When I get up the next morning, I go out and find several people scattered about working the farm. I laugh to myself as it seems odd that it takes so many people to do the work that Bob does every day alone. It's actually only about ten people, but still, when you are use to stepping outside every morning and seeing only Bob out and about, even ten people seems like a crowd.

I head up to the main house to check on Bob, and as I walk in, I find two local women busily working in the kitchen with Bob sitting at the table enjoying a rather impressive feast.

"Hey Ray, grab yourself a plate and come help me eat some of this food the girls made." he says.

"Well, it's good to see you won't go hungry." I say as I sit down at the table.

"He needs to build up his strength." says one of the women as she comes and pours me a cup of coffee.

"I didn't lose my strength, I broke a few bones." says Bob

"Never mind that. Eating a good breakfast every morning is going to help those bones heal, young man." says the woman as she makes her way back to the kitchen.

Bob leans over to me and in a softer tone, "It's a good reminder for me of why I never married." and winks at me with a smile. "Did you get in touch with Gayle?" he asks.

"I did. Should be here sometime today. She said she would plan on staying in one of the other cabins, if that's okay. She figured you wanted her to make sure all the helpers did things the Jacobs Farm way, so she is planning to stay a bit."

"Excellent. I do want her to make sure the crops are done correctly, but I need to talk with her about the future of the farm. And if you're up to it, I'd appreciate you being in on it too so you can write everything down for me."

"You mean like a last will? You only broke a couple ribs Bob."

"I know — it's not a last will. Just going to the hospital made me think that it might be time for me to prepare the farm for the next generation, that's all."

"I'd be happy to write it down if you want. So what do you want me to do today?"

"You'll have to ask Rick. He's a good friend who is taking charge while I mend. He has a farm a few miles from here, but his is bigger and he has a crop manager who runs the place for him. He's taking time off from his EMT work so he can come over here every day and make sure the volunteers are doing the right thing."

"That's awful generous."

Bob laughs, "He knows me too well. He knows that if I see anything being neglected, I'd get out there and do it myself." he leans over again in a lower tone, "That's why he signed up those nags in the kitchen. He knows they will keep a thumb on me to be still. But to be honest, I am a bit sore and my body tells me to take it easy right now. And now that I know Gayle will be here, I'm feeling much better about things. I'll just sit here and eat all day. I'll probably gain

600 pounds and not be able to get out the doors, which I think is their plan." he says, nodding towards the ladies in the kitchen.

"I heard that young man. We're not here to fatten you up, we're here to shape you up." says one of the ladies.

Bob looks over at me with raised eyebrows and a face full of cringe.

When I get back outside and talk with Rick, it appears that I'm not needed much. Dave came over earlier to milk the cows and goats and will be coming back in the afternoon to talk to Bob about his recipe for making the cheeses. He's got four or five volunteers working and preparing the soil for planting later on, and a few others doing odd jobs to keep the place clean and organized as Bob likes it.

It appears that for the time being, I'm going to have plenty of time to work on my book, which is fine with me. My story has developed nicely and I could certainly stand to stay focused on it with minimal distractions. That's why I rented this cabin, after all.

Back to the book.

******

As I get up to get something to drink, I look out the window and see that the day is quickly fading away. The farm looks quiet, as the volunteers seem to have left for the day.

I guess that explains why I'm hungry.

That's what I love about being a writer. When you get into a zone, your story truly becomes you. I've had many nights when I stop to make me some dinner only to realize it's almost three in the morning. YIKES! That's why a writer never worries about writer's block. I've always believed that it was God's way of making me stop and realize that some people actually live a normal life. Guess there aren't too many people eating dinner at three in the morning I suppose.

As I'm fixing myself a sandwich, there is a knock on my door that nearly makes my heart stop. I'm not use to visitors so the knocking scares the hell out of me.

I go and open the door to find a young women that absolutely makes me pause.

"You must be Ray, the writer who cuts women's heads off?" she says with a smile.

"Well I'm Ray, yes. You obviously are Gayle?"

"Correct. I just unpacked next door and wanted to say hi."

"Of course, would you like to come in?"

"I'm not interrupting anything, am I?" she says as she walks in carrying a bottle of wine.

"No. I was just fixing myself a sandwich for dinner. Are you hungry?"

""No I ate with uncle Bob. You're just having a sandwich for dinner?"

"Well sometimes when you're in a zone, you don't want to spend a lot of time cooking, so a quick sandwich is just fine."

"I guess when you write such gruesome stories, you probably lose your appetite anyway, right?" she says with a smile, as she puts her bottle of wine on the counter.

"I don't write just gruesome stories. If you read the book, you know the profile of the murderer didn't exactly make him a boy scout."

Gayle laughs, "I know. I'm just messin' with you. I actually enjoyed the book, and I'm not a big fan of murder mysteries, so that's a compliment. I was mostly speaking from a jealousy standpoint. I read a lot of books and find it so fascinating how writers can make up stories like that and make them so believable. Were you a detective before or something?" She asks as I get a glass out for her wine.

"No. It's called research. If you write non-fiction, you just write the facts. If you write fiction, you can create whatever story you want, but you have to do a lot more research to make sure your story is believable. I did interviews with a few detectives to make sure the profile for my murderer made sense. Apparently, I did a good job."

"You did that."

As Gayle settles into her seat with her glass of wine, and I follow with my sandwich, I am quickly noticing the fluttering about inside of me that takes my interest up a notch.

She's an attractive woman by my standards. On the thin side, but not skinny. Dark, curly hair down to her shoulders that frames a face with warm eyes and an engaging smile that brings a melting sigh into your soul. She carries herself with a strong sense of confidence. She's comfortable in jeans and a tee shirt, but you don't need much of an imagination to know she would carry the night well in a gown and fancy makeup at some extravagant gala event.

"So you were right about Bob. He seems serious about talking to me about the farm. Do you have any ideas about it?"

"I don't. He did say that when he was at the hospital, it made him aware that he needs to start preparing the farm for the next generation. He did ask me to sit in on the talk and write down what he wants to tell you, so I guess I'll be there too."

"Oh great. The Gruesome Murder at Jacobs Farm. Is that your next book?"

She laughs as I roll my eyes, "Ha... ha... ha."

"Maybe it's more than broken bones. Do you think there's something he's not telling us?"

"I don't think so, Gayle. I told him it sounded like a last will and he laughed. Said it wasn't anything like that. He just said there are a lot of stories about the farm that he wants to make sure continues on."

"Well that makes sense. Every time I'm up here helping him out, he tells me bits and pieces about the farm history, but every time I ask for more, he backs off. I know enough about the farm from what he's said, so if that's what he wants to talk about, this is going to be great!"

As she gets up to refill her glass, I get out a glass as well as we settle into the chairs by the fireplace and get to know each other.

I am amazed at how comfortable Gayle is in sharing stories. I have always been on the shy side and it usually takes me a long time before I open up with people. But with Gayle, I'm finding it easy, as we get into conversations about writing, the farm, politics and religion. The usual stuff you cover on a first date, but I remind myself that this wasn't a date. She just came over to introduce herself and within a couple of hours I am completely enthralled by her. I am in no hurry to get back to my book.

"So what are your future plans?" I ask her, as I've heard enough about me.

"I'm not sure. I majored in art at college and really love painting, but it's not exactly the type of major that screams opportunities, really. Maybe I'll find a really rich man who can make enough money to build me a studio in the back and leave me alone to paint." she smiles.

"Well good luck with that." I say

"With the art? Or finding a husband?"

"Oh – both, I guess." I say with a chuckle.

"Well I always believe that you should shoot high for your dreams. Besides, you're doing okay with the book sales, maybe you could be the rich guy I'm looking for?" she says with a smile.

I laugh in humor dripping with nervousness, "Oh I doubt that. I'm sure I'm too creepy for you." she laughs too.

We continue the conversation with neither of us in any hurry to break it up. But at some point, you look at the time and realize it's way past the time you were thinking it was and it puts the breaks on quickly.

She heads back to her cabin after a hug that doesn't say goodbye, but says this was a nice beginning.

******

The next day I go outside and find another frenzy of activity around the farm. Some new faces as well as some I saw yesterday, all busy with various chores. I see Gayle driving the tractor over by the Christmas trees and admire how comfortable she seems handling the tractor duties.

I go talk to Rick, who is again the man in charge – though clearly only in putting the volunteers to work, as Gayle is the one who knows what to do. Again it appears that today will be a good writing day, which is fine with me.

Once again the creative juices finds me totally locked into my story and oblivious to the world around me when I hear a knock on my door. I peel myself off the ceiling and head for the door, hoping it's Gayle, and sure enough, as I open the door I find that warm smile looking at me.

"Gayle, good to see you. Come in."

"I'm a mess, so I'll stay out here. Thanks for all your help today." she says with a smile I'm hoping is an indication that she's kidding.

"I was out there this morning and Rick didn't have anything for me to do." I say with a hint of defensiveness in case she was serious.

"I'm just kidding. How's the book coming?"

"Great. I'm feeling pretty good about it, thanks."

"Good. Listen, I'm going to clean up and then go cook dinner for Bob. He wants you to join us and we can start on whatever it is he wants to talk about. Is that okay with you?"

"That depends. What are you cooking?" I say with a strong dose of teasing.

Gayle smiles, "Whatever you want, as long as it's pork chops, mashed potatoes, vegetables and wine."

"Sounds great. What time?"

"I'm going to take a shower and change. How about I come here on my way to the house. In about an hour?"

"I'll be ready. Thanks Gayle."

"Oh, and bring whatever you writers need for talking. Pad 'n pencil, a tablet, or whatever you take notes with, okay?"

"Got it"

"See you in about an hour then." says Gayle as she heads for her cabin.

******

"I'm really glad you came here Gayle. I hope that when I'm done sharing this with you, you'll appreciate why I asked you to come. I'm also glad to have Ray here to write it all down, but you both must promise me that this will never be shared with anyone else. I want it written down only to have the family record, but only Gayle must know about it. Not even your dad, you understand?"

We both nod in agreement.

"I'll give you the whole story tonight, but I'm sure you'll want to get together from time to time to fill in some of the blanks. But I'm also confident that if you just listen to the story, a lot of it will make sense to you."

"As you know, Gayle, this farm has been in the family going back to the first settlers. Every generation has chosen one relative to carry the story through the next generation. My mother chose me because I loved the farm and your father did not. That's no reflection on my brother, of course. He found his own path and has done very well. I have chosen you for the same reason over your brothers. Once you hear the story, you'll understand more."

"So let me start at the very beginning and if you have questions, don't hesitate to speak up, but I also know you'll learn a lot more by listening, okay?"

We both nod in agreement.

"The first owners of the farm were the Pitmans....."

Legend of the
Magic Christmas Tree

Amity Pitman was a colonial girl whose parents, Lilly and George Pitman, settled into a tough life carving out the wilderness in what is now North Conway, New Hampshire in Carroll County.

Amity was 14 when she lost both her parents within a week to the rough existence of the times, leaving her alone to manage the small farm her father had created.

Her best friend growing up was an Indian boy from the Abenaki tribe who became good friends with Amity when they were very young. She called him Ahano because it means 'he laughs' which was so true. He was a happy Indian boy who loved to play and have fun. He showed her how to farm and survive alone in the wilderness, as well as other men from his tribe.

He died suddenly of smallpox, which broke Amity's heart to lose such a good friend.

But Ahano's spirit continued to visit her after he left for the other side of life. He continued to show her tips for growing good crops and protected her from every danger surrounding a young lady in the wilderness. He also taught her a lot of the values and teachings that would groom her for a successful life.

Take only what you need and give the rest away – either as a mutual need trade, or in charity, but never take more than you need.

Always respect the soil where the seeds land and the earth will always give you what you need to live.

If you see God in everything, you can have no fear in your heart.

The spirits will lift you up as much as you lift up your neighbors.

As Amity became a woman, she married a young Irishman, Patrick O'Brian, who came to the new country to work the land.

They had three daughters.

Amity raised her three daughters to be independent, teaching them all that she had learned from Ahano. She taught them that the farm would be left to them after she and their father died, and it was important for them, as girls, to be strong and work hard to keep the farm in the family.

"Wow. Those girls owned the farm back then?" asked Gayle

"Trust me, Gayle, it gets even better." says Bob.

When Amity died – eight years after Patrick had – the three girls took over the farm, determined to grow the best crops in the region. They worked well together, and as each got married, there would be a simple home built on the land for each family to stay on the land.

"Those are the cabins we are staying in today?" I ask.

"1708 they were built by the girls and their husbands. They have been upgraded through the years, but much of the original cabins are still in the bones." Bob says.

Amity chose her youngest daughter, Eliza – known as Lizzy to most – to be her contact, much as Ahano was hers after he passed away. She chose Lizzy because, of the three, she had the most generous heart and loved working the land.

Amity would talk to Lizzy every day when she was in the fields working. She taught Lizzy the many lessons she had learned from Ahano, but she also added some of her own teachings.

The crops will grow equal to the generous love in your heart.

Your neighbor that struggles the most, gets the best from the first harvest.

Lizzy and her sisters worked well together, but as they began to have families, the two older sisters decided to move off the farm and create their own life with their families. There were no issues between the sisters. The older two knew how much Lizzy loved working the farm and were more than happy to leave it in her care so they could go out and explore adventures of their own.

Lizzy had two children, a boy, Will, and a girl, Laura, and the children grew up learning all the lessons of working the farm from their mother. Will left the farm at an early age, but Laura stayed and learned all the lessons from her mother. Her father, Christopher Miller, died in 1704 when Laura was only six, so her mother taught her how to run the family business until she died at the age of fifty in 1718. She married a Douglas Porter in 1721 and they had four children, two boys and two girls.

******

And so it was. Generation after generation always produced a female who would be chosen by the previous mother to work the farm.
Each mother would teach the chosen girl the many lessons that they had learned, and each mother added two of their own lessons that they had learned from their own experiences.

This was not an easy legacy to maintain, as women had very little rights until after 1900. Each woman had to marry a man who would agree to work the farm and leave it to any daughter they had. Not hard to do in today's world, but in the 17-1800s, finding a man to agree with the terms of marrying these women was quite a challenge.

"How cool is that? Girl power rocks!" says Gayle

This all became part of the magic of the farm.

Every chosen daughter would find a husband who was completely supportive of her running the farm by the lessons passed down through the generations. Some suspected that the mother spirit, or possibly Amity's spirit, would always visit a young man eager to marry their daughter to make it clear what he was getting into. It did seem unusual, especially in the earlier generations, that a woman could find a man who would agree to the terms of this farm at all, let alone every generation without fail. There had to be something at work, but no one knew for sure.

Every generation, a female was chosen.

Every female chosen added to the spirit of generosity established by Ahano and Amity.

Every generation produced the best crops in the region.

******

In 1790, Emma Parker, who was running the farm, established the farm as a good stop for African Americans traveling the underground railway. Her and her husband, Jacob, would provide as much food as they could carry and direct them to the safest areas as they headed north.

In the 1830s, Alice Woodward, who was the woman in charge of the farm at the time, helped many of the Indian families migrating north after the Indian Removal Act. Even though the Act was designed for the Indian tribes of the south, many of the tribes in the north knew that President Jackson would not stop until every tribe was removed from the land. Many tribes in the area knew the Woodward farm was a friendly neighbor that would help them with food and seeds to help them along the way. The Abenaki tribe, especially, understood the history of the farm with Ahano and Amity and that their tribe was always welcome on the farm.

During 1850s and '60s and the Civil War, Charity Wilson – Alice's daughter- established the farm as a neutral site that provided food and rest for any soldiers – Union or Confederate – passing through.

In the 1920s, Harriet Smith, daughter of Charity, was a good friend of Sally W. Hovey, Chair of the New Hampshire Woman's Party who was a leader in passing the 19th Amendment. Harriet donated food, time and money to helping women, especially those recovering from abusive homes.

"Way to go Harriet!" Gayle says with enthusiasm.

During the great depression, Elizabeth Jacobs, ("Your grandmother" says Bob), Harriet's daughter, was very active in helping out locals who were struggling. Her and her husband made jars of soups, sauces and preserves to give out to the families in need. And when WWII broke out, Elizabeth continued her mission of making sure everyone in North Conway had food.

Every generation, the women running the farm added to the legacy of the farm. Strong women, working the land and giving to the community.

The farm changed a little from generation to generation. Emma Parker added a crop of sweet potatoes that were easier to transport through the underground railway. Alice Woodward added the Christmas trees as well as a group of milking cows and goats that would add cheese products to their offerings. Charity Wilson added a lot of different vegetables . Elizabeth Jacobs added a small orchard of apple trees that would create the famous apple cider.

Elizabeth and William had two boys, me and Calvin. Calvin was ten years older than I, but there were two unsuccessful pregnancies between us, both girls, that explained the gap in age.

Mother worried that she had broken the female chain of ownership at the farm, but her mother, Harriet, assured her that there was no rule to be broken. The family tree had strong, generous women in every generation able to carry the traditions of the farm, but there were never any rules that said it had to be a female. She reminded mother that it was the heart of the farm that created the legacy and that one of her two sons would surely have the heart to continue it.

When my dad passed away, I quit school to help run the farm and mother quickly came to understand that I truly had the heart to keep the farm going.

Things got rough when mother died. I was in my early twenties and wasn't sure if I was going to be able to run the farm on my own.

When mothers spirit started visiting me in the fields, as did every mother from every generation did, she quickly moved to explain the heritage of the family farm and assured me that she would remain with me throughout my life to insure that the farm remained a beacon of generosity for the community.

I settled into my life at the farm. I love visiting with mother while I work in the fields.

"So you're talking to your mother when I hear you in the Christmas tree lots? I thought you were just talking to yourself?" I ask Bob.

"Mother always meets me in the Christmas tree lot." Bob says with a smile.

Mother carried on the tradition of not only teaching me the lessons learned from generation to generation, but she told me the stories of every woman going back to Amity Pitman that made the farm history so special and unique.

I loved hearing all the stories and was always eager to hear more. I began to understand why the farm had so much success too. I loved spending my day out in the fields working the land while listening to mother tell stories. I also understood why mother was always so happy to work out in the fields when she was alive as well. She would spend her days working the land while listening to Grandma Harriet. And to think that it has been this way since Amity Pitman and Ahano started it, made me realize why the produce coming from this farm was always the best. Good soil, water and sunshine certainly help make plants grow, but spending your day working the fields while listening to your family stories certainly gave the produce the added ingredient that made them so special. Making the special apple cider wasn't just taking a recipe from a piece of paper, but having mothers spirit at my side explaining each ingredient and how to mix each of the variety of apples in the orchard just right to create the perfect cider.

It was in early August when I was planting gourds and a pumpkin patch that mother explained the magic of the Christmas tree.

It was Alice Woodward who started the grove of pine trees in the early 1800s. She started with a variety of trees to see if there was any potential in the variety of nuts the cones produced. When the Indian Removal Act was passed, Alice built a good reputation of helping the Indians heading out to find new lands with seeds and produce.

One group of Pennacook natives heading towards Maine had a male named Mundoo. He was an older native that had heard of Ahano and the story of Amity Pitman, the original owner of this farm.

Mundoo was given many seeds, sweet potatoes and nuts from Alice, who embraced the stories he told her about Ahano and his tribe that helped her fill in some of the blanks created from the stories handed down from Amity.

Mundoo also helped Alice with tips for her nut farm. Before leaving, Mundoo spent some time going through every row of nut trees, explaining to Alice which trees were worth working and which were not.

He got to one small pine tree that almost seemed out of place from the others. It wasn't very full of branches and didn't produce many cones. Mundoo walked around it a few times, then stopped. He took an eagle feather from his bag and tied it to a branch.

"This is your spirit tree. I can feel it. Be sure and save every seed it

produces. Replace any tree that is removed with the seeds from this tree. Any tree that is grown from the seeds of this tree will be blessed. Any tree or cones that come from the seeds of this tree must be used and ground into mulch to work into your soil. If you follow this, your farm will always be blessed with the best food."

Alice followed the advice of Mundoo. The one small tree towards the back of the lot with an Eagle feather tied to it became the most important tree of the farm, as Alice ditched the nut farm and began to just grow Christmas trees from the seeds of that little tree in the back.

Even after Alice passed away and her daughter Charity took over, the small tree was honored as instructed by Mundoo. Even when a storm blew the Eagle feather away, Charity found the feather and carefully buried it at the base of the little tree, tied to a root with a stone she painted blue placed over it to mark it's location for generations to come.

"So THAT'S what the blue rock at the base of that scrawny little tree back there represents! How cool is that?" says Gayle.

"If you'll remember, I told you awhile back how that tree with the blue rock was the most important tree on our property. You kept bugging me to explain why, but it wasn't time yet." says Bob.

From each generation that followed, the Christmas tree lot evolved. Every time a Christmas tree was cut down for a family, it would be replaced with the seeds of the little blue stone tree in the back. Every tree that was grown from the seeds of the blue stone tree were beautiful and perfect for the holiday season. Every customer who was lucky enough to get a tree from the farm, had to promise to bring the tree back to the farm so we could grind it down to be mixed in with the soil.

It wasn't the biggest or fullest tree on the property, but the caretaker of the farm in every generation understood the magic of the blue rock Christmas tree. It always produced the seeds that made the rest of the farm magical.

Every holiday season, the spirit mother would be responsible for naming the one family in the area that would get to cut down a Christmas tree. It would be the family with the greatest needs, and every year, that family would have a Christmas unlike any other. More than just toys and fun presents, the family would also find the best food available filling their kitchen.

No one knew how it happened, but every year it did. Only the spirit mother knew and she was not to tell the care giver of the farm. It simply came from the spirit world and the generations of mothers who worked the farm.

"So grandma has been telling you every Christmas what family she has chosen for the special Christmas?" asks Gayle.

"Yes, but that's all I know. She just tells me the one family that has to be on the list for cutting down a tree. I can chose whoever else I want, and the chosen family can cut down any tree they want. But every year, the chosen family that mother tells me to include always has a magical Christmas. I can't explain it. All the presents and food don't come from this farm, I know that. Only my mother knows, and all the mothers before her as well."

"How cool is that?" Gayle says as I certainly nod in agreement.

"Gayle, I wanted you to know this history because I feel your passion for the farm. I am the first male to own the farm, but that's only because mother had two daughters that died at birth. I never married, so obviously, I have no one to pass this on to but you. When I spent the night at the hospital, it was made clear to me that it was the right time to share the story of this farm with you."

"It's funny. The day of the accident, I was talking with mother about the future of the farm, and she was the one who told me to pay attention to my niece. 'She has the heart of the women before her' she told me. I know it's a lot to put on you right now, and to be clear,

I'm only fifty six years old and plan to be around a bit longer. But I want you to think about it. I'm hoping that when the time comes, I'll be able to leave this farm in your care."

"Does that mean you'd be bugging me in the Christmas tree lot every day after you die?" Gayle says with a smile.

"I plan to follow you all over this farm and annoy the hell out of you." Bob says with a genuine smirk.

Gayle screams as we all break into laughter.

"Uncle Bob, this is so incredible. It is a lot to think about, for sure, but it also is an honor to think that I've been chosen to follow the women of my family and carry on the legend of this farm. This is really exciting for me. Thank you."

******

I got my book done and it turned out to be even bigger than my first one.

Bob died shortly after his sixty forth birthday and Gayle took over the farm.

For her wedding present, I built a nice painting studio near the main house for her.

I am one male who loves to watch my three daughters and their mother working out on the farm. I appreciate being an anonymous side bar of such a wonderful history full of remarkable women.

Recently, Gayle and I were sitting on the front porch enjoying a glass of wine, when she asked me if we should change the name of the farm since the Jacobs are no longer here.

I smiled as I watched our girls playing in the fields and then looked at Gayle.

"Maybe the 'Headless Women's Farm? Or better yet, we should help the people out down at records and just call it 'Amity's Farm'

"Ha, ha, ha …. we'll go with Amity's Farm." she said with a click of our drinks.

And so it was and will always be.

Amity's Family Tree

1951: Robert Jacobs: son of Elizabeth and William Jacobs. Had two sons, Robert and Calvin. Cal was ten years older than Bob, but there were two births that failed between them, both girls.

1915: Elizabeth Jacobs : daughter of Harriet and Wilbur Smith, along with two older brothers. Elizabeth took over farm after her mother Harriet died in 1927. She and Wilbur made lots of soups and preserves during the depression to help struggling families in the area, and continued to contribute during WWII. Married William Jacobs. Had two sons, with two daughters still born in-between.

1886: Harriet Smith, youngest child of six children of Charity and Frank Wilson, {four daughters and two boys} who grew up a good friend of one of the powerful women of the woman's movement, Sally W. Hovey, Chairwoman of the New Hampshire Woman's Party. Harriet donated food, time and money to women working to pass the 19th Amendment. She also donated same to homes for abused women. Married Wilbur Smith. They had two sons and a daughter.

1850:Charity Wilson third daughter of five children of Alice and Rodney Woodward, established the farm as a neutral site during the Civil War, providing food and rest for any soldiers – Union or Confederate – passing through. She married Frank Wilson. They had six children, three boys, three girls.

1818: Alice Woodward, second of four daughters born to Emma and Jacob Parker ran the farm when it had a reputation as a friendly farm to Native Americans escaping America to reservations in Maine or Canada, giving them seeds for their new homelands and food for their travels. The Indian Removal Act of 1830 affected Indian tribes of the southern states, who had to move west of the Mississippi river. But even the Indian tribes of the north knew that Andrew Jackson would not stop there and began migrating north in the mid 1800s. She married Rodney Woodward. They had three daughters and two boys.

1787: Emma Parker, youngest of two daughters of Rita and Stanley Johnson established the farm as a friendly stop for African Americans traveling through the underground railway north to Canada. Her and her husband would provide them with food and guide them to the safest routes heading north. She married Jacob Parker. They had four daughters.

1756: Rita Johnson, only daughter of Susan and Jake Wilson (They had two older sons who died young in the Revolutionary War) Provided food and clothing for the soldiers fighting for independence. She married Stanley Johnson. They had two daughters.

1728: Susan Wilson, youngest of four children (two boys, two girls) of Laura and Douglas Porter, was running the farm that was known to settlers for helping newcomers with seeds and food as they got started. She married Jake Wilson. They had two sons and a daughter.

1698: Laura Porter was the daughter of Eliza and Christopher Miller (they had a boy in '96). She learned to work the farm from her mother and took over the farm after Lizzy died in 1718 at age fifty. She married Douglas Porter. They had two boys and two girls.

1668: Eliza (Lizzy) Miller was the youngest of three daughters born to Amity and Harry O'Brien. Was chosen by her mother to take over the farm after Harry passed away in 1680. Amity taught her daughters all about the farm until her passing in 1688. The two older sister got married and soon moved away, leaving Lizzy and her husband Christopher Miller, whom she married in 1694. They had a boy and a girl.

1636: Amity O'Brien was the only child of Lilly and George Pitman who settled on the property in 1629, coming from England to start a new life. When she was 14 in 1650, Amity's parents both died within the same week from smallpox, leaving her alone on the farm. A young Indian boy named Ahano, who was Amity's best friend growing up, and some of the males of the Abenaki tribe close by helped Amity work her land until she married a young Irish boy named Harry O'Brien in 1661. They had three daughters.

The End

6

Danny's Christmas Stocking

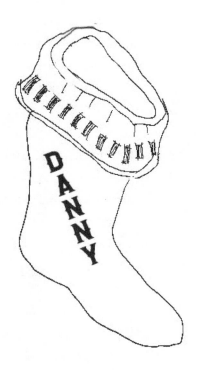

by Paul Gerard Smith Sr
(grandfather of author)
The stars were shining extra bright
That beautiful night
As Danny climb the stairs
To say his prayers

And close his eyes
And wait for every big surprise
That he would see
Beneath the tree
At the dawning of the morning
And in his hand, now this is quite shocking
Danny held his Christmas stocking
To see how it was filled
With the small things the thrilled
Little girls and little boys
The nuts and the toys
And as he slept
He kept
His stocking gripped ever so tight in his hand
As he flew through the clouds into slumber land
Before the night became much older
Danny felt someone shaking his shoulder
He said, "Oh my!"
As he opened one eye
"I must pretend I'm asleep, because
This might be Santa Clause"
Slowly he opened the other eye too
Then said, "Why Horace, it's you"
Now just in case you haven't met
Horace the friendly ghost
He's the kind of ghost you can't forget
The kind that a boy likes most
You can see right through him
He floats through the air
In a manner most uncanny

He goes here, there and everywhere
And his personal boss is Danny
He looked at Danny there on the bed
And said with a bob of his head
"Loads of presents and lots of fun
And a merry Christmas to everyone!"
Danny smiled and said, said he
"And a merry Christmas to you from me"
Horace nodded and said, "My lad
You're bound to get good things when
All through the year, you haven't been bad
Except every now and then
Santa Clause will surely drop
Down the chimney from the top
Without any noise
Without ringing doorbells
Without even knocking
He'll tiptoe in
And fill up your stocking
With the nice things a small boy enjoys"
Danny thought a minute
With his stocking in his hand
There was something about Christmas
He didn't understand
And Horace noticing it cried
"What's wrong?" and Danny replied
"Christmas is such a nice day because
Of all the nice presents from Santa Clause
But why does he do it each year, gee wiz
There must be a reason why Christmas is

There must be a reason
Why everyone's happy
For just one day of the year
It's weird
There's a reason for this
And a reason for that
For eating your breakfast
Or wearing a hat
People don't feel like this in June or July
So there must be some good reason why
They're different when Christmas is here
What was it that made Christmas begin?"
Horace taken aback
Rubbed his chin and smiled and said
"Very well little man
You want to see where Christmas began?
Hop out from your covers and let's go see
Get read, Get set, Come with me"
He took Danny's hand with a smile on his face
With a whish and a whoosh
And a swish and a swoosh
Suddenly they were flying through space
"We're flying backwards!" cried Danny
As he watched the clouds below
"Yes, we're flying backwards" said Horace
"Through time
To where Christmas began long ago"
Everything disappeared, the first thing Danny knew
Everything round them was nothing but blue
With stars hanging in it, some small and some large

But there was one star shining brighter by far
As they got close to it by and by
Wonderful music came out of the sky
With sweet voices singing a heavenly chorus
"What's that?" asked Danny
"That's Angels" said Horace
Through the clouds Danny saw
Lots of hills down below
Some sprinkled with snow
And some men half asleep, tending their sheep
Who wandered about to and fro
Then much to Danny's surprise
Both the men and the sheep raised their eyes
As if they saw something no sheep or no men
Had ever seen until then
Then way down the road Danny saw a strange sight
Three camels making their way through the night
On each sat a man, and each seemed to hold
A box of copper, silver and gold
Their arms were covered with bracelets and rings
Horace pointed and said, "Those are camels and kings"
"Why are they headed for that little town?"
Said Danny, said Horace
"Let's see, we'll go down"
So they did, they slid
Down from the sky to the top of a hill
The whole place was standing still
Except for some singing and din
That came from the Inn
"That's funny" said Danny, "This surely can't be

Where Christmas began to begin"
Then he saw a sign reading no vacancy
Said Horace, "No room in the Inn"
Danny turned his head and saw a little shed
With a donkey tied up to a post
Danny whispered, "Now wait a minute
Looks like there's people in it"
"There are people in it" said Horace
"That's very odd," said Dan, "It's a lady and a man"
Horace smiled and said
"To make the whole thing stranger
There is more than you can see
Not two people, there are three
There's a little baby in the manger"
Danny murmured, "Gee wiz, what a pity it is
To be all alone like they are"
He lifted his head and saw that the shed
Was bright with the light of a star
"Let's go down" said Danny, "We two
And see if there is something that we can do
So they went down the path that led to the shed
There was a man with a beard and a woman of charm and grace
A baby wrapped in a bundle of cloth
With a smile upon his face
Danny walked up to the lady and said
"I have a mother at home in bed
Who's pretty and sweet like you
I was born in a hospital instead
Of wrapped up in straw in an ugly bed"

The lady smiled and said, "Thank you so
There was no room in the Inn, you know"
Then Danny said, "I think it's a shame
But anyhow, I'm glad I came
As long as I'm here, perhaps I could
Help out a little and do some good
Like warming a bottle or picking up scraps?"
The lady just smiled and said, "Perhaps"
Then she laid her fingers on Danny's head
And smiling sweetly, she softly said
"Thank you so much for coming here
Remember this visit from year to year
And as you get older
And the years roll along
When you need a shoulder
When things go wrong
Or maybe just a little favor done
Remember to ask my baby son"
Then she saw the stocking so thin and so flat
And she looked at Danny and said, "What's that?"
Danny said, "It's my stocking I hang up because
It's filled with presents from Santa Clause"
The lady took the stocking, shook it out and said
"Would you mind if I filled it up instead?"
Danny cried out, "Sure" as little boys will
And the stocking began to fill
"These three little presents" the lady said
"Are hope, contentment and love
And this little jewel is the friendly eye
That will watch over you as the years go by

From our home in the sky above
And always to remind you of my son's birth
Here's a big package of peace on earth"
Danny took the stocking, his heart filled with joy
And said, "Thanks an awful lot, and thank your baby boy"
Then the air was filled with the heavenly chorus
As the kings came riding in
And -wish- through the air, he flew with Horace
As Christmas began to begin
He woke up the next morning and oh, what fun
He had cookies and candy and toys by the ton
A Christmas tree that was six feet tall
A bicycle and a big red ball
But his mother and father could not understand
Why he kept that stocking gripped tight in his hand
But Danny knew, and every now and then
He'd think about last night again
The trip through the stars, the shed by the Inn
The little boy there in the hay
The kings, the camels and the Angels songs
And he'd smile to himself and say
"I wonder just who that baby was
I know it wasn't Santa Clause"
Merry Christmas

This poem was written by my grandfather when my Dad was born and has been read every Christmas to every generation of Smith children.

7

Lilly's Song

Lilly DiPaul was one of the most successful songwriters in the music business. Every recording artist knew that if they recorded a Lilly DiPaul song, it would almost guarantee another big hit for their career. She was in demand, making a fortune doing what she loved to do – write songs for other people to sing.

Lilly loved her life. Happily married to her high school sweetheart, Kevin Dukes, and a young daughter, Carrie, Lilly had the best life had to offer. They lived in a quaint home outside of Nashville, Tennessee. She could afford a lot more home, but her and Kevin preferred the simple surroundings and using their wealth for helping others as they could.

After a night out celebrating another song reaching number one status, Kevin, Lilly and Carrie were on their way home when a deer suddenly darted in front of their car. As Kevin quickly reacted to avoid the animal, the car lost control and rolled off the embankment.

Kevin was conscience but in shock. Neither Lilly or Carrie were making any sound, which frightened him. He couldn't move as the roof had crushed on the roll, leaving little room to maneuver. He heard a car stop above him and heard a man's voice calling out.

Then his world went dark.

Kevin opened his eyes and took a few minutes to get his bearings. He seemed to be in a hospital which made him remember the accident that occurred just before his world went blank.

As a nurse and doctor comes into the room, he is quick to ask about his family.

"Where's my wife and daughter?"

The nurse comes and takes his hand with a look that tells him the answer is not going to be good.

"Mr. Dukes, you've been in a serious accident," says the doctor in a very formal tone, "Unfortunately, your wife did not survive and your daughter is in pretty bad shape, but we are doing everything we can to save her."

They pause to let him soak in the horrifying news. He is stunned as his eyes moisten with pain.

"My Lilly is gone?"

"Mr Dukes, it's hard, I know," says the nurse, "But your wife did not suffer. We are doing all we can for your daughter. Right now it's important for you to rest. You have several broken bones that need to mend."

Kevin remained in his hospital room for a week with a broken leg, collar bone and three ribs …. as well as a broken heart. He was told that Carrie had also lost her battle and crossed over to be with her mother, leaving him alone for the first time in his life.

For the most part, Kevin spent the week in silence. Only a few visitors, family mostly, but most respected his privacy as he faced a new world without the two most important people in his life.

******

It's been a tough couple of years for Kevin after the accident. Physically, his bones have healed, leaving him with only a slight limp in his gate. He sold the Nashville home and moved to Leavenworth, Washington. To keep a somewhat private posture, Kevin started using his middle name of Theodore and everyone around Leavenworth knew him as Ted. He owns a quaint photography shop in the Bavarian village just east of his and Lilly's hometown of Seattle.

Ted was always a photography buff and did pretty well as a freelancer back in Nashville, doing many concerts and music industry gatherings on Music Row.

Now that he's in Leavenworth, he does very well selling photos and equipment to tourists passing through and documenting many of the important events in the area.

He has a comfortable cabin outside of Leavenworth where he quietly lives alone. He doesn't need anything, as he continues to post generous royalties from Lilly's catalog of songs that artist continue to want to record. He remains in touch with Lilly's publisher back in Nashville, but for the most part lets the publisher take care of the music issues while he lives his quiet life outside of the music business.

Even though the music business often seeks interviews, book deals and general information about Lilly's husband, the publisher continues to respect Ted's desire to stay out of the spotlight. What made Kevin and Lilly such a great team was his willingness to give all the attention to his wife. He enjoyed being in the background with his camera always in hand to document the many events Lilly was featured in. He made sure the publisher had a file of photographs available for any stories journalists were doing about Lilly.

Losing the love of his life and his precious daughter took a heavy toll on Kevin's heart, obviously, so his ambition is to mostly be left alone to work within his photography business. He maintains his positive nature that he's always had and has built a reputation around Leavenworth as a very generous man always willing to help out with those in need. He would not be considered a happy man, but considering the hand he's been dealt, he is content with his ability to move on with his life in a positive way.

******

As Fall slowly makes its way into the holiday season, Ted is in heaven. This is the time of year a photographer loves to be outdoors documenting the beautiful colors and excitement of the season. He also loves to help out with all the decorations around town that turns Leavenworth into a magical winter wonderland during the holidays.

He is part of a five person committee that secretly reviews local families who are struggling and making sure their holiday is one of magical dreams come true. They meet every Wednesday night to go over their lists of needs and typically meet at Ted's cabin, as it is outside of town where they can do their work anonymously. Ted loves being a part of this secret club and doesn't hesitate to give whatever he can to the cause of helping others.

No one around town knows much about Ted's past. Few, if any, know how Ted is able to be so generous with his money. Only the people at the bank understand his money situation and are respectful to keep his past private. He doesn't talk about his past, and being in a small town, not many people ask him about his past. They just know he's Ted, he's a photographer, and a very generous man. That's how Ted likes it.

One day, as Ted was in his photo shop in town, an older woman comes into the store. Nice looking. Carries herself well. He's guessing a city girl.

"May I help you find anything, or are you just looking?"

"Actually, my daughter and her family are out in the square shopping. I just had to come in out of the cold."

Ted smiles, "You are welcome to help yourself to some hot chocolate over there. Should warm you up in no time." he says as he points out the table towards the back with a big container surrounded by paper cups, a bowl of marshmallows and a couple of bottles of whipped cream.

"Isn't that sweet." she says.

" It's not special, really. Every store around the square offers a hot drink of some sort. Maggie next door has some pretty good apple cider and the bar across the way has a very nice hot buttered rum, if you like. Joe, over at the hardware store has some home made eggnog – and if you're nice to him, he can put a splash of spirits in it, as long as you can prove you're over 21."

"Isn't that nice that everyone pitches in like that. I've always had a soft spot for photography, so browsing around here with a cup of hot chocolate is perfect for me."

"Where are you visiting from?"

"My daughter lives near Seattle and I came up from L.A. to spend the holidays with her. She insisted that we spend at least a day in Leavenworth, and as much as she hyped it up, I must say it does not disappoint."

"Good to hear. We really go all out for the holidays."

"Did you take all these photos?"

"Most of them. I have a couple of local photographers that I'm happy to feature as well. Mary has a bin to your left and Suzie has one over here."

"So it's like a consignment shop then?"

"No not really. If someone has some good shots they want to sell, I'm happy to help them out."

"You don't charge them for space?"

"No. They can sell the pictures for whatever they want and if it sells, they get the money."

"That's very generous of you."

"Not really. This is a small town and we all try to help each other out if we can. That's just how we do things around here."

The woman looks out the window and sees her daughter waving at her.

"Well I better get back before my daughter throws her arm out. It was nice talking to you. My name is Joanne, but everyone calls me Jo"

"Good to meet you Jo. I'm Ted, but everyone just calls me Ted around here."

They smile at each other before Ted finishes.

"If you come back, you're always welcome to some hot chocolate. But if you want my advice, I'd go for that hot buttered rum myself."

"I'll definitely have to try that, Ted. Thank you"

******

The next day, Ted is busy at his shop when a young woman drops in. Young, attractive, with two children in tow that appear to be twins – a boy and a girl.

"How are you doing today?" says Ted as he makes his way to the front of the shop.

"Good thanks. My mom was in here yesterday and said the hot chocolate is great, so I thought I'd get some for the kids if that's okay?"

"Of course. Help yourselves. Your mom must be Jo, then?"

"Yes. She's here for the holidays from L.A. My name is Courtney."

"Good to meet you Courtney. I'm Ted. She says you live in Seattle?"

"Well it's really about half way between here and Seattle. Near the Wallace Falls area."

"Oh yes. That's a nice area."

"Are all these pictures yours?" Courtney asks

"Most of them. I have a couple of others who sell their photos too."

"That's nice. I've been thinking of taking a photography class. Do you have any classes here?"

"Well nothing scheduled, but I'm always happy to give lessons to anyone who wants them. What kind of camera do you have?"

"Oh I'm not sure to be honest with you. My husband died a few years ago and had a lot of equipment. I was hopeful that he would teach me how to use it before he got sick. I didn't want to get rid of the equipment because I always thought that some day I might have the opportunity to take a class."

"I'm sorry about your husband. My wife died a few years back too, so I get it. Next time you're up this way, bring me what you got and we'll set up some time to learn how to use it all."

"That would be great, thank you." says Courtney as the twins gather with their hot chocolate to continue on with their day, "These are my twins, Scott and Susie."

"Enjoy the hot chocolate, kids. Here's my card. I live just outside of town towards Stevens Pass area, so we're practically neighbors I guess. Just call or text me when you want to come by so I can be sure to be here."

"Thanks Ted. It was nice meeting you. I promise to call you soon."

******

The very next day, Courtney calls Ted to see if he'd be available to check out her equipment. She's always been that type. When she decides to do something, she decides to do it now.

When she walks into the photo shop, Ted is humored at her struggles to get in the door and quickly jumps in to help her out.

"Looks like you're moving in Courtney. My classes really aren't that long you know."

Courtney smiles, "I'm afraid to say this is just a sample of what Bill had. I just brought the camera and whatever lenses he had. There are things that look like umbrellas and stands and other stuff that I figured I could deal with later. I hope it's okay – I really don't want to take up too much of your time."

"Not at all. I'm excited to help you go through all this." he says as he starts to look through the luggage of all the lenses and gadgets. "Bill has some nice stuff here. Was he a professional?"

"He thought he was, but it was mostly a hobby that he loved. He worked in the tech world as a programmer in Seattle. He did make a little money from time to time for his pictures though."

"Well he certainly knew what he was doing. This is pretty top drawer equipment here."

"That was Bill. He always spent a lot of time researching all his options before he purchased anything."

"Smart man. I'm always careful to make sure people know what they have before I offer any lessons. Some people come in wanting lessons with a camera that has nothing to offer but point and click – there's your lesson."

Courtney laughs, "Well I certainly had no idea what I had when you offered me lessons."

"I just had a feeling you would be worth the risk." he says as she looks at him with curios eyes and he looks back, quickly scrambling to revise his comment, "About the equipment, of course. It sounded like you had a lot of equipment, so I figured it wouldn't be a point and click lesson." he says with a clear tone of embarrassment as he desperately tries to ignore the fluttering butterflies in his stomach and Courtney smiles.

"Well I know you're a busy man and I don't want to waste your time, but I really am excited to finally get around to learning this. I promise you I'm worth the risk." she says with a slight flirtatious smile.

For the next hour or so, Ted went through everything Courtney had brought him, explaining to her what each object did, being interrupted by the occasional customer wanting to make a purchase. The air of attraction was growing between the two and it was obvious that they both were trying very hard to ignore it.

But it was there.

Both had lost the love of their life, so the attraction wasn't seen as a romantic source of excitement, but more a troubling fear of being unfaithful. They both wrestled with the idea that they were perfectly justified to get involved in another relationship, but could not resolve the notion that doing so would create feelings of being disrespectful of their love lost.

Of course they would work harder to push these feelings away more than they would to embrace them.

"This has been great, but I probably need to get back or my mom will think I've abandoned them." says Courtney, "How much do I owe you?"

Ted smiles, "You don't owe me a thing. I'm happy to help you out."

"Oh please, I don't want to take advantage of your time. Let me pay you something. Maybe I could take you out to dinner?" she says as her heart stops [Did I just ask a man out on a date? …. will he think I'm asking him out on a date? I'm asking him out to dinner and that sounds pretty much like a date. Oh My God. I'm not ready for this, am I?]

Ted hesitates [Is she asking me out on a date? She just wants to pay for the lesson, right? Sure sounds like a date, though. Oh there is no way I'm ready for a date. I need to nip this in the bud.] "Dinner would be great." [What did I just say? Oh my GOD]

"Great!" says Courtney with a smile that isn't as warm as it is dripping with panic of wanting to be anywhere else than standing there, "We can do that after all this craziness of the holidays, right? I know we're both busy."

"Any time you want. You're welcome to come back any time for more lessons. Maybe after you get the hang of it, we could take a hike on some of the trails and take pictures?" [What am I doing? Now I'm asking her out on a date? Am I crazy?]

"I'd love to."

"Great. It's a date."[WHAT?!] "Well not a date, date, I just meant we could do that. It'd be fun. "[God, get me out of this conversation before I make a complete idiot of myself.]

******

Courtney is finding more and more time to get together with Ted to talk photography. It isn't coming in complete romantic overtones, either. She has really become excited to learn photography and Ted is really enjoying teaching. He is starting to think that he would love to start giving real classes, maybe one night a week.

Today, they planned to take a hike on one of the many trails around Leavenworth as Ted has been teaching Courtney how to use shadows and what to look for in different landscapes.

"Now a lot of people come out here in the Fall and take a bunch of pictures of all the colorful foliage. But sometimes they miss the best shots. Sometimes it's way better to take the same picture in black and white. The bold variety of colors can give you such a variance of grays that can be so impressive. When I was in Tennessee, the Fall foliage in the Smokies were so vivid and bold – it looked like God spilled paint all over the place. The color shots were always impressive, but often times the black and white version told a better story. You always have to think of the story your picture is telling you. So today I want you to take both color and black and white pictures every time so you can compare when you download them."

"I never thought of that." admits Courtney who is busy looking around for her next shot.

"That's having the eye of a photographer. It's not just seeing the object before you, but being able to see what might be if you used a different lens or filters to make the object more dynamic or tell a different story."

Of course Ted was teaching Courtney how to take good pictures, but neither hesitates in using the time together to get to know each other better too. They are both becoming more and more comfortable talking to each other, though Ted clearly backs off and redirects the conversations that involve Lilly. Courtney doesn't push Ted to talk about it as she has learned from personal experience that when you lose someone that you love so much, it is always better to let them talk about it as they feel comfortable in doing so.

Ted appreciates how Courtney doesn't push him about Lilly, but he also knows that he eventually will have to get to a place of celebrating Lilly's life. And he understands that his reluctance to talk about it isn't just because of Lilly, but it also involves Carrie, the daughter he loved being a dad for. He knows it would be so much easier having Carrie with him to help him work through the loss of Lilly than it is being alone dealing with the loss of both of them.

Eventually he'll get there, but for now he knows that it's a tall order to ask a heart to heal from a loss like that. Ted knows that part of what makes him open to Courtney is her gracious and understanding of his loss and her willingness to let him share whatever he wants at his own pace.

As they make their way back to the shop, Courtney gathers her belongings to head back home, while Ted gets out a folder of his pictures to give her some examples to take home to study.

"Before you go, let me get you a couple of pictures from my files that you can study to see what I was talking about on the trail."

"That would be great. I appreciate it."

As he's going through his files, he comes across a nice black and white photo of Lilly. He hesitates, but realizes it really is a good example of how a black and white shot can give more emotional insight than color. Courtney can see his hesitance.

"Is something wrong?"

He pulls the picture out, "I'm hesitant to show you this one, but it really is a good one for what we were talking about."

He hands Courtney the picture and she knows why he hesitated, "Is this your wife?"

"Yes. I took a lot of pictures of her and they all came out great."

"That's because you shot them with the eyes of love." says Courtney as she looks at Lilly.

"She was a simple woman in that you wouldn't say she was beautiful, but her beauty was in how she carried herself. It was her strength and confidence, her warmth and kindness that made her simple exterior so beautiful. And when you take away the makeup, the color of her dress and make it black and white, it draws you to that spirit reflected in her smile and her eyes without any distractions. It really is a perfect example of how black and white sometimes is the best choice."

Courtney looks up at Ted and realizes this is a big step for him. "I really appreciate you sharing this photo with me. I know how hard it must be. It really does show her beauty from within – in her smile and in her eyes. I can see why it was important to take away all the colors to give this picture a much better story."

"Thank you. You're welcome to keep any of these other shots, but I would want that one back if that's okay. I'm just not ready to go there yet. I hope you understand."

"Of course. I'll look them all over and guard them with my life. I'll bring them back on our next class, I promise."

"I appreciate you Courtney. Getting to know you has really opened me up in ways I thought I never could. I've got a long ways to go I know, and I hope you are patient with me. But I understand that before I have a future, I have to accept the past."

"I know Ted. We have both had great losses And we both have a long ways to go, I'm sure. My hope is that we can get to a point together where we can appreciate what we had in the past without it taking away from what we could have in the future."

With that, Courtney picks up the folder and steps up to give Ted a hug.

It's a powerful hug that neither wants to let go of. And as they pull away, they stare into the wanting eyes of the other, wanting to find a kiss, but reluctantly making the hug the final word, as Courtney leaves the shop.

******

As Courtney is busy in the kitchen preparing dinner, Jo and the twins come through the front door after an exhausting day in Seattle.

After a blow by blow review of the days activities, Courtney takes charge of the night.

"It sounds like you had a great day with grandma. Why don't you two go change into your jammies while I serve up dinner. After dinner, we'll sit by the fire and watch Christmas movies and have popcorn and hot chocolate."

The twins don't need to be told twice for that action as they head up the stairs.

"They really are great kids, Courtney. You've done a great job with them since Bill passed. They seem so normal – in a good way of course." says Jo as she sets the table.

"It's funny how parents are always trying to rescue their children from the bad experiences, when in truth it's the children who adjust much better than the parents do. If I didn't have the kids, I'd be a basket case for sure. They really do keep me grounded."

During dinner, the conversation elaborates on all the adventures they had in Seattle. With the plates nearly empty, one of the twins asks mom about her day.

"So what did you do today Mommy?" asks Susie.

"I had a great day too. I went to Leavenworth for another photo lesson with Ted. We went on a hike on one of the trails and I learned so much about how to look for different ways to take pictures. It was fun."

"So you seem to be enjoying your photo lesson a lot." says Jo.

"I really am. Ted's a really good teacher."

"He seems like a very nice man. Is he single?"

"Mother, really."

"I'm just asking. I can see that your interest seems a little more than just taking pictures, that's all."

"Mom, we get along very well. His wife died a few years ago, so we both understand how it is. I wouldn't read much more into it than that."

Jo seems to let that be the last word for now as dinner is wrapping up and the kids are excited to get the movie night started.

After a fun day in Seattle, two holiday movies, a big bowl of popcorn and plenty of hot chocolate to keep them warm, Courtney can see that the twins have clearly missed the ending of the second movie.

"You grab one and I'll grab the other. I think these kiddos are done." says Courtney to her mom.

When they return, they get busy cleaning up, when Jo notices the folder of photos Ted gave Courtney on the dresser. She opens them to take a look.

"Are these your pictures?" she asks.

"No they belong to Ted. He wanted me to study them for various shading effects we were talking about on the trail. It's my homework, I guess." says Courtney with a smile.

As Courtney heads back to the living room, she notices her mom seems frozen.

Jo looks up at Courtney as she pulls out the picture of Lilly.

"What is this?" she asks mysteriously.

"Mom. It's Ted's late wife. He wanted to show me how a black and white photo can often times tell a better story." Courtney is confused at her mothers reaction to the picture. "Is there a problem?"

"Honey, if this is Ted's wife, then he's not Ted. His name is Kevin Dukes. This is Lilly DiPaul."

Courtney has no idea what her mother is talking about, "Okay. And who is Lilly DiPaul?"

"She is a legend in the music business. One of the greatest writers of all time. Artist are still recording her songs. He hasn't said anything about his past?"

"Well Mom, our relationship hasn't gone that far. Neither one of us talks much about our painful past. I had no idea about all this, but it doesn't really matter."

"Doesn't matter? Maybe for you, but I've been writing for Billboard magazine and the Los Angeles Times for years and this is one of the saddest stories the music industry has had. Kevin and Lilly were one of the really great couples in the music business. They put on charity events in Nashville that people are still talking about."

Jo pauses as she sees Courtney looking a bit overwhelmed as tears gather in her eyes.

"They went out to dinner a few years back and a deer ran out in front of them. Kevin tried to avoid it and ended up over an embankment. Lilly died instantly. Their daughter – Carrie, I believe was her name – died a few days later. Everyone in the music business was crushed. Kevin recovered, sold their home and left. No one has heard from him since. Everyone keeps asking what happened to Kevin. Lilly's publisher is the only one who knows and he's not saying anything."

"Honey, this is a huge story that would be so welcomed in the music business. They need to hear that Kevin is doing well. It will bring a lot of comfort to people."

Courtney shakes her head, "Mom, I'm sure there is a reason why Ted changed his name. I now understand why it's so hard for him to talk about his past. (She pauses in tears) I didn't know he lost a daughter too? I hear what you're saying about the music business needing to know, but I'll be honest with you mom, Ted and I are growing pretty close lately and I wouldn't do anything to hurt him or ruin what seems to be a very promising future for us. You may have to decide between the music business and your daughter's happiness, so you need to be careful."

Jo goes and hugs Courtney and doesn't rush it.

"Courtney, you have to trust your mother. I don't write for the National Enquirer you know. I have built my reputation within the industry as a writer who is fair and works hard to keep my stories positive. I'll talk to Kevin tomorrow and I'll promise him – and you – that I will not submit any story without showing it to him first. I'm a good writer and I know I can write the story that the music business needs to hear and still honor Kevin's need to live quietly in Leavenworth."

******

As Ted enters his shop from the back, he sees Jo standing at the door. It's not every day he finds someone waiting to get in, and he works quickly to put his things down and unlock the door.

"Jo. Getting an early start on the Christmas rush I see."

Jo walks in quickly and cuts to the chase.

"Ted, we need to talk."

"Okay. " he says suspiciously, "Is it about Courtney?"

"Oh no Ted. But she certainly seems to enjoy her times with you, but I think it's mutual so I'll leave that up to you two."

She turns around and takes a deep breath. "Listen Ted, last night after dinner I saw your folder of pictures you gave Courtney to study. When I asked her how you got a nice picture of Lilly DiPaul, she looked confused and told me that was your late wife. You're Kevin Dukes."

She pauses to let Ted have a moment. He seems void of any response or feelings as she continues.

"Ted I am a writer for the music business with a column in Billboard and the Los Angeles Times Entertainment section. You and Lilly are legends in the music business, especially in the Nashville family of songwriters. The whole industry was crushed when your wife and daughter passed away. Everyone has been asking about you. What happened to Kevin? Everyone understands the total grief you must be burdened with, but there are so many who just want to know that you're okay. You were a big part of Lilly's life and the music scene in Nashville. I think they need to hear that you're okay."

Ted looks away. He was afraid this day might come. His emotions are rudely breaking his peaceful existence that he so embraces.

"Listen Jo, Lilly was really good with the press. Early in her career a story came out about some wild affair she was having with an artist. Of course it wasn't true and Lilly handled it with grace, but it really had an impact on me. I could never understand how writers could throw these stories out there with no regard for the truth. That's why I moved here. I used my middle name, Theodore and became Ted- a quiet guy who just wants to live my simple life."

"I understand Ted. There are a lot of writers who only care about selling papers and making headlines and they know that the easiest way to achieve it is through controversy and negativity. It seems nobody cares about the truth any more. But those writers never last. They get the scoops that are juicy and throw stories at the public with complete disregard for the truth. They may achieve the fame, but in doing so they develop a reputation of hurting innocent people like yourself. They don't last because editors don't have an apatite for supporting writers who don't do their due diligence in reporting the truth."

"Ted I have no desire to hurt you or disrespect your life here in Leavenworth. That's not my story. My story is to tell the music world that Kevin Dukes is doing well. He's living a quiet life alone, but continues to be one of the most decent, caring people that we knew in the music business. They need to have that closure. They deserve to hear that you're okay. They lost Lilly too Ted, and even though I completely support your need for privacy, I think you're wrong to keep the music industry that was such a big part of Lilly and your world in the dark. I'm asking you to trust me as a writer."

Ted feels as if he has nowhere to go.

"I'm sure I can't force you to keep quiet and I know you can throw the freedom of the press at me with some notion that you have a right to tell my story. But I want you to know that I'm just now getting to a good place in my life. Your daughter has taken me to a place in my heart that I thought I'd never go again. When you write your story, you damn well better think of Courtney. Is the music business and your headlines more important than your daughter?"

Jo gets upset as she heads for the door, "Ted, that's not fair. I'm disappointed you would go there." as she leaves upset at the response.

******

For the rest of the day, Ted keeps himself busy at the shop. Luckily, being close to Christmas, his shop was very busy. He kept pushing away the conversation he had with Jo, but there definitely was an awareness that what Jo had said was true. He knew through his publisher that everyone was asking about him. He seemed to turn down requests for interviews every time he talked to his publisher and he knew he didn't make life easy for him.

But it was more than just Lilly and the music business. Carrie was only seven years old when the accident happened. He loved being a Dad. He and Lilly were talking about getting a little brother or sister for Carrie because they both loved being parents so much. He couldn't imagine doing an interview and talking about Lilly and her music without talking about his daughter. It seemed so wrong, and he felt his daughter deserved more.

But he also thought about the life he had in the music business. They made a lot of friends. Good friends too. They had so much fun throwing parties and events that raised money to help so many under served people. The more he thought about that, the more he understood where Jo was coming from.

Meanwhile Courtney and Jo kept busy too. Courtney took the twins to a different location near Monroe to shop, play and enjoy the festive surroundings while Jo stayed back to work on her story.

That evening as Courtney was busy preparing dinner, the twins gave grandma a complete rundown of their fun outing with mom. The kids seemed to be the only ones on this day that embraced the holiday season with any enthusiasm.

When Jo went into the kitchen to refurbish her empty glass of wine she knows Courtney is avoiding her. Courtney knew she was going to talk with Ted but was afraid to ask anything.

"Sounds like you and the kids had fun today."

"We did. Your day went well?"

"It was okay. I talked to Ted and then spent most of the day working on the story."

"He's okay with that?"

"Not really, but I think once he sees what I've written, he'll come around."

Courtney puts down what she is doing and looks at her mom.

"Mom, I'm really falling for Ted. It's been a while since I felt this way about someone."

Jo interrupts, "Honey I know. Ted made it clear to me that it's a mutual attraction. I understand that. I won't do anything to get in the way of those feelings between you two."

Jo pauses as she looks deeply at her daughter in frustration, "Courtney, I'm a good writer and you need to understand that there will not be one word in my story that doesn't start with you and Ted in my heart. I think I deserve your trust."

They hug without another word about it.

******

The next morning as Ted walks in from the back of his shop, he gets to his routine of preparing for what he hopes to be another busy day. When he goes to unlock the front door, he notices an envelope laying on the ground. He picks it up and as he walks back in, he notices that it's from Jo. He pulls out the contents which is three pieces of paper. He knows right away that it's the story she wants to submit.

On top, the first page is a letter to Ted.

Dear Ted;

Enclosed is the story I have written about you that I would appreciate your approval for. Please know that I will not be submitting it for publication until the Spring, as I do not want anyone associating my story with my Christmas vacation to Seattle.

I do respect your privacy and I hope you find the story respectful of that as well as being a nice comfort for those who shared so much in your loss. I strongly believe that there are many within the music world who will benefit greatly from reading this.

I'm not looking to disrupt your life, I'm hoping to enrich the lives of those many who care about you, Lilly and Carrie.

Best regards – Jo

He's Doing Well

A few years ago, the music world lost one of their brightest stars. Not an artist, but a writer who made so many stars shine.

Lilly DiPaul was one of those writers that only comes around every now and then. Her ability to tell us stories in lyrical motion made every artist always look to her whenever they needed a hit. Her songs truly connected to the every day people. Her songs can be found on all the great artists albums of our time. They are still being recorded today.

It's not fair when life takes away someone like Lilly at such a young age. She died instantly in a car accident, and her beautiful 7year old daughter Carrie died a few days later. Her husband, Kevin Dukes , survived with several broken bones and one horribly broken heart.

Within a year, Kevin sold their house in Nashville and he moved away. It has become the sixty million dollar question : Where is Kevin Dukes and is he okay?

Lilly and Kevin were one of the great couples in the music business. Their willingness to host charity events and fund raisers for those less fortunate were legendary in Nashville. If you saw an event with their name on it, you knew it was going to be a first class event and help out a much needed charity.

Lilly was loved by everyone who spent any time around her. Her positive attitude and bright smile inspired everyone and left you believing that she was the happiest person on earth. She loved her work, she loved her family and she loved to help others.

Kevin was her perfect match. Her rock. Always with his camera. Kevin was much less outgoing than his wife and gladly let the spotlight always fall on her. Kevin was comfortable taking the pictures that were famous in their own light. He took wonderful pictures and for those in the know, he was a creative mover who made so many of Lilly's charity projects work.

It was a tremendous loss when we heard about the accident. The whole music world seemed to come to a silent stop. The numbing sadness was so thick throughout the industry that many wondered if we would ever hear music again.

And in the center of all this sadness, we thought of Kevin. The music world lost a legend, but Kevin lost a wife and daughter that he loved so dearly. Lilly and Carrie was his life.

When he moved away, no one questioned his reasons. We all understood. Kevin never enjoyed the press and with all the requests for interviews and stories, it only made sense for him to move away and start his own path.

Since the accident, people have asked about Kevin to no avail. Lilly's publisher was the only one who knew anything about Kevin and he was not talking. Even when the CMA wanted to do a special feature on Lilly and desperately wanted Kevin to make an appearance, the publisher stood firm to honor Kevin's privacy.

Recently, I was doing some work and driving through a small town and by luck, happened to cross paths with Kevin. At first, he looked familiar, but being that most of my work comes out of L.A., I admit it was merely a passing thought at first. But it bugged me and when I asked him if he was in movies (I'm so L.A.) He assured me he wasn't.

It wasn't until that night in my hotel room that I saw a piece on Lilly DiPaul and it clicked immediately.

I found Kevin Dukes.

The next day I went to find him again and luckily, it was a very small town which made the search quite easy.

When I told him who I was, he had a look of fear that was obviously not welcomed. I assured him that I was working on another story and would never divulge his whereabouts, so help me God.

But I did tell him that there were so many people in the music business that would love to know how he's doing. He agreed to join me for a cup of coffee, as long as I promised not to disrupt his private life.

It was a delightful conversation with a man who was dealt a pretty bad hand in life. He spoke fondly of Lilly and Carrie and the difficult road of life without them.

But all things considered, he was the same Kevin we all knew before. Friendly, generous and more than happy to turn the spotlight on Lilly.

I will honor Kevin's desire to be left alone, so don't even try to get it out of me.

I just wanted my music world family to know that Kevin Dukes is doing well.

That's all we wanted to hear, after all.

******

When Ted was done reading her story, he felt that maybe he hadn't given Jo a fair response. She truly wrote a good story and kept her promise. And he felt her story would bring some closure to many of the friends that he and Lilly had. She was right to tell the story and he felt bad about giving her a bad time about it.

As he considers everything, he gets a text from Courtney.

'Photo class later today?'

'I'd like that. Maybe we could hit another trail?'

'Great! How about I show up there about 3?'

'I'm looking forward to it.'

Ted feels good about seeing Courtney again. He really is falling for her and is thinking it may be time for him to take a risk with love again.

Meanwhile, Courtney – who is unaware that her mom dropped off her story to Ted – was happy to know that Ted is at least responding to her. She's not sure if she needs to apologize for her mom or not, but she is sure that she is ready to take her relationship with Ted to a new and more serious level. She is nervous and concerned as she has the kids to think about as well. But hearing about his daughter makes her think that Ted would be okay with their situation.

As she comes into the shop, Courtney finds Ted busy helping a customer, so she puts her camera on the counter and quietly goes through a bin of pictures near the front. She's not sure what to expect today and is a bit nervous.

"Hi Courtney" says Mary who startles Courtney from her thoughts.

Mary is called the town's pinch hitter, as she can be found in many of the small businesses around town covering for the owners when they need to be away. She's a retired teacher who has a deep passion for her Seattle Mariners baseball team, so picking up some extra cash around town helps her be able to make a few trips to the ballpark in the Summer.

"I'm sorry, did I frighten you?" says Mary, a bit humored.

Courtney laughs as she gathers herself, "No – well yes – I wasn't paying attention. How are you Mary?"

"I'm good, thanks. I'm helping Ted out this afternoon because he has another photography class. You must be his student again?"

"Yes. I'm really getting into it. I hope it's not tying you up too much."

"Are you kidding? I hope you're a slow learner. Ted's really enjoying teaching you and if you keep it up, I might be able to buy season tickets this year."

They both laugh as Ted comes over.

"Hi Courtney. Ready for a hike?"

"Sure am. What are we going to learn today?" Courtney asks.

"Photography. This is a photography class you know." Ted says with a smile.

"Ha, Ha, Ha." responds Courtney, happy to see Ted in a good mood.

"Mary, are you okay for a bit?" Ted asks Mary as he puts on his coat and grabs his camera.

"I'll be fine. Take your time."

As they head out towards the trails outside of town, the air is cautious. This is the first time they've been together since the 'secret reveal', so they are both guarded in their approach to each other.

Courtney is unclear how much her mother may have affected Ted's feelings about her, while Ted is unclear if his secret past has had an affect on Courtney. Their chit-chat is painfully slow and uninspired, until they arrive, get out of the car, and begin their journey down the trail.

The fresh, crisp air and beautiful scenery seems to loosen their spirits. It's a good day for taking pictures, yet there is a sense that today's class will be more about being together and less about taking pictures.

"Ted, I'm really sorry about my mom. When she told me about

your past, it really took my breath away. I can't imagine what you've been through losing your wife and your daughter like that. I'm really sorry."

"It's okay. When your mother talked to me, I wasn't upset. I figured the truth would eventually come out. I'm not trying to hide from my past, I'm only trying to live with it. I was only afraid that it might push you away."

Courtney looks at Ted, "No Ted. It made me appreciate you more."

They both pause and look at each other with reassuring eyes that today's hike will lead them on a path to their hearts.

"I know my mom wants to write a story, but I want you to know I'm trying to discourage her from doing so. I'm guessing that was the reason you left Nashville and changed your name."

"It's okay Courtney. She already wrote the story and dropped it off this morning."

"Really? Well I'm glad she took some time to think about it." Courtney says with a strong dose of displeasure.

"Actually Courtney, your mother is a really good writer. Her story was really well done and appropriate. And she promised not to publish it until the Spring so no one can trace it back to her vacation with you here."

"So you're okay with it?"

"Yes. I suppose a lot of why I moved out here and changed my name was because of my dislike for writers. Lilly was always great with the media, but not me. We barely got done with the funeral and writers were already trying to get me for a story. I had to leave so I could just deal with it on my own without a lot of writers bugging me. Your mother was right when she told me that there are writers who are like that, but most writers really do care about the stories they tell. Her story made me see that."

Courtney shakes her head, "I guess I was pretty hard on her too" she stops and turns to Ted, "I was so afraid. I'm having feelings for you that I never thought I would have again. I know it hasn't been long, but I can't deny that I think I'm falling in love again and I didn't want that to be ruined by my mother's career ambitions."

Ted and Courtney fall into a hug that is remarkably painful as they break into laughter, realizing having big cameras around your neck doesn't make for the most romantic embracing. They both remove their equipment, lay them on the ground, smiling at each before they try again. This time they melt into a warm affectionate kiss. A kiss they both knew would come. A kiss they both knew would take their hearts down a glorious new path of love.

******

Ted walks into the local diner that is off the main tourist section of town that the locals love to start their day at. He finds a seat and greets the many locals as he settles in and gets his cup of coffee.

It isn't long before Jo walks in and sees Ted, making her way to their table.

"Hope you didn't have any trouble finding this." says Ted as Jo settles into her seat.

"No problem at all. I'll be fine once I get a cup of hot coffee to melt some of the ice." she says rubbing her hands together.

"I guess they don't do cold very well in L.A., right?"

"No. If it dips into the 50s, everyone panics." as she wastes no time taking a sip from her cup of coffee that has arrived and continues to hold the cup to warm her hands.

As the server takes their order and heads off to post it, Ted is anxious to get to the conversation.

"I wanted to thank you for the story you wrote … and apologize too. I guess it only takes a few bad writers to create a bad environment of distrust. I'm sorry that I put you into that category."

"Oh don't worry about that. There's a lot of good writers who spend way too much time fighting for their reputations that a handful of idiots have ruined. I'm sure Lilly felt the same in the songwriting world."

"She did. And I got an ear full many times about it."

Jo smiles, "So you approve of my story?"

"Of course. You really did a nice job and I appreciate that you won't publish it until the Spring. You know, both Lilly and Carrie had birthdays in April. Might be a good time to publish it then."

"That would be great. It would nicely distract the vultures from trying to find you." Jo says with a smile. "I'm really glad you liked it."

"It really got me thinking. A lot of what you said is true. Lilly and I made so many really good friends, especially in Nashville. I've been so focused on surviving my own grief without giving much thought about all those friends who lost Lilly too."

"I think those friends understand Ted. But I also know they will appreciate hearing that you're doing okay."

"You're right." he pauses, "I was wondering if you might want to help me with a project?"

Jo sits up ,"I'd be happy to …. I think."

"I have more money than I'll ever need and every quarter, I get even more money. I'm happy to help out around here when I hear of families in need, but it's a pretty small town. I was thinking of all the events Lilly and I put on and was thinking it would be nice to start a foundation dedicated to helping the people in the music business in their time of need. There are so many people who make the shows so special. Engineers, set designers, costume designers, musicians of course. They work hard and get paid well when they're working, but they all know how to bartend too. That's why Nashville has so many good restaurants. That's what Lilly and I loved about living there. So many people with such a passion for music. It's a real feast AND famine lifestyle that you don't see in many places. Everybody helps each other out, though. I want to start the Lilly's Song Foundation that we can set up with a lot of the money I make from Lilly's songs. It should be available to help music industry and food service industry workers in their time of need, since they're both pretty much the same industry."

Jo shakes her head with a smile, "That is such a wonderful idea, but not surprising. I'd love to be a part of it. What can I do?"

"Well I want to remain Ted. I want to stay here in Leavenworth. I don't need to tell you that my future includes your daughter – I hope. I'm happy to fund the foundation, but I was thinking maybe you would be good for getting the right people with the right heart to run the foundation."

Jo smiles at Ted as she considers her response.

"You know Ted, if you're serious about me helping out, I will tell you that I've been looking at my options for a while. I've been in journalism for a long time and I've been feeling like making a change. I would love to get involved with something like this. Maybe I could make my story about you in April be my last column. That would be a great way to go out. Tell the music world that Kevin Dukes is okay and start the Lilly's Song Foundation. And since I've helped others before setting up a foundation, I know what to do, so if you're okay with it, I'd love to start getting it set up."

"That would be great Jo. If you and our publisher in Nashville can work out all the details, I'll make sure the funding is there to get things started. My hope is to have the foundation taken care of by others so I can just stay focused on my life here in Leavenworth."

"Well my goal is to build a foundation that reflects the spirit and legacy of Lilly while providing you with the time and environment you need to be with Courtney. I really love the thought of working for a foundation that helps the people who make music, but I also like the thought that somewhere down the road, I may become your mother – in – law?"

Ted smiles, "Let's do one thing at a time. Right now you concentrate on the foundation, and I'll concentrate on Courtney."

As they get up to leave, Jo hesitates in thought.
"I think this has been the best Christmas ever."

"We still have two days until Christmas, Jo ... but I'm thinking you might be right."

"Ted, I'm always right, get use to that."

8

Christmas of '82

(non-fiction)

Being a single parent, one grows use to adversity, but it always seems to hit the hardest during the holidays. Nobody wants to do more for their children over the holidays than the single parent, but the reality of living from paycheck to paycheck makes the magic of the holidays more wishful thinking than anything else.

It was Christmas, 1982, and I was coming into the season a tired, frustrated young man trying to balance a world of being a father, mother, breadwinner, bill juggler, cook, maid and friend to my two little girls, Tracy and Kelly.

As the holiday spirit began to warm the hearts of anticipation, I found myself feeling kind of down and not very excited. I usually love this time of year with all the lights, rat-race of shopping malls, no parking spaces, waiting in lines, crowded churches and all, but when you're a single parent on a low income budget, these things only serve as a reminder of all the nice things in life that are so out of reach in your world. It's an empty, lonely feeling to walk through a store and have your kids asking you if Santa will bring them this toy or that toy, knowing the answer will be no, but your love for them compels you to simply reply with a soft, "Maybe so".

It was just after Thanksgiving when I sat down with my girls and tried to explain to them that Santa would be leaving his presents at their Grandparents home, since they would be spending most of the day with their mother. I told them that all I could afford this year was to buy each one of them a present and, as much as I hated to tell them, I was not going to be able to even buy a Christmas Tree for them to decorate. I tried hard to downplay the hardships and instead assured them that they would have a great time when they went over to their grandparents house that morning.

They seemed to take this all pretty much in stride. That's what I love so much about my girls. As hard as times got for us, they always seemed to understand that daddy was doing the best that he could and if he said he couldn't get a Christmas Tree, they knew that it really was a matter of no money and not desire. Sometimes, I wished that they would throw a fit or start whining when I gave them the old, 'I can't afford it' routine. Their acceptance of the way things were only made me more frustrated. There were nights when I would literally cry myself to sleep as the frustration became too much for me to handle.

I worked at a large residential facility for emotionally disturbed children at the time. During the holidays, I would volunteer to work extra hours so that many of my coworkers could go home for the holidays – not to mention that the extra cash came in very handy for me. I worked every day but Christmas.

It was Christmas Eve and I was at the center frantically trying to get the kids ready for their passes with their parents. It was an atmosphere full of anxiety and busy chaos, but I was an old pro at this and was more than up to the task. Besides, the chaos kept me from feeling sorry for myself as I faced Christmas day sending my girls off to be with their grandparents while I spend the day on my own.

My supervisor came into the cottage that I was working to see how things were shaping up and make sure that I had all the festivities set up for those few kids who would not be going home.

He pulled me off to one corner and asked me how my Christmas was going with the girls. I told him that it was going to be a lean Christmas, but I thought I did a pretty good job of convincing them that Santa would be dropping off his presents to them at their grandparents.

He shook his head smiling and asked me to go with him to his office for a few minutes. I told my coworker to hold down the fort for a few minutes and started out the door with my supervisor.

"You know Andy, we only have two girls here at the center, and both of them are almost too old for most of the stuff we had donated to us." he told me.

I made a futile attempt to show interest in what he was saying, but frankly, my mind was somewhere else. As we got to his office, he opened the door and I noticed that his office was full of toys.

"Andy", he said as we entered the cluttered room, "I've been trying all morning to find another agency that could use this stuff, but everyone else seems to be in pretty good shape, too. I thought you might take some of this home to your girls and help me get rid of it." he said with a smile.

I looked at him with amazement as he put his hand on my shoulder and continued, "Besides, you don't think they really bought that story about Santa dropping off his presents at their grandparents, do you?"

With a big lump in my throat and my eyes heavy with appreciation, I began to fill bags with stuffed animals, dolls, coloring books and other goodies. For the first time in a long time, I began to feel as if Christmas truly was a season of miracles.

That night, as I was tucking in the girls, I reminded them that there would only be two presents for them when they got up in the morning and how they would get all the good stuff when they went to their grandparents.

My youngest daughter, Kelly, smiled and told me not to worry. "I'm sure Santa will help you out, daddy". A big hug and a kiss from daddy and they were off to dreamland, unaware that 'Santa' would be up most of the night wrapping the many wonderful gifts that had been so generously provided earlier that day.

It was getting late that evening when I heard a knock on the door. It was Bobby, my next door neighbor. Now Bobby is the kind of guy that society looks down on, for the most part. He's a real biker type with the long hair, beard, black leather jacket and boots, old jeans and a colorful vocabulary that was not ideal for raising kids with.

We lived in a duplex that shared the same yard which consisted of engine parts and motorcycles on his side and tricycles and Barbie dolls on mine. We were different as night and day, but really got along great.

Underneath that rough cover was a gentle man who seemed to really respect my world of raising those girls on my own. I really don't believe that there was anyone else at that time who treated my girls better than did Bobby.I invited him in and offered him a beer, but he seemed anxious to get right to the point.

"Hey Smitty, I noticed that you didn't have a Christmas Tree up when I came over to use the phone the other night@, he said. Bobby had no phone and was known to come over to use mine from time to time.

"Well you know that I'm lucky to get the rent paid on time. Bills don't take holidays, ya know." I said, a bit surprised that he should even ask.

He quickly fired back, 'Well hell, don't you think that the girls deserve more than just the rent?"

He started back out the door as I stood there trying to figure out what the point was to his questions. He came back in the house with a huge Christmas tree, six-pack of beer and a smile from ear-to-ear.

"Merry Christmas, pops!"

I asked him where he got it, and immediately withdrew my question. With a guy like Bobby I knew that the less information I had, the better off I was.

The two of us got busy trimming the tree and got all the presents arranged underneath it.

As the morning drew near, we sat down to have one last beer and take in the beauty of what was shaping up to be a real Christmas of miracles for my two little girls. We both laughed at the thought of the girls coming out of their room in just a few hours expecting to only find two presents sitting on the dining room table.

What a feeling to look at the tree with all the presents underneath it, knowing that it was all because of people who cared enough about me and my girls to lend a simple hand.

I'll never forget the look on those two girls when they came out of their room that Christmas morning. As if to be walking into a Disney fantasy world, their eyes lit up with excitement as their mouths fell open in disbelief. It was very hard for me to hold back the tears as the miracle of the season unfolded before me.

And as we walked outside later to head for grandmas' house, Bobby was sitting on his steps next door.

"Did Santa come to leave you presents, girls?" he asked.

The girls ran over and began telling him about all the presents and how Santa had even brought a Christmas tree!

As they spoke, Bobby looked over at me smiling and winked as if to tell me how great it was that he was a part of the miracle of that Christmas in '82.

9

Magic Photo Files Project

"Please come in and have a seat." says Santa as four of his elves walk in.

"Thanks for coming. I have a new project I'm starting and you four have been chosen because I'm too busy, I don't want to do this, and you four would be a much better choice to handle this project than I, So I took a vote and voted you in. You're Welcome."

The four elves look at each other not sure if they should be excited or not.

"It's called the Magic Photo File Project and I think it's going to be fun, so stop looking at me as if I'm about to tell you that we're having liver and beets for dinner tonight."

The elves raise their eyebrows in a horrified expression as Santa laughs.

"Loosen up, this is going to be fun. I chose you four because I knew you would love the project, so relax and pay attention."

Elves love to have fun, but can be rather touchy and timid when Santa starts a new program. Of course Santa knows this and loves to tease them in a good hearted way.

"I came up with this Magic Photo File Project because, as you know, I spend a lot of time reviewing families during the course of the year to get ideas for the kids and all. Many times, I come across families that are struggling emotionally. Could be any number of reasons, but emotionally, these families have hit a wall. The love tank seems to be running on empty, and it always makes me sad because I know they have good hearts.

"What I usually do when I come across a family like this is to pull up their Photo Files on their computers and start at the beginning, pushing the slide show viewing option and sit back to enjoy. It never fails to give me a history of a very good family." Santa pauses in thought before sharing a side thought, "You know, I'm always amazed at how the earthlings take so many photos of events in their life, stick them in a file and never look at them again. What's the point, right?"

The elves look at each other nodding in agreement with Santa.

"So anyway, I was looking through a photo file and it occurred to me that this might be a good project for us here at the North Pole. What if I sent you, the members of the Magical Photo File Project, a family that is struggling, some general information and any specific photos to look for and you all could put together a nice slide show for the family, put it on their opening screen with a title of 'Open Before Christmas'. The hope is that as they watch the slide show, they will see what I see when I do it, and their struggles will gain a whole new perspective and hopefully re-ignite the spirit of Christmas for them."

Santa looks around at the elves who are much more relaxed now and even have a hint of enthusiasm.

"Yes, Focus Freddie." Santa calls on one of the elves who has a question.

"What if they don't have any pictures. A lot of families don't take photos any more you know."

"Good question with a really good answer. I talked to God and he gave me full clearance in situations like that to call on the Guardian Angels at Earth Operations Headquarters and they have full access of the families life and would be happy to assist you in developing a nice slide show. And if the family has no computer, we simply make it a Christmas gift for them. Maybe have a tablet with instructions to turn it on and have it open to the slide show we have created. God has also encouraged me to have you notify the guardian angels of anyone we do a slide show for so they can help us out on their end as well. I know you elves are going to have fun with this, and I encourage you to go wild with it. Remember, these will be families that are struggling and need to be lifted up and we have Gods full support to do whatever it takes to cheer them up, so don't hold back. But do run any really crazy ideas by me before you implement it, just to be safe."

"Any other questions?... yes, Patty Pixel"

"Do you want each of us to take a family, or all of us work on one family at a time?"

"Another good question. You all work together. I chose you four because I thought you made just the right mix. Focus Freddie and Patty Pixel are exceptional at looking at the details and editing a photo to maximize the quality of the shot. Digital Dave is an excellent computer technician who can put together a wonderful slide show, and Frieda Framer has a keen eye for capturing the emotional content perfectly. The four of you working together should be able to put together some really good slide shows that will pull these families back to the emotional compassion that they have been missing. I think you elves are going to do great work."

"This is going to be so much FUN!" says Frieda Framer who is always the emotional one. "I can't wait to get started."

"Well it just so happens that your first project will be a rather tall order for you. As you know, the world has been dealing with a pandemic for over a year now. Safe to say that every family in the Santa delivery zone has been struggling. People have lost their jobs, families have been in isolation, working from home, children doing on-line schooling without being with their friends, and that's not counting the many who have had to deal with the virus within their own families. Needless to say, the world could use a lift this holiday season, so I have put together a list of all the people who have struggled due to the pandemic with no added issues that you can put together a simple slide show of encouragement for. I've listed them on your computers and linked you to their photo files already. I'm asking you to choose about twenty or so good photos that you feel will encourage them to hang in there and be positive. I will have these slide shows posted on their computers three days before Christmas. The first and last slide will have the same message of encouragement for everyone, so it will basically be a fancy Christmas card."

"Wow. That's a lot of slide shows for just four elves? We're good, but not that good, Santa." says Patty Pixel.

Santa smiles, "Ah yes, but Santa has you covered. I got the 'pause' button that God lets me use every Christmas Eve to pause time and let me catch up in a busy neighborhood before I start up time again. It will be used in this room for you all to create these slide shows without using up any earth time."

"That's awesome!" says Focus Freddie as the others agree with enthusiasm.

"Awesome indeed. So I'll leave you to your project and if you have any questions, please don't hesitate to call me. I'm sure after you do a couple and get the hang of it, you'll be cranking out these encouraging slide shows in no time at all. Thanks for your help."

As Santa leaves, the elves are busily pulling up their list and getting started as the Magic Photo File Project begins to take shape.

Santa was right, of course, as the four elves quickly get into a rhythm that is making beautiful, uplifting slide shows for everyone in the Santa delivery zone on earth.

Frieda Framer pulls up the file and goes through every picture, looking for the 20 or so pictures that best trigger an emotionally positive response. She returns the file to the earthling computer and attaches the 20 pictures chosen to the link and passes them over to Focus Freddie and Patty Pixel who crop and tweak the pictures to give each one the maximum emotional impact. Then they pass the 20 photos with the link on to Digital Dave who is a master at putting the pictures in just the right order to create the perfect slide show.

They have no idea how long it has taken them because of the pause button Santa gave them. Every day when they get together in their work place, they push the pause button. After they have created a large group of slide show greeting cards and are a bit hungry, they push the pause button and leave, only to find all the other elves are just starting their day. It takes a little time to get use to the tricks of working at the North Pole, but every elf will agree that you simply can't get a better assignment in the elf world than working at the North Pole. Santa has such a great connection to God, who is always more than happy to help Santa out with awesome tricks that make the work at the North Pole so much easier.

The elves of the North Pole are truly happy elves.

******

"Good to see you, please come in." says Santa as the four elves enter Santa's office after having completed the rather large project of creating encouraging slide show greeting cards for everyone in the Santa delivery zone.

"That wasn't such a hard project, right?" he says as they take their seats and laugh at the comment.

"If it wasn't for that pause button, we wouldn't be anywhere near done, that's for sure." says Frieda Framer as the others agree whole heartedly.

"Ah yes, but you did have the pause button. If I didn't have access to the pause button, I would never considered having you four take on a project like that. So tell me what you think about the project before we move on with it."

"I thought it was a great experience. My problem was in narrowing all the good picture down to the 20 we used for the slide show. I agree with you Santa, that the earthlings take so many great pictures that capture the emotions of the events in their life, but then just stick them in a file never to be seen again. I had to bring a lot of tissue boxes every day because there were so many touching photos to go through, and I don't even know these people I'm looking at." says Frieda Framer.

"It is amazing how these earthlings pay so much money for therapy when they have files full of memories that would better serve to build their confidence and fill their hearts with love, and they never open them." says Santa in agreement.

"And these people spend a lot of money on really good camera equipment. I'm sure Patty Pixel will agree with me that there were a lot of really good pictures that we barely had to do anything to." says Focus Freddie.

"That's no joke," Patty Pixel agrees, " Those earthlings are very good at documenting their special moments in life, you'd think they'd be good about using them to help appreciate what their life is all about."

"Maybe that will change when they open up our awesome slide shows we created." says Digital Dave.

"I certainly hope so. I checked them out and you four did a really good job. But let's not beat up the earthlings for what they don't do, let's appreciate that they do take pictures that gives us another opportunity to promote love in their world. The pandemic has been rough for so many earthlings. I think you did a great job of using their pictures to cheer them up again. It would be nice if they learned from this what pictures are for, but if not, we are here to help them out. Thank you." Santa agrees.

" So now that you fully understand what this program is all about, I think we can move on to the next phase of it." says Santa to get them on to the point of this meeting. "I have some special assignments already lined up for you to take on. These will be different in that I don't want them to be cookie-cutting slide shows. I want them to be unique to their own situation. I'll give you a full report of the situation that has brought them to this point in their life and some ideas of what I think is needed. From that, I want you four to create your slide show. I only have one rule in doing these slide shows –

Whatever it takes to reach their hearts! If you can reach them in one photo, great. If you need thirty, great. We need to use this program to create slide shows that will take the earthlings deeper and deeper into their hearts until they surrender to the answer right in front of them and change the direction they are headed in a more positive direction and outcome. God and I encourage you to feel free to call on the guardian angels of the earthlings you are working with if you need anything cleared up for your project. And remember that if you can't find the pictures, the guardian angels always have access to their life too. The guardian angels can always capture pictures of tender moments that advance love, so don't hesitate to use them. They are busy angels, of course, so if you can create the slide show on your own, do so. But don't hesitate to call on them if you get stuck on something."

Santa stops as he can see in the faces of his four elves that they understand and are anxious to get started.

"So unless you have any questions, I have a file here for you to start with …"

Before Santa can finish, Patty Pixel jumps up, grabs the file from Santa's hand as the four elves bolt out of his office without another word, leaving Santa frozen, smiling and shaking his head as he talks to himself, "Okay then… you're dismissed…. (then in a louder tone) Thanks For Coming!" he says to the open, empty door.

"Looks like I chose the right elves for this program." He says as he goes to close the door laughing.

******

"Wow, this couple is in sad shape." says Frieda Framer as she reads through the report. "This guy even has the divorce papers ready to go after the holidays. What a chump. It says here they haven't had a tender moment in months and according to Santa, they both have been so busy avoiding each other, they have no chance of getting back to the love that's in their hearts unless we can create a slide show from the pictures of their past."

Frieda Framer sets the report down and looks at her fellow elves with a bright expression, "This sounds like fun!" she says with a bit too much enthusiasm.

"Yea, we'll have these two gushing in cheesy love within twenty pictures for sure." agrees Focus Freddie.

"I bet we nail it in fifteen pictures." says Digital Dave with confidence.

"I don't know, " says a cautious Patty Pixel, "He's already got the divorce papers ready. It's not easy to move the heart of a man who has already given up on love, you know."

"Let me pull up their photo file and see what I can find." says Frieda Framer as she stares at her screen, quickly scrolling through the pictures.

"Oh look at this one." says Frieda Framer as she posts a picture from the file of the man and wife in a very romantic setting."You can see the absolute love in their eyes, can't you?"

"I think we should pile on the pictures of his wife doing wonderful things. Playing with the kids, fixing up the garden, being a pillar of beauty at special events with him. We want this guy to really feel small. We want him to think 'This is the woman you want to dump? Like YOU can do better? What a dirt bag!' says Patty with obvious attitude.

"Woe, woe, woe little firecracker. We have to remember, Patty, that the objective here is to melt the guys heart into an emotional sea of compassion and love, not drive him into a pit of worthless depression. We want to encourage him to appreciate how much he has with loving memories, not condemn him for getting off track a little. Tender moments, Patty, tender moments." says Digital Dave.

Patty sighs, "I suppose you're right. But I think we need to remember that this is a guy who already has the divorce papers ready to go. This is a guy looking for the easy out to avoid having to do the work to get back on track. A little dose of guilt wouldn't hurt, that's all I'm say'n."

"The guilt will come when he looks at the love. Every picture has to reflect the love." says Frieda as she continues to scroll through the files, sending the really good ones to Focus Freddie and Patty Pixel to start working on.

As Frieda gets to the end of the files, she seems completely satisfied that they have enough pictures to turn this love around. While Focus Freddie and Patty Pixel freshen up and enhance each picture, they agree. And when Digital Dave shows them the final product, there is not a dry eye in the room.

******

'Open Before Christmas' the tag on the file says.

Doug is suspicious and annoyed that someone has been messing with his computer. He tries to think who it might be that would leave this file on his desktop. Probably Sue, his wife, which makes him even more upset. She's probably looking through his files to get the goods on him, but she would have been disappointed. He's always been very careful not to leave anything in his computer that could damage his spotless reputation. He chuckles at the thought of how long it took his wife before she realized she wasn't going to find anything.

Reluctantly, he opens the file:

'When it comes to LOVE,

it's always good to look at the past
in order to find the focus you need
as you move towards your future.
We wanted to help.'

says the opening screen. There's a 'Start' button that Doug pushes hesitantly.

As Doug watches the slide show, he is becoming more nervous and concerned. He tries to look away. He thinks he'd like to delete it. But with each slide, he finds himself unable to do anything but look at the pictures. The tender moments captured. The look of pure joy on Sues face. Look at how she's looking at me. Wow – I remember that night. I never laughed so much. Every pictures pulls him deeper.

The last frame has a final message:

'You and Sue have really good hearts.
For Christmas, Santa would rather you both
open your hearts instead of presents.
You both deserve the LOVE that your hearts carry.
We know you can do it, Doug.
Merry Christmas
Santa's Elves' at the North Pole

Doug quickly closes the file and sits back. Was this some kind of a joke? Where did those pictures come from? It doesn't seem like Sue to do something like this. That's just not here style. Who else would have pictures like that?

He shakes his head. He's over thinking it. It doesn't make sense.

Out of curiosity, he opens his pictures file and finds a folder that has pictures of one of the events reflected on the slide show and opens it. There is the same picture of Sue that was on the slide show. He looks at the surrounding photos which together takes him back to an evening spent with Sue that they enjoyed so much.

From there, Doug spends quite a few hours into the late night, traveling through the files of pictures that reflect a good life.

The next day found Doug a bit tired, understandably, and a bit subdued. He can't get his mind off of the slide show he received, and refuses to even think about where it came from. The Elves at the North Pole made me that slide show? Right – I'm sure no one would have a problem believing that one.

Meanwhile Sue seems a bit subdued as well. Not tense and edgy as she normally is. Doesn't seem to be interested in conversation, but thankfully, neither is Doug. There seems to be a clear reluctance to make eye contact between them.

Luckily, the morning routine of getting the kids off to school and yourself off to work serves them both well this morning. Any parent knows that having children can be part of the solution and part of the problem at the same time.

And being the holiday season, both Doug and Sue have no problem keeping themselves busy between the shopping for the kids, holiday events and regular routines.

But it's still there.

Every night after everyone else goes to bed, Doug stays in his office and watches the slide show. And afterwards, he always pulls up his picture files and spends some time looking through so many folders that have documented his life. For the first time, Doug is asking himself, 'How did our love get off track?'

It happened the next morning. They were getting the morning routine going and Sue was putting together the children lunches when she casually said, "I'm going grocery shopping today after work. Is there anything special you'd like to have for Christmas dinner?"

Doug nearly chokes on his toast. Wow. It's been a long time since Sue asked him what he wanted for dinner, let alone Christmas dinner. He hesitates, then smiles.

"Why don't you get a leg of lamb and I'll cook it?" he says.

Sue stops and slowly looks towards Doug, "Really?"

Sue use to love cooking with Doug and she especially loved it when he made a leg of lamb. It was her favorite. Of course, Doug knew this as well.

"Sure. It's been a long time since I helped out in the kitchen It'd be fun to do it again."

Sue desperately tries to keep her composure. She was expecting the usual, 'Whatever' response as he grabbed his things and walked out to work. It's been a long time since she saw this side of her husband.

Of course, they both quickly got back to their morning routines and went to work without any further conversation.

As Christmas morning came, there was a noticeable calm between Doug and Sue that had been growing stronger every day since Doug opened his slide show from the supposed Elves of the North Pole. They were both clearly guarded in their response to each other, but the holidays usually increase the tensions within families and this was clearly not the case this year.

After the kids opened their presents and were busy taking over the room with all their toys, Doug handed Sue a present.

With a look of uncertainty, she begins to open the gift. As she takes the lid off, she freezes as she sees the divorce papers staring up at her. Her heart sinks and her eyes fill with emotion as she slowly looks to Doug with an expression of absolute pain.

Doug sees that she doesn't get it and quickly encourages her to read the note with it.

She looks back inside the box and pulls out a small envelope.

Sue: I did some research and discovered that if you throw divorce papers on your Christmas log on Christmas morning, it will bring your family the warmest, happiest Christmas of all time.

Merry Christmas

I Love You

Doug

Sue looks back at Doug, who has tears falling from his eyes as well.

"Sue, I'm sorry." He says, then points to the papers inside her box, "That will never happen, I promise you that. Please throw those on the fire."

Sue stands up and nearly leaps into Doug's lap as they embrace in a passionate kiss that seems to melt their hearts together.

When they come up for air, Sue gets up and takes the divorce papers, rips them in half and scatters them onto the fire.

After a wonderful Christmas day of the kids playing with new toys while mom and dad cook a fabulous feast in the kitchen, the kids are carried off to bed and are sound asleep before the lights are turned off.

With the children quietly sleeping and the fire place slowly burning out, Sue and Doug settle into the couch to enjoy one more glass of wine.

"What made you change your mind?" asks Sue about the divorce papers.

Doug smiles, "Oh, it was crazy. I don't think you would believe me if I told you."

Sue perks up and looks at Doug, "Santa's Elves at the North Pole?"

Doug perks up and looks at Sue, "You did that?"

"No. I thought you put the slide show on my computer." Sue says.

"Wait…. you got one too? Was it the same one?"

"I hope not. Mine was a bunch of pictures of you. What was yours?"

"A bunch of pictures of you during some of the great moments we've had. Wow! Do you think they really came from Santa's Elves? I mean the pictures came out of our own files. Who could do that?"

Sue puts her hands on each side of Doug's face and looks into his eyes with passion.

"Whoever it was that did it, I'm glad they did." and she kisses him.

******

"Now that's what I was looking for when I started this program." says Santa as he stops the video and looks around at a table full of tissues and four elves sobbing.

As they slowly gather their composure, Santa looks at them with a big smile. "So I'm guessing you four want to continue in this program?"

"I just love happy endings, Santa. That's why I love working at the North Pole." says Frieda Framer, who is trying very hard to gather herself.

"Well hopefully you four will create a lot of happy endings. Are you ready for another one?"

Quickly, the four sit up and put their game faces on as Digital Dave says boldly, "Let's do it!".

Santa smiles, drops another folder on the table as he walks out, "Keep up the nice work, my friends. Oh, and making two separate slide shows for them was a nice touch. That really nailed it. Keep it going!"

"Heather is a thirteen year old girl desperately trying to break away from being a girl and heading for a world of being a teenager. Needless to say, her relationship with her mother is anything but charming. Her mother, Beth, is a good mother who doesn't try to hold her daughter back, although if you talked to Heather, she would give you the impression that her mother is completely smothering her and controls her every move." reads Frieda Framer to the others as they look at a new case.

"It's frustrating for Beth because she's always been a very supportive mother in every stage of Heathers life. But now Heather is moving into the world of being a teenager, and she is really good at it."

"I knew when Santa told us about this project we would be getting a lot of cases involving teenagers." says Focus Freddie as the others agree.

"Well it sounds like Heather has a good heart and Santa gave us the link to Beth's photo files as well as a link to Heathers computer. I've got the photo file up. [Frieda Framer pauses] WOW – there are a ton of pictures here. This lady has so many pictures of Heather. Geeze, lady, did you take pictures EVERY day for thirteen years? [Frieda Framer looks up to the others] Should be no problem finding some good pictures with this one!" she says brightly.

As Frieda Framer goes through the files and sends the good ones to Focus Freddie and Patty Pixel, she gets into a rhythm of being absolutely focused on the pictures as she scrolls through them, and is constantly blurting out [without looking away from her computer] "Oh my God, throw the one with the blue dress out. This one is way better."

Focus Freddie and Patty Pixel look at each other and decide to sit back and just wait for Frieda Framer to finish, as they seem to be deleting a lot of pictures they worked hard to get perfect, so it seems to be a lot of wasted effort on their part.

But Frieda Framer is a fast worker, and before long she sits back and looks to the others.

"That should do it. How many do we have?" she asks.

Focus Freddie and Patty Pixel look at their screen, then at each other, before looking to Frieda Framer, "147 pictures." they say without emotion.

"YIKES!," says Frieda Framer, "That's way more than twenty." as she scoots over to look at Patty Pixels screen and quickly starts deleting pictures.

"There, that should do it." says Frieda Framer as she scoots back to her computer feeling much better.

Focus Freddie looks at Frieda Framer, "Fifty four is still too many Frieda Framer. You have to understand that Heather does not have the pause button like we do. We do not want to keep her up all night, we just want to give her enough to soften her heart and get her headed in a better direction, that's all."

Focus Freddie looks at Patty Pixel who smiles at him, then he looks at his screen at the fifty four pictures. He highlights one and looks up to Patty Pixel, "Delete?"

"Yup." says Patty Pixel as she follows him on her screen.

This continues at a quick pace, with Frieda Framer constantly trying to jump in with a protest, only to be cut off with both Focus Freddie and Patty Pixel holding up their hands to stop her every time.

Finally the two get down to the twenty pictures or so needed and send the pictures over to Digital Dave, as they look over to Frieda Framer and smile.

Frieda Framer, ever the optimist, smiles back, "Wasn't that fun?" as Patty Pixel and Focus Freddie look at each other shaking their heads.

******

Heather always likes to sit at her desk in her room and watch some videos or check out the social media scene before she heads to bed. This has been one of the issues between her and her mom.

Beth knows that she has to be the bad guy because if she didn't go into Heathers room and remove the laptop and take it with her on her way to bed, Heather would likely be up all night.

Of course, Heather sees it as a prime example of the world of suppression she has been forced to live unjustly with.

As she opens her laptop, she sees a file that is tagged, 'Open Before Christmas'.

She quickly pulls it up and finds the first slide that says:

> *We know you are quickly moving forward*
> *to becoming an independent adult.*
> *But it's always good to look back first*
> *at the foundation your parents gave you*
> *When you were so dependent on them*

Heather pushes the 'Start' button and sees a picture of her mother holding her on the day she was born. Then a picture of her mother running next to her cheering her on enthusiastically when she was learning to ride a bike without training wheels. Twenty pictures that reflect a mother involved. Twenty pictures that trigger the memories of a mother who was always encouraging her. Twenty pictures of a woman who always gave up her own agenda to be a part of her daughters agenda.

Then she gets to the last slide:

> *Your mother doesn't want to stop you from becoming an adult*
> *She wants to help you become a good adult – like she is.*
> ### Merry Christmas Heather
> *Santa's Elves at the North Pole*

Heather stares at the final slide and reads it over and over, bouncing between the first two lines about her mother, and the last two about Santa's Elves at the North Pole? She's not sure what to make of it. Did her mother make this slide show? She doesn't think so. That really doesn't seem like something her mother would do.

She goes back to the beginning and plays the slide show again.

And then again.

Every time, she looks at the expression on her mothers face as she remembers the event that it represents. But after a while, she hears the familiar sound of her mother coming up the stairs to go to bed. She quickly turns off her laptop, unplugs it and stands to meet her mom who is quietly knocking and opening her door.

"Here you go mom. Goodnight" she says as she hands the laptop to her mother and turns towards her bed.

Beth raises her eyebrows surprised. This is the first time she hasn't had to wrestle the laptop away from her without a barrage of protest.

"Goodnight, honey. Do you want me to read you a bedtime story?" she asks.

Heather looks back at her mother with an 'oh, please' look on her face.

Beth smiles warmly and shrugs her shoulders, then with a strong dose of appreciation, says "Thank You." as she turns to leave.

For the next few days, Beth sees that Heather is being much more receptive to talking with her. There hasn't been any battles to get simple tasks done. She even wanted to talk to her about those touchy issues of what it's like when your body goes from a girl to becoming a young woman.

They agreed to go Christmas shopping together the next day, and Beth promised to take her by a woman's apparel shop and look at girly things.

As they walk into the mall, they notice a woman standing with a microphone and a guy standing next to her holding a camera. They recognize that she is a young reporter for one of the local stations.

"Hi, I'm Jessica Thomas, and I'm doing a story about having a female President and how it affects teenage girls today. Would you mind answering a few questions for me?" says the reporter to Heather.

Heather looks to her mom who shrugs and smiles, before saying 'Sure' to the reporter.

"Great. This will just take a minute. Mom, you can stand over by the camera man and you can stand next to me. What's your name?"

"Heather."

"Okay" The reporter waits for the camera to signal that they are on.

"This is Jessica Thomas. I am talking to teenage girls about having a woman in the White House, and today I'm with Heather. So tell me Heather, what do you think about having a woman being your President?"

"I think it's great. It's about time, really."

"Do you think a woman can handle the many issues of being the President as well as men?"

"I think a woman can handle anything better than the boys – except being stupid. Boys are much better at that."

Jessica laughs and jokingly says "Sorry boys" to the camera before she continues.

"So Heather, does having a woman President change your outlook of what you want to be when you grow up?"

Heather pauses a bit then shrugs her shoulders, "Not really. I want to be a good mother like my mom was for me." she says.

Jessica obviously sees this is not a keeper interview and moves quickly to exit.

"That's so sweet, Heather." as she turns to the camera, "This is Jessica Thomas reporting."

As Jessica moves quickly to thank Heather and move her out, Heather asks her when is it going to be on the news.

"Oh, well you know Heather, these stories take time. You do a lot of interviews like this and then you go through the editing and getting it down to the right time set and then it's still no guarantee that they will even air the piece, so there's no telling, really. But thanks for helping out Heather."

Beth can tell that Jessica was blowing off her daughter, so she moves quickly to get her back into shopping mode.

"That was so nice of you to say about me Heather." says Beth as they are walking away.

"Oh Mom, don't get all cheesy on me. I have no idea what I want to be when I grow up and I just said boys were stupid. I said that about you because I'd rather be cheesy than stupid."

Beth thinks about it and decides she loves that response and laughs out loud.

"You have lots of time to figure that out so don't worry about it.

And it's much better to be cheesy than stupid. [Beth looks over at Heather and smiles] It just takes boys longer to figure that stuff out."

They both laugh.

That evening as Heather hears her mom coming up the stairs, she decides not to close up her laptop.

Beth softly knocks on Heathers door and slowly opens it, finding Heather at her desk with the laptop open.

"Mom, can I show you something?"

"Sure honey." says Beth as she walks over to the desk and looks at the empty screen.

Heather points her mouse to the folder that says 'Open Before Christmas' and looks to Beth, "I got this about a week ago and at first I thought it was from you. But I don't think it is. I watch it every night and I just don't know what to think about it."

Heather pushes the 'start' button as Beth looks on.

With each picture, Beth becomes more emotional. After a few, she pauses the slide show and asks Heather where she got those pictures from.

"Mom, they're in the slide show. I didn't make the slide show."

Beth turns back to continue the show, "Those are from my files. They're beautiful."

"I know, really." says Heather as they both follow the slides reflecting a mother and a daughter creating thirteen years of wonderful memories.

When they get to the final slide, Beth seems frozen as she stares at the last slide for what seems to be a quarter of eternity, then looks at Heather.

"Santa's Elves?"

"I know. It's crazy. But who else could have done this with your pictures?"

"Is there a new band out named Santa's Elves?"

"Mom, really?! Do you think I would listen to them if there was? Besides, how would they get into your picture files?"

Beth looks off in thought before Heather redirects.

"Mom, let's watch again without trying to think of who did it, okay?"

Beth turns her attention back to the screen as Heather starts the slide show a second time. This time they both watch it in silence. This time Beth gets pulled into the slide show with more focus as she watches these pictures that reflect such wonderful memories. As the show ends, Beth looks to Heather.

"That really is a beautiful slide show."

"I know. I've watched it a hundred times and it just gets better. It makes me want to look in your picture files at the other photos." she pauses then looks at her mom, "I know I've been a hand full recently and I'm sorry mom. I know they always say they're cute now, but wait until their teenagers. But I don't want to be that teenager. I want that mom on the slide show to be my mom as I'm a teenager."

"I'll always be that mom for you Heather." says Beth as the two embrace.

As Beth wraps up the cheesy mother/daughter hugging, she says, "You know, I have a ton of pictures in my files. Maybe that would be a nice project for us?"

"That would be great. From bedtime stories, to looking at files of family pictures. Can't think of a better way to end the day." says Heather as she climbs into bed.

******

"Another great outcome. You elves are great!" says Santa as he looks around the table full of tissues and elves sobbing once again. "But I'm thinking I should get an extra supply of tissues before we continue." he says with a laugh.

"Santa, do you think we should leave off the Santa's Elves at the North Pole at the end? Seems like it's confusing people." asks Digital Dave.

"Don't worry about that. I only concern myself with two things – being truthful and getting a positive outcome. This was another great outcome, and you are Santa's Elves and you are from the North Pole and you are the ones who created the excellent slide show. You'll learn that being confused is pretty much a normal state for earthlings anyway. Nice work." says Santa as he drops another assignment on the table and leaves.

******

"Wow, this one is going to be tough, listen to this." says Frieda Framer as she reads through their next assignment. "This lady is actually thinking of taking her own life."

"No way" says Focus Freddie, as the others sit up to hear more.

"Way. She was thirty years old and engaged to the love of her life when she got sick. She had to have an operation, which saved her life, but she was told that she wouldn't be able to have children, so her boyfriend calls off the engagement because he wants to have a family." Frieda Framer reads as she's shaking her head.

"What a dirt bag! That guy doesn't deserve her." says Patty Pixel with obvious attitude that the others do not challenge.

"Oh wait, it gets worse." says Frieda Framer as she continues, "This girl, her name is Becky Brownstone [she looks at the others] she goes by BB, is a nurse. During the pandemic, she has been working twelve hour shifts non-stop, having to choose which patients to help and which patients to let die."

"That sounds so unreal. How can anyone make decisions like that?" says Digital Dave.

"It's a numbers thing. Too many sick people, not enough nurses. That's why they call it a pandemic." says Focus Freddie.

"So nurse BB is at a snapping point. It's not that she's planning to kill herself, but when she prays, she tells God she is more than ready to go." Frieda Framer reads.

"Talk about burnout." says Patty Pixel, "Who can blame her, though. Her life sucks"

"We're going to have to do something special for her." says Digital Dave, "Maybe we could talk to her guardian angel?"

"Santa encouraged us to call on them any time, but never told us how." says Patty Pixel as the others agree.

At that moment, the door opens and in walks a short little lady who is dressed in a green skirt, red and white stripped long sleeve shirt and a red pointed felt hat. It appears she was trying to look like an elf, but didn't really come close – the elves are very precise about their attire after all.

"Can we help you?" says Frieda Framer as the others watch the lady come in and take a seat with pained looks on their faces.

"Hi! I'm BB's guardian angel and you wanted to talk to me, so here I am." says the angel with confidence, as the others look at each other.

"Guess that's why Santa didn't give us any contact info." says a bewildered Digital Dave.

"Yes," says the angel, "I am BB's guardian angel so I monitor not only what is going on with her, but any other conversations about her as well. I heard Digital Dave say you should contact her guardian angel, and since that's me, I came right over." she says with a smile.

Patty Pixel, never the elf to be shy, breaks the silence, "Do all the guardian angels dress like that?" she says with an unflattering face.

The angel laughs, "Oh no. The angels are spirits, so we don't have any specific look. Whenever we are required to go to earth for any reason, we can take on any physical presence that best suits the situation we are going into. Do you like it?" says the angel as she stands up and spins around proudly.

The elves look around at each other, as Focus Freddie shakes his head negatively, indicating no comment needed – let's move on.

"Great," says Frieda Framer, "So do you have a name?"

"No, we don't need names in the guardian angel program. I'm BB's guardian angel until she passes into the spirit world and then I'll be assigned to the next child born and be their guardian angel. But you're welcome to call me whatever you want if it helps any."

"Well since we are working for a girl named BB, why not call her BA for Becky's Angel?" says Patty Pixel as the other nod in agreement, not so much because they like it, but because they are anxious to move on.

"So we have been assigned to make a slide show for BB using her photos, but as I'm looking through them, there isn't a lot to go on. Since she seems to be in pretty bad shape emotionally, we would love to have any ideas you might have." says Frieda Framer.

"Of course," says BA, "Thank you for wanting to help. BB has had a tough time the past year or so and her spirit is really down. She has a really good heart, which is nice, but it also can work against you. This pandemic can be very brutal for a nurse with so much compassion. She feels like she's drowning in sadness every day she goes to work. I don't think she's had any time to relax or laugh in months."

"I can only imagine. It must take a lot of compassion to be a nurse under normal circumstances, but in a pandemic, it must be overwhelming." says Patty Pixel as the others agree.

"It is." agrees BA, "There is so much sadness, it's hard to imagine how tough it is. That's why I don't think BB is suicidal. I don't think she wants to die, I think she just wants this world she's living in to end. I'm not sure that making a slide show with a bunch of pictures from her happy past would work either. I'm concerned that seeing pictures from her happy past might depress her more about her present situation. She keeps saying her job is to save lives, not watch people die who could live if only there weren't so many people sick. It's really sad."

"How long has BB been a nurse?" asks Focus Freddie.

"Well let's see…. she's thirty two years old, so I'm thinking she's been a nurse for about eight or nine years. She's always wanted to be a nurse and went right into nursing school from high school." says BA.

"Now you have access to every moment of her life, right?" Focus Freddie continues.

"I can pull up any moment of her life and give you a snap shot or video."

"In the years that she has been a nurse, how many lives do you think she has saved?"

"Well that depends on what you're looking at. Obviously you can say that there are patients every day that a nurse works with that would likely die if they didn't come to the hospital." says BA.

"Okay, let's narrow the group. How many patients did BB work with where she had a significant moment that turned their life around. Something BB said or how she treated them that made them pivot into a more positive direction in their life?' asks Focus Freddie.

BA looks at her screen and does a quick calculation, "Thirty seven." she says.

"Good … I was hoping you wouldn't say 147." he says as he looks at Frieda Framer and smiles.

"What are you getting at?" asks Frieda Framer.

"Well maybe it would be better in saving BB's life by showing her how she saved other lives as a nurse. You know, show her what an impact she's had on others."

"That might be a good idea." says Frieda Framer.

"But that won't be easy with just pictures." cautions Patty Pixel.

"It would be easy. I could add an audio thread to the slide show." says Digital Dave.

"Get out of here. No way!" says a surprised Patty Pixel.

"It's easy. I could add an audio thread or a music thread. There's a lot you can do with a slide show, ya know."

"Well that's a little information we could have used, YA KNOW. Why didn't you tell us before?" says Patty Pixel a bit annoyed.

"Didn't need to. The other projects worked perfectly with just the pictures. And the purpose of this program was to get people to look at their photos for the answers to their struggles. We only needed the photos. But in this case, it might help to add the audio to show BB how much impact she has had as a nurse."

"I like it." says Focus Freddie who turns to BA, "Do you think you could put together about eight patients. Maybe ones with really good stories that will leave no doubt that BB made a big impression on them?"

"I'm already ahead of you." says an excited BA who is busy typing on her computer, "I'm sending you eight pictures with the stories for the audio. Then I contacted the patients guardian angels to send me a current picture that we can use on the following slide that reflects how their life changed because of her."

"Oh this is going to be so cool." says Patty Pixel as she gets busy pulling up pictures on her computer as the others do as well.

The room becomes an explosion of creative energy as the elves work feverishly tossing ideas back and forth as they create the slide show for BB. Digital Dave is working with Frieda Framer who volunteered to be the voice on the audio stream, while Focus Freddie and Patty Pixel work on the photos to make each picture pull in the maximum emotional response, as BA works through her computer with other guardian angels to find the best pictures to use.

"Okay, we have sixteen slides ready to go. Do we need any more?" asks Digital Dave as a calm comes to the room.

"One more story," says BA as she sends another photo to the elves. "This girl is named Rosemary. Her guardian angel approached me a few days ago and we've been working together on it. She's seven years old. Lost both parents three years ago. There's not much family, and what there is doesn't want to take on the responsibility, so she is up for adoption and will live in foster care until she can find the right family.[BA looks up at the elves] Trust me, children do NOT want to get lost in the foster care system. You don't want to force feed a story like this, so I'm thinking we should have the eight stories of BB's life as a nurse, then show her the picture of Rosemary and keep it really simple. Say this is Rosemary. She's in room 3204 on the 3rd floor of your hospital. We think it would be great if you dropped by and said hello to Rosemary. And leave it at that. Don't say anything else. Knowing Rosemary's heart and BB's heart, I think if we do this right, we may create a situation where Rosemary can save BB's life and BB can save Rosemary's life. And in the guardian angel program, that's an outcome we want to celebrate."

The elves look around at each other with looks of excitement ready to explode.

"This is going to be so awesome!" says Patty Pixel as she pulls up the photo of Rosemary and gets to work.

******

"Open Before Christmas?" Says Becky as she turns on her laptop and finds the folder staring at her after another long day at the hospital.

"Oh great. Just what I need. Now someone has hacked my computer." She deletes the file on her screen shaking her head.

Within a few seconds, it pops back on her screen, this time it says, 'Please Becky, Open Before Christmas.'

"What the …." Becky deletes it again, gets up and goes to the kitchen to pour herself a glass of wine.

"I don't need this."

As she heads back to her chair, the file is back up on the screen and says, 'BB Please. We Promise It Will Make Your Day'

"WHO ARE YOU?!?" Becky says as she stares at the file and takes a sip of her drink.

"I swear to God if my computer goes crazy when I open this, I'm taking it out on my balcony and tossing it!" she says as she carefully points to the file and double clicks it.

We know it's been rough for you recently
We wanted to make this slide show for you
Thinking it might encourage you
Because we care

She reluctantly pushes the start button and grabs her glass of wine.

The first slide is a picture of her at the bedside of a patient and she's holding her hand talking to her.

Remember this patient? Her name is Betty. She was asking you to 'pull the plug' and let her die. She was in bad shape, but you stayed with her for a long time and talked to her.

The next slide is of the same woman a few years later, looking healthy and having a warm smile as she plays with children.

This is Betty now. She volunteers as a cook at a children's home and the children absolutely adores her. Because you didn't pull the plug. Because you spent the time with her. The children are thankful that you were there in Betty's critical time. Thank You.

Seven more stories with the same impact.

Eight stories of patients at a crossroad in their lives. Eight patients that she encouraged and spent time with.

By the time she got done with the eight patients, Becky's eyes were overflowing with emotion. She remembered each patient and was so pleased to see that things turned out so well for each of them.

Then the slide show brings her to Rosemary. This little girl triggered no memory. She never saw this girl before. What a cutie, she thought.

This is Rosemary. She's in room 3204 on the third floor of your hospital. We think it would serve you well to drop in and say hello to Rosemary next time you're at work.

The slide show reaches the final page.

You have a very compassionate heart, Becky
Your past reflects such a giving heart
We know your future will too
Merry Christmas and Thank You
for all you do for LOVE
Santa's Elves at the North Pole

Becky is overcome with emotion. Today was such a rough day at work, so the timing could not have been better. She's not sure how it came about, or who sent it to her, but she can not deny the emotional response in her heart. She would spend the better part of the night looking at the slide show. Over and over again. Each time drawing her deeper into it's message. It truly has been a rough couple of years, but for the first time in a long time, she is looking towards the future. For the first time in a long time, she is seeing hope.

The next day, Becky decides to leave early to go to the hospital, being anxious to drop by room 3204 to see what the connection Rosemary has in the slide show. One of her best friends is a nurse in the children's unit, so she can talk to her first.

"Hey BB, what brings you to the 3rd floor?" says Shirley at the nursing station.

"Hi Shirley. I wanted to see someone before I start my shift."

"Great. Who?"

"Room 3204. Her name is Rosemary." says BB.

"Of course. She's one of my favorites. How do you know her?"

"I don't. I got a note that said there was a girl named Rosemary in room 3204 that I should meet. I have no idea what this is all about, but I thought I'd go see her anyway."

"Who sent you the note?"

BB pauses in thought and decides that this is not the right time. "Listen Shirley, it's a long story that would be best told with a glass of wine. I know this probably breaks several regulations, but I'm hoping you can just trust me and know that I will explain it all later. Right now, I have no idea who this girl is or why I have been told to go see her. But something tells me it's going to be okay."

Shirley looks at her friend and smiles. She knows BB has never done anything crazy, so she trusts her to keep this from becoming a bad situation.

"Okay, girl. She never has any visitors except her social worker, so it would probably do her good. But if the social worker comes in, please just pretend you're a nurse and get the hell out of there before she can ask you any questions." says Shirley as she and BB heads towards room 3204.

"What about her family?" asks BB.

"Doesn't have one. Parents died about three years ago and she's been in foster care since." says Shirley as they arrive at room 3204.

Shirley knocks on the door gently and opens it, signaling to BB to stay while she checks on Rosemary.

"How's my girl today?" she asks as she walks over to the bed .

Rosemary is laying quietly, looking out the window.

"Hi nurse Shirley. I'm okay." says the girl as she sits up expecting the normal routine of taking vitals.

"Oh honey, I'm not here for vitals. I have someone who wants to visit you."

"Someone wants to visit me? Who is it?"

"She's a nurse on the 5th floor and a good friend of mine She wanted to meet you."

"Why?"

"Honey, you'll have to ask her. Mind if I let her in?"

Rosemary shrugs her shoulders, "I guess so."

"If she gives you any trouble, just ring for me and I'll throw her out, okay" says Shirley as she heads to the door.

"She's all yours, but remember – if the social worker comes in, you have to bail. You know how social workers are a bit touchy about privacy matters."

"Got it." says BB as she heads into room 3204 and Shirley heads back to her station.

BB walks over to the bed and finds the innocent little girl staring at her. They know nothing about each other which makes it a bit suspicious, but BB knows how to break the ice.

"You must be the Rosemary I've heard so much about." she says with a warm smile.

Rosemary raises her eyebrows, "Are you here to take me for more tests?"

"Oh no. I can do the test right here." BB leans in and looks very seriously at Rosemary's face, "I need to find out how long it takes you to smile." says BB as she pulls out her watch from her pocket and studies Rosemary's face.

Rosemary looks a little confused, but breaks into a big smile.

"Wow! Your smile muscles work great! You must do a lot of smiling."

Rosemary shakes her head, "I guess so."

"My name is Becky, but my friends call me BB. So I only need to know if you're my friend."

"I don't even know you." says Rosemary who is smiling and quickly relaxing more.

"Well that is a problem, isn't it. Let's see. My favorite food is spaghetti and tacos."

Rosemary smiles, "Me too."

"Crunchy or soft tacos?" BB asks curiously.

"Both... but I really like the crunchy ones."

"Me too.... I love going on walks and being outside... especially in the SNOW."

"I do too. I've always wanted to build a snowman." says Rosemary with a hint of sadness.

"Well there you go. We just have to be friends now, so you can call me BB, okay?"

"Okay" says Rosemary who is enjoying the company.

Just then the intercom comes on as Shirley announces that the social worker is coming.

"Okay, well it looks like I need to leave, but I enjoyed meeting you Rosemary. Can I visit you again?"

"Sure." says Rosemary without hesitation.

"Great. And don't say anything to the social worker about us, okay. They ask too many questions."

Rosemary nods in agreement as the social worker walks in and BB heads for the door.

"How's our Rosemary doing today?" says the social worker who looks at the unfamiliar nurse heading at her with a hint of suspicion.

"She's doing great. I was just checking her smile muscles and I must say, they are in excellent shape." says BB as she gets to the door and turns back to Rosemary. "Have a great day Rosemary, and keep working those smile muscles." she says as she winks and Rosemary giggles.

"Thanks for the heads up, Shirley." says BB when she gets to the nursing station.

"No problem. I know social workers need to do their job, but this one seems a bit too stuffy, if you ask me. So did you figure out why you needed to meet Rosemary?"

"Not really, but she certainly is a cutie. She likes both soft and crunchy tacos, though, so maybe that was it." says BB with a smile, "I've got to go start my shift. Thanks again Shirley."

As BB starts to leave, Shirley speaks up, "You know, they're looking for a family for Rosemary."

BB turns and laughs, "I live alone, that's not a family."

"You live alone and she's alone too. And you both love crunchy and soft tacos. What more do you need?"

BB walks away, blowing Shirley's comment off, but in her heart, she doesn't deny it crossed her mind. When she heard Rosemary had no family, she felt her heart skip. And while she was talking with Rosemary, she admits she was looking at her more than just as a patient she was visiting.

That night, after another tough shift at work, BB found herself again looking at the photo of Rosemary on her slide show. She still doesn't know what Santa's Elves at the North Pole is all about, but she finds the idea of getting to know Rosemary pulling on her heart more and more.

Every visit with Rosemary pulls Becky deeper. Every time she sees Rosemary laugh pulls Becky deeper. Every day she goes without seeing Rosemary pulls her deeper more.

Even the stuffy social worker has taken notice that Becky and Rosemary have the chemistry that creates an interesting prospect.

★★★★★★

"Thanks for coming, Becky." says Mary the social worker who asked Becky to come by her office to talk. "Rosemary talks a lot about you and you both seem to be connecting so well. I wanted to get a sense from you for where you see this relationship going?"

"I really love that girl. When I look to the future, I only want to see Rosemary."

Mary thinks for a moment, "You do seem to have a special chemistry. The only thing I don't understand is how you came to know about Rosemary in the first place?"

Becky knew this would come up and takes a deep breath.

"I have always believed that telling the truth was the most important part of being a nurse. What I'm going to tell you comes from a very frightened heart because I know it's the truth, and I also know that it could completely ruin my relationship with Rosemary, and I don't want to lose her."

"Mary, I was in a very dark spot in my life. The pandemic was certainly taking a toll on me, but it came shortly after I had surgery and the doctors told me I would not be able to have children, which ended my engagement to a man who couldn't bare the thought of living with a woman who could not pass his precious genes to a new generation. I was, as you could understand, in a very dark spot in my life."

Becky stands up with her laptop in her hand and places it in front of Mary and turns it on.

"Mary, it was after another rough day at the hospital, when I opened this laptop and found that file you see there. It said Open Before Christmas. It was not my file and I figured someone hacked me, so I deleted it. It came back, this time with a tag that said, Becky Please Open Before Christmas. I deleted it again. It came back a third time with the tag you see there, and I opened it."

Mary looks at the file, then to Becky who nods to encourage her to open the file.

> *We know it's been rough for you recently*
> *We wanted to make this slide show for you*
> *Thinking it might encourage you*
> *Because we care*

Mary looks up at Becky with a puzzled look.

"Please push start"

Mary pushes the start button and watches the slide show. She looks up at Becky after every story. Becky has a look of complete hesitance and uncertainty. She has no idea if this is going to have an impact or more importantly, a positive impact, but it's the truth and she feels she has to stay with the truth.

When Mary gets to the picture of Rosemary, she becomes even more cautious.

This is Rosemary. She's in room 3204 on the third floor of your hospital. We think it would serve you well to drop in and say hello to Rosemary next time you're at work.

Then Mary gets to the final slide.

You have a very compassionate heart, Becky
Your past reflects such a giving heart
We know your future will too
Merry Christmas and Thank You
for all you do for LOVE
Santa's Elves at the North Pole

Mary sits back and considers what she has just witnessed.

"You have no idea where Santa's Elves at the North Pole came from?"

"That's why I brought it to you, because I have no explanation." says Becky.

"And you deleted it twice before you opened it?"

"Yes. It came back every time."

"Do you mind if I delete it?" asks Mary.

Becky hesitates, but confirms.

Mary sits up and deletes the file. It instantly pops back up with a new tag on it.

Mary, you know better than that
You're a social worker after all
You can't delete other peoples files
You want to end up on the naughty list?

Mary sits back in her chair with a look of horror on her face. Becky gets up and looks at the screen. She too is speechless.

After a very uncomfortable time of silence, Becky looks at Mary, who slowly looks to Becky.

"For the record, I never saw this, but clearly, you and Rosemary need to be together. I can start putting together all the paper work right away if you wish."

Becky smiles with tears streaming down her cheeks as she nods in enthusiastic agreement.

******

"Now that's an outcome I'll take every day!" says an excited Santa as he turns off the video feed and turns to his elves. "The Magic Photo File Project is clearly everything I thought it could be. Thank you all so much. I showed this to God and he loved it. He is going to present the program to his Guardian Angels at Earth Operations and encourage them to contact the Magic Photo File Project at the North Pole if they ever need a slide show, so you four should be quite busy I would guess." says Santa as he looks around at the four elves emotionally drained once again, as he smiles.

"Be strong, my little helpers. I'm thinking it's going to be like this for a long time. You've done a great job and I really do appreciate you." says Santa as he heads out the door, leaving the Magic Photo File Project in good hands.

10

Assignment Santa

"You call for me sir?"

"Ah yes, indeed. Please come in."

The angel comes in and takes his seat in a simple office of Earth Operations Headquarters.

"I think I have an assignment that would be just perfect for you." God says

"Always happy to help where I can sir."

"Great. You've always done good work, but this one may be a bit more challenging, but definitely a nice fit for you."

"Always like a good challenge, sir."

"Yes, well this one involves a couple that lives in the city of

Chicago in the USA. Both of them came from really good families and they both were consistently on Santa's Nice list throughout their youth, so I know they have good hearts. They met in college, got married and started their careers working in the stock markets. They make a lot of money, live a very comfortable life with their two children – a boy Todd who is 9 and a girl Mary who is 7."

"Sounds like the American dream, sir. Do they have a dog, too?"

God smiles at the angel, "I don't worry about the dogs – all dogs go to heaven after all."

"Of course. So what do you need me to do here?"

"Santa contacted me and told me that he put the children on the Naughty list, not because the kids are any trouble – in fact, he tells me they're actually pretty good kids. Their on the Naughty list because the parents are so bad all year long until Christmas when they try to out-do each other with buying gifts for the kids. The gifts are not from a loving heart, but from a heart of guilt, which according to Santa will never end, as they both go right back to their world of making money and ignoring relationships as soon as the holidays are over."

"Santa has asked me to have someone here at Earth Operations help him out and see if we can get these two adults back on track. I've looked it over and feel strongly that they have a great foundation – good, loving parents growing up – but they've just been consumed by the money. They have abandoned any appearance of a relationship between themselves or their children, and have taken on the posture of elitists who think that money can make all their issues go away. I chose you because I know how much you love working with the 'snooty' population, as you like to call it."

"Indeed I do sir, and I appreciate the two for one on this project. This will be fun."

"Great. I've got a slide show in conference room B that should give you plenty of ammunition to work with and then I have some suggestions at the end that you can use if you're so inclined. If you need another angel to help you out, feel free to get one. The main thing is that we want to win their hearts over. It would be easy to just put them through a financial valley to wake them up, but as you know, I never want to give a message that money is a bad thing. I want them to understand that relationships have more value than money. Making money is never the sin – until it takes away from the relationships."

"I hear you, boss. " says the angel as he gets up to head for conference room B, "You can tell Santa that he can make a special delivery to those kids this year. I'll have those parents believing in Santa and the magic of Christmas by Christmas morning with time to spare."

"I thought you'd like this one." says God as he stands up, looks out the window down at all the guardian angels busily monitoring their Earthlings as they prepare their hearts for the holiday season and smiles, claps his hands and turns to leave.

"This should be another great holiday season."

******

Katie Johnson is hanging out with some of her girlfriends by the bar at the firms annual company Christmas party. It is loud and reflects an event where everyone shakes off the office persona and takes advantage of the open bar service.

The company always hires a Santa Clause for their party to handle the secret Santa portion and to be available to those who are brave enough to go sit on Santa's knee and tell him what they want for Christmas. There are no children of course, which makes it an easy payday for Santa, although few Santas want this gig because of the annoying adults with a tad too much to drink make for an embarrassing series of worthless conversations.

"Look at them. They're all hammered." says the angel Santa to his angel Elf helper whom he recruited for the assignment because the angel Elf has not done an assignment for Earth Operations yet and wanted to show him how things work with Earthlings.

The angel Santa does not look like a Santa because he comes from the spirit world, as does Santa, so he figured he could make his physical appearance pretty uneventfully normal. The outfit they gave him was rather baggy as it was intended for a much larger figure, which only made Santa angel look more ridiculous standing next to his angel Elf assistant, who is also rather baggy in his attire.

Katie puts her drink on the bar, "I'm going to go sit on Santa's lap and tell him what I want for Christmas. Do you think he'll deliver?" she says in an seductive tone, as her friends laugh and she marches up to Santa.

"Hi Santa. Mind if I sit on your lap and tell you what I want for Christmas?"

The angel Santa looks at his angel Elf assistant, who has a pained look and very unconvincing smile, then at Katie.

"Sure little girl. And what is your name?"

"Awe, he's so cute." she says as she tugs on his beard which does not give way as Santa smacks her hand.

"Hey, don't do that. You don't want to hurt Santa when you're telling him what you want for Christmas do you?"

Katie turns to her friends at the bar, "The beard is real. We must have the REAL Santa this year." she says with a strong dose of humor as she turns back to Santa and stares at him with a smirky smile.

After a frozen pause, Santa finally breaks the silence, "So are we done here?"

Katie sits up surprised, "Well no, you silly old man. I haven't told you what I want for Christmas yet." she says humoring herself.

"Oh, well go ahead, but it doesn't make much difference because you're on the Naughty list anyway." he says matter-of-fact-ly.

Katie sits back and turns to her friends in pretend shock, "He says I'm on the Naughty list." They all laugh as she turns back to Santa, "Just because I pulled your beard, Santa? That's not very nice."

"Oh no. You've actually been on the Naughty list for quite some time." he pauses in thought, "Let's see, the last time I dropped anything off for you was – (he's thinking) – I guess when you were about ten. That doll house. You really loved that doll house, didn't you?"

Katie's jaw drops as she stares at Santa in disbelief.

Santa smiles at her innocently, then turns to his angel Elf assistant who shrugs his shoulders, then back to Katie.

"But you're welcome to tell me what you want if it will make you feel better."

"How did you know that?" she says, almost tripping over every word.

Santa smiles, "You're the one who said they got the REAL Santa this year. You'd think I would know what I've dropped off for you through the years. If I remember right, the year before the doll house, it was a pair of roller skates, right?" he says with that innocent smile.

Katie stands up and shakes her head in disbelief, "Time to cut me off. This is getting too freaky." as she turns, goes to check out her coat and heads out the door without another word, as her friends watch bewildered, then up to Santa who smiles and waves, "Next?"

Nobody bothered the funny looking angel Santa for the rest of the evening.

******

This time, angel Santa and his angel Elf assistant are at the food court in a Mall ringing his bell to collect the change from all the hungry holiday shoppers.

As Bob Johnson is leaving the food court with a sandwich to go, he stops at the Santa to drop some coins in the bucket.

"Thanks Bob!" says angel Santa brightly.

Bob pauses and looks at Santa closely.

"Do I know you?" he asks.

"Well just about everyone knows Santa Clause, Bob. Really." he says a bit surprised.

"But you know my name." Bob says confused.

"Well you know Bob, that's one of the myths that most people get wrong. They think I only know the names of those on the Nice list, but I also know the names on the Naughty list as well. In fact, I spend a lot of time working up to Christmas Eve trying to get some of those on the Naughty list back on the Nice list. It's not easy, but well worth the effort if I can get just one back on the Nice list."

"I see." says Bob somewhat humored as he turns to walk away before turning back to Santa. "So you're saying I'm on the Naughty list then?" he says a bit sarcastically.

"Yes, but I really think you have a lot of potential to get back on the Nice list Bobby." Santa says with a smile.

Bob – who hates to be called Bobby – turns to walk away when angel Santa stops him.

"And Bobby," Santa says as Bob turns back to him with a look that is none too friendly, which angel Santa ignores of course. "When your Mom calls, you should say yes. That would be an excellent place to start." he says with a big smile.

Bob stares at Santa. His mother seldom calls. At that very moment, his phone rings and gets Bob's attention. As he pulls his phone out of his pocket and looks at the caller ID, he sees "Mom", then looks back at Santa who gives a very silly smile and exaggerated thumbs up as Bob answers his call.

"Mom?" he says in a tone of concern.

"Hi Bob, this is your mother."

"Yes, I know. Is there something wrong?"

"No, honey. (she pauses) Well yes there is. Your father and I were hoping that you and your family could come out here for Christmas this year."

Bob looks again at Santa who has an even sillier smile and holds up his bell and rings it in a very animated manner.

Bob takes a deep breath, turns and walks away, talking to his mother.

Santa turns to his angel Elf assistant, "That went well don't you think?"

"Yea, but do you think he'll go to his Moms?"

"I don't know. He's not on the Naughty list because he makes good choices, you know."

"Well it sure is fun working with the Earthlings." says the elf.

"Well let me tell you that any time you get a call from Earth Operations Headquarters, you've got to take it. The Earthlings think they know everything, but they're really kinda stupid. But they have really good hearts, so your assignments with the Earthlings almost always has a happy ending."

"Good to know." says the elf as the two head out the door to plan their next adventure.

******

We are now at the entrance of a food market where angel Santa and his angel Elf assistant are ringing their bells and singing Christmas songs quite poorly, which bothers angel Santa because he thinks he has a beautiful voice – which he does not – and doesn't appreciate the people laughing as they walk by.

A young woman comes up to put some money in the bucket.

"Does that really help?" she asks angel Santa.

Confused, angel Santa responds, "Does what help?"

"I think I heard somewhere that if you sing really bad people will put more money in the bucket. Is that why you do it?"

Angel Santa stares at the lady as the angel Elf assistant scrambles to recover, "Yes, of course. We could do much better, but hey, if it helps the cause, we'll do it."

The young lady walks away laughing, "Well you should make a lot of money today, that's for sure.."

Angel Santa continues to stare off without expression as angel Elf assistant tries to recover the moment.

"Ah don't worry about it boss. She's probably on the Naughty list anyway. Come on, let's sing that one about twelve days of Christmas."

"I refuse to sing another word!" says the disgruntled Santa.

"Well do something, here comes Katie!"

As Santa and Elf regroup, Katie makes her way out of the store with a basket full of groceries.

"Hi Katie." says angel Santa.

Katie looks over and realizes it's the same Santa as the Christmas party last week.

"What are you doing here?" she asks in a not so friendly manner.

Angel Santa looks at his outfit, then over at the red kettle and bell in his hand, then back at Katie.

"Just trying to raise some money to help those in need, Katie."

Katie walks over to them, "If I put in a dollar, well that get me back on the Nice list?" she says with a terrible tone of sarcasm as she puts a dollar bill into the slot.

"Actually Katie, money is never used to measure a person for the Nice list. It's all about relationships. Being a wife, a mother, a co-worker. Those relationships are what is used for the Naughty or Nice lists."

"Well I'm a very good wife, mother and friend, so you can put me back on that nice list." says Katie as she starts for her car.

"Well I'm thinking you'll have to get rid of David first."

Katie freezes and turns back at angel Santa.

"WHAT?!?"

She marches over to angel Santa and glares at him.

"Well I'm just saying your relationship with David doesn't exactly scream wife of the year or anything close to it." says Santa with a smile.

Katie hauls off and belts angel Santa as he goes flying backwards and she storms off with her groceries.

"Are you okay Santa?" says the angel Elf assistant as he scrambles to help his friend.

"I'm fine. We have no feelings you know. But I'm guessing I hit a pretty soft nerve with Katie on that one."

"She sure didn't like that one, boss. We may want to steer clear of her for a bit."

"Oh it's nothing. Earthlings always think they are getting away with their secret lives until someone busts them. They always go crazy, but it almost always works out well in the long run. She'll lose a lot of sleep tonight and guilt will take hold of her. She has a good heart as God says, so I'm thinking we may have made some really good progress today."

He pauses as he gathers himself, "Besides, the thing that saves her the most is that Bob is certainly no candidate for husband of the year either. They both have done a lot to hurt each other. We just have to dust it all off and get them back to their beautiful hearts."

"Well it sure is a good thing we don't have feelings. That was one fine smack down she gave you that's for sure."

"God knows what he's doing." says the angel Santa, "You take an assignment in Earth Operations, you better be ready for a few smack downs."

They both walk off laughing.

******

Angel Santa and angel Elf assistant are back at the Mall ringing their bells but not singing as angel Santa still seems to be a bit too touchy about his singing abilities, so angel Elf assistant just wishes people a Merry Christmas as they walk by.

They see Bob walking by and angel Santa calls out to him.

"Hey Bobby. How's it going?"

Bob looks over and stops and sees that it's them again and walks over.

"How did you know my Mom was going to call the other day?" he says with a huge dose of suspicion.

"Well I'm Santa and I kinda know stuff like that." he says casually.

"You're not Santa. You're some old man picking up a little extra cash for the holidays."

"Oh, well if that's what you believe then I can understand your being freaked out about me knowing your mom was calling I guess."

"And how did you know my name?"

"Well Bob isn't exactly a wild guess you know. So are you, Katie and the kids going to your mothers for Christmas?"

"How do you know my wife's name? You know, you're really beginning to give me the creeps, pal."

"Well Bobby, let me help you out. I know you have a really good heart. Katie does too. You both have gotten swept up with your careers and all the money and stuff, but you've lost touch with the relationships in your life that are most important to you."

"Is that why I'm on your so-called Naughty list?" Bob asks with a mound of sarcasm.

"Yes it is. You see, Bob, the Naughty and Nice list depends completely on the relationships you have in your world. Santa doesn't really care about the money people have"

"And you're saying I have bad relationships? That's not true."

"Oh it's true alright. You and Katie are so terrible throughout the year and then at Christmas you both buy tons of presents for Todd and Mary with some idea that this will make it all better. But it doesn't work that way Bob. Santa had to put Todd and Mary on the Naughty list because you and Katie are so busy trying to buy your way out of your guilt, so Santa has no reason to make a stop, even though both Todd and Mary are really good kids that Santa would love to visit."

"Old man, I'm not sure how you're getting all this information, but you've got it all wrong. Katie and I are fine. The kids are doing well.

I'm sure there are a lot of other people you can help out, so why don't you go annoy someone else and leave us alone."

"Okay Bobby. But first I want you to do something for me. I want you to go into that store over there (he points out a gift shop across the way) and on the right, on the second shelf down you'll see some snow globes. If you go look at them, there is one of Paris to the right – I believe it's the next to last one. Remember the one you bought Katie when you were both falling in love at college? It's the same one, so you should recognize it."

Bob looks at Santa very suspiciously as angel Santa continues.

"Remember how you promised to take her to Paris once you both got settled into your careers? You both were so in love with each other (he pauses with a dreamy sigh) That trip never happened did it Bob?.."

Bob looks at Santa as his eyes moisten.

"Go in there and shake that snow globe for me Bob. Let the snow flakes flutter about in your heart. Remember that time of love you and Katie had together. It's still there Bob. You and Katie have great hearts. It's time for you both to stop hurting each other and start loving each other again. I just want to see your kids back on the Nice list, but it won't happen until you and Katie come clean and let your hearts win the day again."

Bob stares at Santa then turns to walk away. He pauses at the gift store and looks in, then back at angel Santa who is smiling.

He walks in.

About ten minutes later, Bob comes out the door and pauses, looks over at Santa who smiles and rings his bell as Bob, who has a gift bag from the store in his hand, turns and walks off the other way.

"You think he got it?" asks angel Elf assistant.

"I think he did. You know, when you are working with

relationships like this you always think the women would be the easiest to turn around, but often times it's the man. It's a good thing too. If we have been successful in getting Bob turned around, he'll be much more successful at turning Katie around than we could be. This is looking very promising, my friend."

They head out with a subtle bounce in their gait.

******

Today we find angel Santa and angel Elf assistant in a school gym. The elementary school always has their Christmas festival on the last day of school before Christmas break. There are many stations for the kids to make decorations, a Christmas story telling section from the library, and various other fun activities for the children. Of course they have a nice set up for those kids who want to visit Santa. Of course angel Santa makes the most of the situation with all the kids by working a little extra credit with those few children who are on the fence between the Naughty and Nice list.

"So who do we have here?"

"Dale"

"So Dale, what do you want Santa to bring you this Christmas?"

"I want a scooter!" says Dale with great enthusiasm.

"Well you know, Dale, Santa would love to bring you a scooter, but first you have to stop teasing Ellen."

Dale sits up in protest, "Hey, did my teacher put you up to this? That's not fair!"

"Woe, hold on there buddy. Do you think Santa needs the teachers to know what's going on? I'm just say'n that you need to be nice to Ellen. She doesn't have all the advantages that you and the other kids have. She has to work so hard to stay up with the rest of you and she sure doesn't need you annoying her all the time, that's all. Be nice Dale."

Dale pauses in consideration, then collapses into Santa crying, "I'm sorry Santa! I'll try harder, I promise." as angel Santa scrambles to save the moment.

"Come on Dale, loosen up here. (Dale sits up with a very long face of sadness) You're a wonderful boy. I'm sure Santa is going to bring you that scooter. I'm just saying that you should treat Ellen like you treat your other friends. You really are a good friend, Dale, and Ellen needs all the friends she can get. If others see you being nice to Ellen, then they will say 'Gee, if Dale can be nice to her, why can't I?' and pretty soon Ellen will have all kinds of friends. And it will be all because of you."

"Okay Santa, I'll try to be nicer."

"Now Dale, I can't let you go until I see a smile. It's Christmas! I need to see that…"

Dale breaks into a big, warm engaging smile.

"There it is! Now go have some fun Dale."

As Dale scurries off the stage, angel Elf assistant whispers, "Nice recovery Santa."

Angel Santa leans over to angel Elf assistant, "Remind me to tell Santa that Dale better get a scooter or he'll be in institutions the rest of his life."

"He did seem a bit touchy. " says angel Elf assistant.

"A bit?" says angel Santa as another boy approaches.

"So what's your name fella?"

"Todd."

"Oh yes – Todd Johnson. What would you like Santa to bring you for Christmas?"

Todd shakes his head, "I don't really believe in Santa. I just came because my friend Dale wouldn't go unless I did."

"Awe, yes Dale. Nice boy. A bit touchy, but a good boy. Nice of you to support your friends like that Todd. So why don't you believe in Santa Clause?"

"Well it all seems to be crazy. A big fat guy in a red suit who hangs out with flying reindeer? I just don't see it."

"Good point Todd, but maybe you're looking at it all wrong."

"How so?"

"Well the image of a fat guy in a red suit that hangs out with flying reindeer seems a bit crazy, I'll grant you that. But maybe that image is what we created to understand the spirit of Christmas. The magic that only happens at Christmas. The emotion of Christmas. People believe in God and say that God is love, which is fine. But the image of a God with long hair and a big beard is just an image we have to help us believe. We see God in the acts of kindness of others, birds singing, rainbows after a storm. The spirit of God or the spirit of Christmas comes in many shapes and forms. We create an imagine simply to give us a better understanding of something we can't see."

Todd nods his head in understanding, "I guess that makes sense. But it doesn't matter because we never get presents from Santa Clause anyway."

"Oh yes, I know. But that's my point Todd. You and Mary don't get presents from Santa because Santa doesn't need to give you presents. Your mom and dad always go way overboard buying you two everything you want and more. Santa knows your parents have got you covered, so he can concentrate on the children who are more in need of presents. That's the spirit of Christmas Todd."

"I guess you're right. You're a pretty good Santa you know."

Angel Santa sits up in a proud posture as angel Elf assistant chimes in, "He is good, but don't ask him to sing for you."

Angel Santa snaps a glare at angel Elf assistant, who has a deflating smile through a panicked expression, as Todd leaves the stage.

After several more children visit with angel Santa, Mary makes her way to sit on Santa's knee.

"So who do we have here?" asks angel Santa who is having more and more fun talking with the kids.

"I'm Mary Johnson."

"Awe yes, I believe I spoke to your brother Todd earlier. It's so nice to have a big brother like Todd isn't it?"

Mary has a half smile with a hint of painful expression as she looks away in thought, then back to angel Santa, "I suppose."

"So what would you like Santa to bring you for Christmas?"

"I don't really need anything, but I would like to know why my parents are acting so weird?"

"Excuse me?"

"Todd and I always get whatever we want from mommy and daddy, so Santa can give our presents to those who need it more. But I would like to know why my parents are acting so weird lately."

"That's very sweet of you Mary and I'll pass that along to Santa. But what makes you say your parents are acting weird?"

"Well they use to work all the time. We almost always eat dinner with our nanny because they both work late. We see our nanny a lot more than we see our parents. But suddenly, they seem to be hanging around the house more. They eat dinner with Todd and me and want to talk about school and stuff. I even saw them kissing in the kitchen the other night – I almost screamed! And then the other night they told us that we were going to spend Christmas at grandma and grandpa's home. It's really creeping me out."

Angel Santa is desperately trying to keep his composure, "Well that all sounds wonderful Mary, not weird."

"But I don't understand what got into them?"

"Well Mary, that's the magic of Christmas. It's the spirit of Christmas that has been going on for a couple thousand years. People get so wrapped up in careers and making money, but then Christmas comes along and reminds us that it's not about making money or having a fancy career – it's about relationships. It's about being family. It's about caring for one another. It sounds to me like the spirit of Christmas has finally got into your parents hearts, and that's a good thing Mary."

Mary thinks for a moment, "I guess so, but are they going to be like that after Christmas?"

"I hope so Mary. I mean if it really grosses you out to see your mommy and daddy kissing in the kitchen, you might want to try a fake cough or something to let them know you're coming, but to be honest, seeing your mom and dad kissing is a good thing. It means they have love, and everybody needs to have love. I think you and Todd should be thankful any time you see your parents kissing. A family can never have too much love."

Mary seems to understand. "Well I know you're not the real Santa, but if you could tell him that even though Todd and I don't need anything, we'll still leave out some cookies and milk for him so he can take a break, okay?"

"That's very nice of you Mary. I'll make sure Santa drops by then."

And as Mary gets up to leave, she finishes, "Nice talking to you – have a nice Christmas!"

As the day finds the buses hurrying to deliver the children off to Christmas break, angel Santa and angel elf assistant head towards the exit sign.

"Well my friend, it looks like we can put that assignment to bed. Nice work."

"We don't have to follow up and make sure it works out well?" asks the angel Elf assistant confused.

"Nope. God gave the Earthlings a free will and he's pretty strict about staying with it. Our job was to get Bob and Katie back on track so Santa can put Todd and Mary back on the Nice list as they deserve to be. If Bob and Katie are freaking out the kids by kissing in the kitchen, I would say we got them back on track, my friend. It's up to Bob and Katie to stay on track and which direction that track leads them. But our job is done."

"Working with Earth Operations has been a great experience. I wouldn't hesitate to take more assignment like that." says the confident angel Elf assistant as they walk out the gym doors.

"It's the best. Earthlings are great to work with. But before we put this to bed though, be sure and contact Santa and remind him to get that scooter for Dale, okay"

"You got it."

"That kid is touchy." says angel Santa as they both leave with a bounce in their feet and laughter in their heart for a job well done.

Assignment Complete.

11

A Wish For Grandpa

Ernie and his son, William had a blowout argument when William was about to head off to college that ended with William leaving his home and never looking back. William didn't come to his mother's funeral when she died a few years later because he didn't know she had died. Ernie made no attempt to keep up with his son, missing his wedding and later the birth of his grandson. He knew his son lived in San Francisco, but had no idea what he did there. They were two stubborn men to be sure. Two men who refused to make the first move.

Turns out that Williams wife, Anna, has an aunt who lives in Park City UT, near where William grew up in Snyderville. On this particular holiday season, Anna insists that they accept her aunts invitation to spend the holidays in Park City.

Anna's parents both died when she was a teen and her aunt Carrie took her in until she went off to college. When Anna left the nest in Pasadena, CA to go to college, Carrie sold her home and moved back to her home town of Park City, Utah to get away from the southern California rat race and simplify her life with her passion for writing and skiing.

Anna has never understood her husbands refusal to connect with his parents. Whatever happened between him and his dad happened a long time ago and being very much a family person, she has tried many times to reach out to William so their son, Bobby, could finally meet his grandparents, to no avail.

Understanding that Anna wasn't giving him a choice, William reluctantly agrees to spending two weeks in Park City with Aunt Carrie, as long as Anna promised not to bug him about his family that he assumed might still be living in Snyderville.

The plans confirmed, the family heads to Park City Utah for a real Christmas of snow in the magical winter wonderland of Park City.

As they settle in at aunt Carries very nice home in Park City, William, Anna and Bobby are very excited about the prospects of having a real festive holiday. Being from the San Francisco Bay area, this will be their first white Christmas with all the trimmings, and William, who grew up in the area, could certainly attest to the fact that there are few places that does Christmas better than Park City.

On the first night, after William and Bobby crash in their guest rooms, Anna and Carrie catch up with a glass of wine near a crackling fireplace. The conversation leads to talk about Ernie and the failed relationship between her husband and his father. Carrie, being an established writer known for being very thorough in her research for every story, agrees to help her niece investigate to see if Ernie and his mother, Maggie, are still living in Snyderville. If they are still alive and there is any window of opportunity to work some Christmas magic, maybe they could get the two stubborn men back together again so Bobby can have grandparents.

For the next few days, Carrie runs into many dead ends regarding Ernie and Maggie, as Anna makes a few cracks in her stubborn husband, trying to convince him to at least go to Snyderville so his son could see the place where he was born and raised.

When the family heads out to spend the day ice skating and enjoy some family time exploring the town, Carrie decides to head off to Snyderville . She's made little headway on the phone and knows that the best way to get answers is to go and talk to people.

Her efforts are rewarded as she talks to a couple of locals who know Ernie well. Quiet man. Lives alone outside of town on a small farm, his wife having passed away about twenty years ago. Stays to himself for the most part, but is always friendly. Not one to engage with conversations much. They hesitate before adding that the only time they see much of Ernie is at Christmas time, when he volunteers to play Santa Clause for the kids at the local rec center.

That night, Carrie and Anna compare notes after the boys go to bed. Anna is excited that Carrie was able to get so much info on Ernie, but is saddened to hear that Williams mother had passed and he didn't even know it. She was excited to hear that Ernie plays Santa at the rec center, though. This could work well for their plans to get William and Ernie together.

The next day, William agrees to take Anna and Bobby to Snyderville to show them where he grew up. He takes them by the elementary school he went to, the high school, the place where he got his first job and the diner where he and his buddies use to hang out for shakes.

As they are eating lunch at the diner, one of Williams old buddies notices him and stops by their table to visit.

After a warm trip down memory lane, his friend, George, brings up Ernie.

"I see your dad every now and then. He comes to town for supplies and doesn't talk much. He has one word answers for everything. You just can't get into a conversation with that man. Everyone loves Ernie though. You hardly see or hear much from Ernie until the holidays. He plays Santa for the kids over at the rec center every year and the parents love him because he never promises the kids anything. He just tells them to be nice to their parents and be thankful for what they have."

"My dad is Santa Clause?" asks William, totally surprised.

"Yea, didn't you know that? He's been doing it for years."

"Well, we kind of lost touch after I went away to college."

His friend looks a little surprised, "Really? I always thought you were really close to your dad when we were kicking around. I guess after your mother died, shortly after you left for college, he really shut down. Stays pretty much to himself now. I don't think anyone knows if he even has a phone. But he's a good Santa."

"Yea, he wasn't much of a phone guy. Neither am I, I guess."

"Well I better get going or my wife will start worrying. It was really good to see you, Willie, and meet your great family."

"Good to see you too, George." says William as his friend makes his way out the door.

Anna can feel the weight of emotions from her husband as she gently takes his hand, "Do you want to head back to aunt Carries? We can come back maybe some other time." she says in a very supportive way.

It's a quiet ride back to Park City.

As they get back to aunt Carries, Bobby is quick to dominate the conversation about their day, seeing all the places his dad grew up in and then he pauses in thought.

"I found out I have a grandpa, too." he says a bit subdued.

Carrie is quick to redirect, "I was just thinking of baking some Christmas cookies. How would you like to help me out?"

"Sure." he says with enthusiasm.

Meanwhile, up in Anna and Williams room Anna apologizes.

"I'm so sorry William. I just wanted Bobby to see where you grew up. I didn't think that you might run into an old friend and dig up some of those memories. I should have thought about that."

William looks at her with eyes full of emotion, "I didn't even know mother died. I've sent her a Mothers Day card every year and never heard back from her. I figured dad told her not to talk to me either."

Anna goes over to her husband and embraces him as he weeps.

The next day while they were out and about Park City, Carrie asks to take Bobby to do some Christmas shopping without the parents. Anna and William go to a restaurant for a quiet drink. William has been understandably a bit subdued today.

"A penny for your thoughts?"

William looks at his wife with a subdued smile, "I didn't realize how heavy guilt is."

"So what do you want to do about your father?" she asks gently.

He looks down at the face inside his drink, "I know what I need to do. I just don't know how to do it." he says as he slowly looks up at his wife.

Anna has been married to this man for fourteen years and never seen this face looking at her now. So broken. So empty, yet so full of emotion. And as she looks deep into his eyes, she slowly breaks into a warm, compassionate smile.

"I know exactly how we're going to do it."

For the next hour, William and Anna are tossing ideas back and forth. With each idea, Anna can see William getting more and more comfortable in his commitment to making this a Christmas to remember.

That night, Anna fills in Carrie with the plan her and William have, as Carrie is overcome with emotional excitement.

"William is going back to Snyderville tomorrow and set everything up with his friend, George, while you and I take Bobby Christmas shopping for his grandfather. We hope to do this on Christmas Eve and hopefully, we'll be able to have Ernie join us here on Christmas Day?"

Carrie lifts her arms with tears rolling down her cheeks, "Yes, of course!" and falls into an emotional hug with her niece.

Christmas Eve comes and all the plans seem to be falling into place nicely. They are to meet up at the Snyderville Diner at noon, then to the rec center at 1 to surprise Santa.

As they get comfortable in their booth, Anna takes Williams hand, "Are you ready to have a dad again?"

William smiles with a confident "Yes", as the weight of guilt has been lifted from his heart and made room for plenty of compassion.

Anna looks over to Bobby, "You know what you've got to do, right?"

Bobby smiles at his mom, "You bet" he says enthusiastically.

Anna looks over to aunt Carrie who smiles and pulls out a box of tissue, "I'm ready."

George walks into the diner and quickly makes his way to their booth.

"Okay, everything is all set. I think everyone in town is going to be there. Even Pat said she's closing the diner as soon as we head over to the Rec Center because she doesn't want to miss it." George looks at Anna, "When we get there, you and Bobby get into line to meet Santa. Willie and I will stay back out of view." he pauses as he looks at Carrie, "I'm not sure who you are…"

Anna interrupts, "That's my aunt Carrie – we're staying with her in Park City."

"Oh, great! Well aunt Carrie you are welcome to stand with Bobby and Anna or whatever you want to do."

"At around one o'clock, the elves will tell the kids that Santa needs to take a break and they already know what's up, so they'll go back to their parents. You and Bobby will go talk to the elf whatever you want to say – she already knows what's going on – then she'll go ask Santa if he can see one more before he takes his break. Since Ernie seldom takes his breaks anyway, I'm sure he'll say yes." he looks over to Bobby, "That's when you do your thing, okay?"

Bobby smiles and shakes his head positively.

"Okay then." George looks at his watch, "We have about ten minutes, so let's finish up here and head on over. I can't tell you how excited I am about this." he looks over to William, "I'm so happy that we were able to do this for you and your dad."

William smiles, "I am too. Long overdue."

They get up and head for the door as they hear Pat back in the kitchen "Time to close down this joint. Let's make sure everything is good to go!"

As they walk into the rec center, they see that George was right. There are a lot of people there mingling about the many booths set up with Christmas goodies.

Anna and Carrie take Bobby and make their way to the line waiting to see Santa as George and William stay back and out of site.

At one o'clock sharp, the elf gets the signal and tells the kids in line, "Santa needs to take a break right now, so mingle about and he'll be back in fifteen minutes."

The kids all break off to their parents with many working to control their giggles.

Anna, Carrie and Bobby approach the elf.

"We need to get back to Park City by two. Do you think Santa could see him before his break?"

The elf winks at Bobby and turns to go ask Santa if he can see just one more.

"Of course." says Santa as the elf signals Bobby to come.

As Bobby sits on Santas knee, Santa starts, "So what's your name, young man?"

"Bobby" he says.

"I don't believe I've seen you before. Are you visiting?"

"My family is visiting my aunt Carrie in Park City."

Santa looks up at Anna and Carrie who are desperately fighting to keep their composure.

"I see. Well why don't you tell Santa what you would like for Christmas."

Bobby looks at Santa with a smile and says, "I want to meet my grandpa."

Santa looks a little puzzled, but has heard many odd requests through the years, so he goes along with it.

"Well Bobby, does your grandpa live around these parts?"

"Yes sir."

"What's his name?"

Bobby hesitates, "Grandpa Ernie."

Santa looks at Bobby, numb with the response. He's the only Ernie he knows of. He looks at Anna and Carrie who continue to maintain their composure, then back at Bobby.

He hesitates, "What's your Daddy's name?"

Bobby thinks for a second then smiles at Santa, "William."

At that, Santa is overcome with emotion. He looks up at Anna and Carrie and then sees William making his way to Anna and takes her hand, smiling at his dad with tears running down his cheeks.

He looks over at Bobby, who smiles, "Merry Christmas Grandpa."

With that, the rec center explodes with emotions as Anna, Carrie and William make their way up the ramp to Santa.

As Santa stands, William looks at his dad. "Merry Christmas Dad"

The townspeople break into singing, "We whish you a merry Christmas, we….." as William and Ernie embrace for the first time in years as Carrie realizes that she did not bring nearly enough tissue.

The rest of the day was a blur of catching up, hugging, and celebrating the magic of Christmas.

The next morning, as they gather around the tree, the door bell rings.

"That must be grandpa." shouts Bobby as he runs to open the door.

"Merry Christmas, young man." says Ernie who is loaded down with gifts and food.

They make their way into the celebration as William stands to hug his father, "Dad, you look ….." he pauses as he looks at his dads suit which obviously has not seen daylight in several years, not to mention an iron, "Awful" then smiles at his dad "awfully great!" and hug.

It's a magical Christmas day where presents are a side dish while the family spends this moment catching up and telling all the wonderful stories that have been missed because two stubborn men refused to make the first move.

Some sad tears talking about Maggie, and how Ernie opened every Mothers Day card William sent and didn't have the heart to reply to him that he no longer had to send them. Some laughter, especially when neither one could remember what their argument was about – politics likely, but not sure. And of course, an effort to see who could apologize to the other more.

But Anna was able to get the last word. As they gathered at the table full of wonderful food, she made the toast.

"Let us give thanks to the magic of Christmas. Christmas love that has taught us that the greatest presents are never found under a tree, but in our hearts. Bobby now has a grandpa. Grandpa has a grandson and a daughter-in-law. William has a dad- again. And my dear aunt Carrie has a home in complete shambles – which I promise we will not leave until we help you get your home back."

"To Santa, who made a little boy's wish to meet his grandpa come true."

"CHEERS!"

12

The Christmas Snow Bird

The little snow bird soars through the forest until she comes to a clearing and finds God sitting near a campfire keeping his hands warm. The snow bird gently glides to a landing on Gods knee.

"There you are little lady. Thanks for coming."

"Chirpchirp chirp chirp, chirp"

"Well I appreciate that. Listen, I called on you because I need you to help me out."

"Chirpchirp"

"I was reviewing the Christmas holidays here and have become quite concerned about the spirit of Christmas getting lost in all the selfish material attitudes of the people around here."

"Chirp chirpchirp chirp…. chirp ….. chirpchirp!"

God laughs a hardy laugh, "That's no joke little lady." as the bird sings in humorous tones. "I was thinking that we could get the spirit of Christmas back on track, but I'll need your help."

"Chirpchirp, chirp chirp chirp chirp?"

"They have a Santa in the town square that the kids always go to. I think it'd be great if you found a nice spot on a branch of the Christmas tree right behind Santa and listen to all the children. Every time you hear a child ask for something that is unselfish, regardless of what it is, I want you to come back here and let me know. Think you can do that?"

"Chirpchirp, chirp chirp chirp chirp …. chirpchirp chirpchirp ?"

"Yes anything at all." God pauses in thought, "Well if they ask for world peace, don't tell me that – I've been asking for that since I created this place and I have to admit that giving these people a free will has it's down side. Everything but peace on earth requests. Just bring it to me and let's show these people what the Christmas spirit is all about."

"Chirpchirp, chirp… chirp chirp chirp chirpchirp?"

"Oh don't worry about that. If it comes from an unselfish heart, bring it to me and I'll look at it. I hope to make a lot of dreams come true and I only ask that those dreams come from unselfish hearts, okay?"

" chirpchirp"

"And remember, I don't work on the clock. It would be nice if you and I created a very busy work load with this, but something tells me we are going to be more frustrated than busy."

"Chirpchirp …. chirp chirp chirpchirp chirp chirp chip."

God laughs, "Good point. Be off with you now. And remember, anything from an unselfish heart comes back to me."

"*Chirp chirp.*" says the snow bird as it flies away.

******

The next day finds the snow bird perched on a lower branch, close enough to hear the children talking with Santa, but in towards the trunk of the tree so as not to be noticed. She is pretty bored and a bit disappointed as child after child asks Santa for toys they want for themselves. She figures that's the point of seeing Santa, but she also understands the problem God is seeing about everyone being selfish.

Finally, a good prospect comes along.

"Welcome young lady. What is your name?"

The shy girl speaks softly, which makes the snow bird have to move up the branch a bit.

"Laura."

"Well Laura, tell Santa what you want for Christmas."

"I want Santa to get my Mommy a new car."

Santa sits back a bit surprised, but he's heard many unlikely requests before so he knows how to deal with it.

"Well Laura, why does your mommy need a new car?"

"Because the one she has is old and keeps breaking down, and her work says if she's late any more, she'll be fired."

"I see. Well Santa will do what he can, but that's a pretty tall order, so don't get discouraged if it doesn't happen right away."

With that, the snow bird darts out of the tree and heads back to the forest where God is.

"*Chirp chirp … chirpchirpchirp chirp, chirp chirp chirp … chirp chirp chir, chirpchirp.*"

"Oh splendid little bird, that's a very nice request to start with. Now what kind of car did she request?"

"Chirpchirp?"

"Well yes. I'll need to know what kind of car and where to send it. Did you get any information that will help me out?"

"CHIRP!CHIRP!CHIRP!CHIRP!CHIRP!CHIRP!CHIRP!CHIRP!!!!."

"Okay little friend, calm down. Her name is Laura. That's all I have to work with?"

Snow bird looks down and quietly says, *"chirp chirp."*

"Okay. Maybe we need to establish a few ideas here. We need to get Santa involved in this too. Does he have a helper?"

"Chirp chirp."

"Okay. I want you to talk to his helper and let her know what we're doing. I'll make sure she has the ability to understand your chirping. Every time you hear a request that fits what I want to do, you will signal the helper – maybe a little singing or something so she'll know to get more information. We only need her first and last name and maybe a street name. Then I can contact the guardian angel to work out all the other details, Okay?"

"Chirpchirp. … chirp chirp chirpchirp chirp chirp?"

"Oh I can find out who Laura is and get her angel to help me out with it. That's a good start though, so don't be discouraged okay."

"Chirpchirp."

"Okay, off with you. Go talk to the helper and make sure she's there whenever Santa is so we don't have any further delays, got it?"

With that, the snow bird flies off as God appears in Earth Operations Headquarters where all the guardian angels are monitoring their earthlings.

"Would the guardian angel for a Laura girl who lives around Milford Massachusetts and asked Santa for a new car for her mom, please report to

the main booth to speak with God." calls out the head engineer angel at the headquarters control booth.

The angel appears right away, "You need me sir?"

"Ah yes, come in and have a seat. So you're Laura's guardian angel?"

"Well I'm not sure if it's the same one, but I do have an earthling named Laura Spalling. She's eight years old and lives alone with her mother Mary Spalling and she did visit Santa earlier and asked him to get her mother a new car."

"That sounds like the one." God turns to the engineer and makes another request, just to make sure.

"God would like any guardian angel who works with a little girl name Laura and lives in the vicinity of Milford Massachusetts to raise your hand please."

God looks out the window down at the floor of angels and sees about six hands go up. He tells the engineer to refine the search.

"Of these guardian angels with a girl named Laura, if their mother needs a new car, keep your hand raised."

Only one hand remains up, so God has the engineer call that angel to the booth.

"You call for me sir?" says the angel who enters the room.

"Yes, yes, have a seat. Now tell me why your Laura's mother needs a new car."

"Well sir, I've been encouraging Laura to bug her mom to get an upgrade, ya know. She drives a nice SUV, but really, everyone has the same SUV and she can do wayyyyy better. Maybe a nice Volvo or Cadillac or even a Mercedes would be swwweeet."

God stares at the angel without emotion, "I see. Is the mother late to work or in jeopardy of losing her job?"

The angel laughs, "Oh no sir. She doesn't need to work. Her and her husband came into a killer inheritance, so they are set for life. I just want my Laura to ride in style. They can afford it, so I'm thinking she should go first class, right?"

God stares at the angel, certain that this is not the right Laura, "Riiiight….. Well it sounds like you have it all under control, so I'll let you get back to your work. But remember, going first class involves more love than money you understand?"

"Yes sir. She's a great kid and her parents are awesome. The money hasn't taken the place of their love, I assure you."

"Okay, well thanks for the info."

As the angel leaves, God turns to the other angel who was the first one called.

"I'm guessing you have the right Laura. Now, is her mother in danger of losing her job because of her car situation?"

"Yes sir. She's a single parent and she works really hard. She's got a great heart, sir. The car she has now really is a piece of junk and it really is sweet of Laura to ask Santa to bring her mom a new car."

"Well let's do it for her. What kind of car do you think she would like?"

"Oh sir, she's really not a picky person. I'm sure if it starts on the first try, she'd love it."

"I don't do cheap miracles, buddy. How about one of the cars the other angel was talking about?"

"Oh sir, those are very expensive cars."

"Well my credit is pretty good you know. How about the Volvo? I like the sound of that name. Volvo. Has a nice ring to it. So I'll have it parked in her driveway tomorrow morning. We'll make sure the title is all in her name and paid in full. We'll also make sure her insurance is paid for the life of her ownership. Anything else I should include?

Oh yes, and I'll give her my own lifetime warranty – if anything goes wrong, I'll fix it before she can get out of the car."

"That's very generous, sir."

"Well I've learned that when you do miracles for the earthlings you better go big, or no one is going to buy it. I want you to make sure that Laura and her mom understands that God is always on their side as long as they put love first."

"I will sir. This is going to be a great Christmas for them."

"Just remember to let Laura know in your own way that God appreciates how unselfish she was in asking Santa to help her mom like that. She needs to hear that, okay? And maybe it'd be a nice touch to have a nice gift for her too as a thank you of sorts?"

"I know just the right gift, sir."

As the angel gets up to leave, God turns to the engineer.

"What about that other angel that was in here? How long has he been in the guardian angel program?"

The engineer smiles, "He's fairly new sir."

"Why Am I not surprised. You keep an eye on him, you hear? And be gentle – he has a good heart. Expensive heart, but a good heart."

With a hardy laugh, God leaves Earth Operations Headquarters and returns to his place in the forest.

******

The next morning, as Mary and Laura quickly leave their home to start their day, they come to a screeching halt as they see the brand new Volvo parked in their driveway. It has a big red bow on the roof and an envelope on the windshield.

"Mommy, did you get a new car?" asks Laura.

"No honey. If I did, I certainly couldn't afford a Volvo."

As she walks over to the car, Laura starts exploring the inside as Mary takes the envelope from the windshield. As she opens it, she finds the keys to the car, the title in her name and a note;

Mary

When Laura asked me to get you a new car, I told her it might take a little doing. I sent the request higher up the request ladder and was happy to hear that God would be delighted to help out. The title is in your name and it is paid in full. He also paid the insurance for as long as you own it (insurance cards included here) and gave his own personal warranty – if anything breaks, he'll fix it right away.

God wants you to know that he is doing this for you because your daughter was so unselfish when she spoke with me. God always has a soft spot for unselfish children, especially at Christmas, so he is more than happy to help your family out.

Enjoy the car and remember that love will always win the day.
Santa

PS: Tell your boss to stop threatening you about your job or I'll put him on the naughty list … but do get to work on time, please.

Mary, with tears streaming down her cheeks looks at the beautiful new car. It is everything that she would want right down to the grey metallic color. It even comes with a booster seat in the back for Laura who is already buckled in.

"Come on mom, you don't want to be late for work, right?"
******

"Hello young lad. What is your name?"

"Joey."

"Well Joey, what do you want Santa to bring you this Christmas?"

"I want you to get a puppy dog for my grandpa." says Joey in a very serious manner.

"Really? Has he been asking for one?"

"Not really, but my grandma died a few months ago – she was grandpa's wife. I think it's sad to see grandpa living all alone now. I think a puppy would cheer him up."

Santa laughs, "Well I'm sorry about your grandmother, Joey, but I agree with you that a puppy might be a nice present for your grandpa. That's very nice of you to think about your grandpa like that. You go to my helper and give her a few more details so we can make sure it's a happy Christmas for you and your family, okay?"

"Okay Santa. Thanks!"

Santa's helper gets Joey's last name and the grandfather's full name and after Joey leaves, the snow bird flies over to Santa's helper, gathers the info in her beak and heads out to the forest.

"Chirpchirp chirp chirp chirpchirpchirp chirp"

"I see. That is very thoughtful of Joey. And you got all the information here. Even the type of dog. So it should be no problem making this wish come true."

"Chirp chirpchirp chirp chirp chirpchirpchirpchirp chirp"

"I know little buddy, you did fine this time. And you got everything squared away with Santa's helper all right?"

"Chirpchirp chirp, chirpchirpchirp chirp chirp chirpchirp chirp."

"So she told Santa about our plan too. Excellent. Just remind her that we only want the information from the unselfish hearts. All the kids who ask for toys they want is Santa's problem. If he promises them the toys, he's got to be responsible to handle the mothers, not me. I only want the unselfish hearts."

"Chirp chirp chirpchirp, chirp."

"Okay, be off with you and find me another good request." says God as the snow bird flies off.

This time, God doesn't need to go to Earth Operations

Headquarters as he always has a direct line to the engineer angel in the booth.

"Could you get the guardian of Joey Powers for me?"

Would the guardian angel of Joey Powers please report to God immediately.

As the angel appears at God's campsite in the forest, he looks around and is impressed, yet not surprised, at how simple the site is. A fire ring with a warm fire crackling and two simple, but very comfortable looking chairs with God relaxing in one.

"You call for me sir?"

"Ah yes, have a seat."

As the angel takes his seat – which truly is comfortable and in no way suggests 'roughing' it.- God gets right to the point.

"Joey asked Santa for a new puppy dog for his grandpa, so I want you to go to the rescue center and get the one in cage #3. I've already done everything and that's the dog grandpa would want."

"That Joey is a great kid, sir. I'm glad we are doing this for him."

"He sounds like a good kid. I want you to take the dog to his grandpa's house and ring the doorbell and I'll have the dog run right into the house before grandpa can react. I'll have a note on the dog's back to assure grandpa that this is a gift requested by Joey. Then I want you to make sure Joey understands that his unselfish request was honored and make sure he gets a special toy under the tree as a token of my appreciation, okay?"

"Yes sir! This is really a great gift. Grandpa Powers has been very lonely since his wife died. They were together for 53 years, so he will truly appreciate having a new best friend for sure. Anything else?"

"That should do it. An easy assignment I'm happy to give you."

"Yes sir. I'll take care of everything. This will be fun. Thank you sir."

******

The next morning, as grandpa Powers is having a cup of coffee and reading his paper, he hears some barking and scratching on the back door. He gets up and opens the door as the little pooch runs in wagging his tail as grandpa Powers laughs.

"Well hey little fella, what have we here?" he says as he looks again out in the back to see if there is any human connected to this dog, which there is not, so he shuts the door and notices that there is a red bow and a note on the dog's back.

Grandpa Powers;
Your grandson Joey asked me to get you a dog for Christmas. He tells me your wife of 53 years passed away recently and he didn't want to see you living all alone.

I am sorry about your wife's passing.

I don't have any dogs at the North Pole, so I moved the request up the line and God was delighted to help me out. He also left plenty of dog food and treats in your utility cabinet by the washer, so you should be all set. (And FYI – since it's from God, you should know that the bag of dog food is the finest and will never run out, so you won't have any added expense)

God is helping me out this year with children who make unselfish requests, so Joey certainly is a boy we are happy to help out.

Merry Christmas
Enjoy your new roommate
Santa

Grandpa Powers puts the letter down and picks up the small dog, who is clearly the happiest dog in the world.

"Hello little fella. Let's see, I'll have to come up with a name for you I guess. How about Sparky because you have brought me a spark of sunshine into my life. Let's get you some food you must be hungry, right Sparky?"

He puts the dog down and heads for his laundry room to check out the food as Sparky closely follows his new boss.

"Oh my." he says as he opens the storage cabinet and finds a nice bag of dog food, two nice bowls for the food and water and a nice red ball for them to play with. He finds a note in one of the bowls:

Dogs are created in my image in that they understand unconditional love.
Enjoy Sparky
God

******

"Hey snow bird, come here." shouts Santa as he stands behind the Christmas tree in the town square. He has a few minutes before he has to visit with the kids, so now is a good time to talk to the snow bird.

"Listen, I know you work for God and I know he wants to help out kids who have unselfish requests. But my helper that you talk to every day needs some help and I was wondering if we could help her out too?"

"Chirp chirpchirp chirp chirp chip. Chirp chirp chirp chirp?"

"She's in danger of having to quit college because her dad passed away this past Summer, and they don't have enough money any more to keep her in college. She wants to be a nurse and she'd be great. She's such a generous person and I would love it if God could help her out. Do you think he might help her?"

"Chirp chirp cirp chirp chirp … chirp chirp chirp chirp chirp?"

"Heather Simpson. She is a server at the Pub over there at night after she works during the day with me. She's working so hard to finish up nursing school so she can go to work helping others and help her mom out too."

"*Chir chirp chirpchirp chirpchirp chirp chirp chirp.*"

"Okay, that would be great. I'll let you know if there are any requests that God could use while you're away."

With that, the snow bird flies away into the forest.

******

"Well what do you have for me today? It's a bit early to have something for today, isn't it?"

"*Chirpchirp chirp chirp chirp chirp. Chirp chirpchirp chirp chirpchirpchirp chirp chirp chirp? Chirp chirp chirpchirp chirp chirp chirp.*"

"I see. That's a very interesting prospect you have."

"*Chirp chirp chirp chirp chirpchirp chirp chirp.*"

"Well buddy, I wouldn't worry about the rules. I make up the rules so I can always rewrite them. If it furthers the spirit of Christmas love, I'm happy to change the rules."

"*Chirp chirp chirpchirp chirp.*"

"Her name's Heather Simpson?"

"*Chirp chirp.*"

"Okay great. You go back and listen to the children and I'll take care of Heather – and thanks! It's good to bring me anything like that if you think it might help, so don't be afraid to stir up the rules a bit, okay?"

"*Chirpchirp.*"

As the snow bird heads back to the town square, God requests Heather's guardian angel.

Would the guardian angel for Heather Simpson please report to God immediately.

"Did you call for me sir?"

"Yes, yes, please have a seat."

The angel takes a seat and is impressed with the comfort of the chair.

"Talk to me about Heather. I understand she's studying to be a nurse, but she's run into some financial problems?"

"Yes sir. Her father passed away this past summer leaving her mom, two younger siblings and Heather. It's been rough on them all. Her mom is doing okay but Heather is trying really hard to help her mom by paying her own way through school so her mom can only worry about the two younger kids."

"How far along is she in nursing school?"

"Again sir, Heather is trying so hard to help her mom out. She wants to take a full load this Spring, take a couple classes in Summer and graduate after the Fall session. That plus working so hard to pay her own way is a pretty tall order, sir."

"No kidding. So what can we do to help? Is paying her school off enough? Does she have a reliable car?"

"Her car is okay. She takes good care of it."

"Good to hear, but I'm still going to give her my special Lifetime Warranty – if anything goes wrong, let me know and I'll fix it in a snap" God says as he snaps his fingers and is tickled at his humor.

"Anything else for Heather?"

"No sir. Paying off her college and keeping her car running would be a great help, sir."

"Okay, here's the plan. I want you to go to the Pub she works at tonight and have dinner. I want you to leave a tip with a note – the tip will cover all her school needs and I want her to also know about

....[he snaps his finger with delight] ... God's unlimited warranty on her car so she doesn't have to worry about it. I want to be clear that I am doing this for her because of her generous, unselfish heart. Think you can handle that?"

"Yes sir. How would you like me to appear tonight?" says the angel with a serious tone.

God smiles, "I could care less. Have fun with it."

"Have any suggestions?"

"Oh I always like to go in as an underdog of sorts. Unmatched socks, horrible color coordination, kinda baggie, oversized look you know. It's so much fun when others look at you like you're a loser, only to find out later – I paid off her college tuition with my tip, what have you done lately? Any time you can help someone out and pass around some humble pie is a win-win assignment, I always say."

They both laugh.

"Well I'm not sure about the attire, but I'll certainly have fun with it. Anything else?"

"How's the mother doing?"

"Well sir, that's why Heather is working so hard. It seems as though the husband ran up a large debt before he died that the wife knew nothing about. She has a really good heart like Heather, but it turns out the husband had a bit of a betting problem, so now she's left trying to get all her bills caught up that fell behind because he was using the money to make bets."

"That poor woman. I'll take care of her myself. She is going to start the new year with zero debt and I'll let her know that an unselfish heart is the best credit rating in my world."

With that, the angel leaves as God warms his hands over the fire in thoughtful consideration of how best to help the mother.

******

The angel walks into the Pub that night in very simple attire – jeans, sweater and coat. Not God's choice, but the angel believes only God could pull off stunts like that, so he decided to go the simple route without drawing much attention from the 'humble pie' crowd..

"Hi, my name is Heather and I'll be your server tonight. Can I get you something to drink?"

The angel thinks about it. He hasn't had to be an earthling in quite some time, so this is basically new territory for him. "What do you suggest Heather?"

"Well I don't know your tastes, but we have 32 beers on tap, a wide selection of red and white wines, any hard liquor you want or on the back of our menu here we have some specialty drinks if you like fruity type drinks."

The angel looks over the selections on the back of the menu. A fruity drink sounds much safer for an angel on assignment he thinks.

"I think the Rainbow Sparks sounds like a festive drink, so I'll try it."

"Okay, but let me warn you. It has a pretty good kick to it, so if you're driving I'll only serve you one – with a glass of water too."

"Good to know, thank you Heather. I'm taking a cab, so there is no issues there." says the angel grateful that in the guardian angel program, when you have to be an earthling in an assignment, eating and drinking will have no affect on you at all.

The angel gets his drink, which is quite tasty, and then his meal of Fish 'n Chips and enjoys the time of watching earthlings do what earthlings do at Pubs.

"Can I get you anything else?" asks Heather as she takes his empty plate.

"No Heather, that should do it, thank you."

"Okay, I'll leave the bill." She says as she lays the bill on his table.

The angel pulls out an envelope from his coat pocket and leaves it with enough cash to cover the bill. He gets up and heads out the door.

"Thanks Heather. Good luck in nursing school." says the angel as he leaves.

As Heather heads to clear off his table, she pauses and thinks to herself, 'How did he know I was in nursing school. I've never seen that guy before'. She shakes it off and continues with her work.

She picks up the cash, which is enough – and more- to cover the meal, then the envelope and heads back to the servers station to pay out his order.

She opens the envelope and finds two pieces of paper – one that appears to be a receipt that is stamped *Paid In Full*, then she looks at the letter with it.

Heather;

Enclosed you will find the receipt showing that your nursing school has been paid off completely. God wanted you to know that he took care of it because of your unselfish heart as you work so hard to help your mother out after your dad passed away.

He also wanted you to know that he is providing you with his own unlimited warranty for your car – if anything goes wrong, he'll fix it with a snap of his fingers (he likes to say that, but he doesn't really have fingers). He's going to help your mom out too.

Have a Merry Christmas

Santa

PS: You make an excellent elf, but you should probably stay with the nursing goals.

Heather looks at the nursing school bill marked *'Paid In Full'* as tears begin to fall. As she gathers her composure, she thinks about what Santa this came from? The one she works with in the town square is an old man she's known for years who is in no position to pay a bill like this. Maybe he knows someone? Maybe it's just an anonymous angel who likes to help nursing students?

She can't dwell on it right now as the couple at table 6 looks a little impatient.

******

The next day as Heather's mother, Stephanie, goes to get her mail, she finds an envelope on top that doesn't look right. It has no postage, no markings at all that would indicate it came through the postal services, just her name.

As she gets back inside, she opens the letter and finds several receipts marked *'Paid In Full'* with a letter.

Stephanie;

Enclosed you will find the receipts that show all your bills are paid up and you are officially debt free. Congratulations.

When I found out that your husband left a pretty large debt when he passed away and that you were unaware of his betting problems, I felt it only right that I should help you and your family out. I have already talked with your husband who truly regrets his actions, I assure you.

I am doing this because I had a talk with Heather's guardian angel who informed me of how unselfish Heather has been in her efforts to helping you and get through nursing school. You have done a great job with Heather and I am always happy to help those people who are so unselfish in their hearts.

I sincerely hope that this will give you a much more positive outlook for you and your family moving forward.

Heather will become a valued nurse in your community and you will be able to be a loving mother to your children without worrying about the sins of others.

It's a gift I only give to the unselfish hearts of love.

If you need anything, you know where to find me.

God

Stephanie doesn't know what to do. She looks at the other mail sitting on the table. Mostly bills she can see.

She opens them one at a time and each one says the same; 'Thank you for your recent payment. You are paid in full and will receive no further statements from us. We appreciate your due diligence in clearing this up in a timely manner. We have notified the credit companies to reflect your good standing with us.

******

"Welcome young lady, what's your name?"

"Sarah"

"Well Sarah, what would you like Santa to bring you for Christmas this year?"

"It's not for me – Is that okay?"

"Well it depends. Tell me what you need."

"It's for my best friends brother Johnny. He really needs a train set."

"He does, does he?"

"Yes. He gets teased a lot at school because he stutters. His dad died about a year or so ago in the war. He promised to help Johnny build a train set in their barn when he came back. He even got a lot of the wood for building it, but he never came back. Nobody goes into the barn any more."

"Well that sounds like Johnny really could use some help, Sarah. That's very nice of you to come ask for something like that. Why don't you give my elf here a little more information so we can see what we can do to help Johnny out, okay?"

"Okay Santa. Thanks a lot."

Santa turns to the tree and winks at the snow bird who is anxiously waiting for the elf to write everything down.

As soon as Sarah walks away, the snow bird swoops down and grabs the information and heads off to find God.

"There she is. Well little snow bird what do you have for me now?" asks God as the snow bird lands on Gods knee and drops the paper with the info on it in his lap.

"Chirp chirp chirpchirp chirp chirp chirpchirp."

"I see. So this Johnny Ellis needs a train set and they have a barn in their back yard with wood in it to build a nice track for it, right?"

"Chirp chirp chirpchirp."

"Oh that sounds like a fun project indeed. Now who is the girl who asked Santa for this?"

The snow bird looks down at the paper and then to God.

"Chirpchirp."

"Sarah ….. does she have a last name?"

The snow bird stares at God with a blank expression.

"The elf didn't give you Sarah's full name?"

The bird stares blankly at God, *"Chirp chirp"* she chirps in a blank look manner.

God holds up his hands and smiles, "No worries, little fella, I'll figure this all out with my angels. This is an excellent prospect, so I appreciate your bringing it to me. You can go back to Santa and I'll get right on it."

With that, the snow bird flies away as God contacts the engineer angel at Earth Operations Headquarters.

Would the guardian angel for Johnny Ellis please report to God immediately …. as well as the guardian angel for Johnny's sister's best friend named Sarah who spoke with Santa earlier, please report to God as well.

"Did you want to speak to me sir?"

"Yes, you're Johnny's angel?"

"Yes sir."

"Good … please have a seat." The angel has a seat and is impressed with the comfortable accommodations.

After a few more moments, another angel appears with a slightly more confused look on his face. "You want to see me sir?"

"You must be Sarah's angel?"

"Will I have a Sarah who spoke with Santa earlier this morning and her best friend is Becky Eillis, which I believe is Johnny's sister, yes."

"Sounds about right. What's Sarah's last name?"

"Johnson sir. You know sir, it would really help us out if you could get that information up front so we don't do a lot of guessing … sir"

"Understood. It would help me out as well, but my snow bird helper gets excited sometimes about a project and leaves out a few details. It's all good. Please have a seat."

"Okay. Sarah asked Santa to bring Johnny a train set for Christmas and it sounds like a good project for us. What can you tell me about Johnny?"

"He's a really good boy, sir. His dad died in the war about a year and a half ago. He's been struggling ever since. He stutters – not a lot, but enough that other children tease him. He's falling behind in his school work too."

"Is it a lot of the children teasing him or just a few?" God interrupts.

"Mostly two boys … Billy James and Brian Rockford."

"Hold on." says God as he contacts the engineer angel at EOH.

Would the guardian angels for Billy James and Brian Rockford please report to God immediately.

That very moment two angels appear by the fire ring as well as two more chairs.

"You call for us sir?"

"Sit down and listen."

God turns to Johnny's angel, "Go ahead."

"Well as I was saying … Johnny gets a lot of teasing by Billy and Brian mostly, [God looks over at Billy and Brian's angels with an expression no angel ever likes to see pointed at them, then he looks back at Johnny's angel who continues] and he's fallen behind in his school work – which is unfortunate sir, because he was really a good student before his dad died."

"Sounds like Johnny needs our help. Now Sarah asked Santa for a train set for Johnny. What can you tell me about that?"

"Yes sir. Johnny's dad promised to build a big train set in their small barn in the back, behind their house. He even bought a lot of the wood for it. But then he was shipped out to war and was killed shortly after he arrived. Nobody has gone in that barn since. So Becky and Sarah wanted to see if they could cheer Johnny up by getting some help to build the train set."

God sits back in thought before he speaks.

"You know, the earthlings do a lot of crazy stuff I suppose, but the one thing they do that I've always wanted to try out is building a great train set." he smiles, "So here's what we're going to do for Johnny, [he looks to Johnny's angel] What about his mother?"

"She's a really good mother, sir. Both Johnny and Becky are great kids. It's been tough for her since her husband died, but she has a good job and works hard to provide a loving environment for her family."

"Excellent. Okay here's what I want you all to do. [he looks over at Billy & Brians angels] Do Billy and Brian have dads?"

"Yes sir."

"Are they good dads?"

The angels look at each other with a pained look, then back at God.

"Not really sir. They have good mothers, but the dads are pretty much worthless."

"Not surprising. Okay, I want you two to work with the fathers guardian angels. These fathers are going to work with me in the barn building Johnny an awesome train set."

"How are we going to do that, sir?" asks the angels.

God smiles, "Not sure. Their angels might have some good ideas and probably would love to help you out. Scare the hell out of them. Don't give them a choice. Tell them they really, really, really don't want ME to have to come get them and they'd be well advised to cooperate and just show up at the barn when we tell them to. I'll coordinate everything with you guys later."

God looks at Sarah's angel.

"I want you to visit Sarah. Maybe take over one of her stuffed animals or something so you don't scare her to death. Let her know how much I appreciate her unselfish heart and I really do want her to know what we are doing. I also want you to make sure she has a nice present under the tree that reflects my appreciation. Johnny's going to have an awesome Christmas because of Sarah's unselfish heart, and she needs to understand that."

God looks to Johnny's angel.

"I want you to hang tight with Johnny. I want him to have a good day every day until we get the train set completed. I'm confident that Billy and Brian will be no problem for Johnny in short order and I just need you to make sure he sees those little acts of kindness every day instead of the negative junk."

"I can do that sir." says Johnny's angel.

"Great. I'll be visiting Johnny's mother tonight. What's her name?"

"Erin, sir."

"I'll meet with Erin to let her know what my plan is. She's a good mom and I don't want her to be afraid of anything. After we talk, I'll let you all know so you can get started."

God looks around at the angels and smiles.

"I can't believe I finally get to build a train set! I am totally pumped about this assignment. Thanks for coming. You can go back to your stations and watch over your earthlings and I'll let you know when to get started. I'll have the engineer refer to you all as the Angel Train, so he doesn't have to call out each one of you separately. So when he calls for the Angel Train, you'll know to meet me here, got it?"

"Yes sir." says all the angels.

"And remember angels – this is a great assignment, so have fun with it…. but don't screw it up."

"Yes sir." They says as they all disappear and God sits back with a big smile.

******

"Erin .... wake up Erin."

Erin bolts up and looks at this strange man in her room and lets out a powerful scream, which of course, God mutes immediately so as not to wake up the entire neighborhood.

"Erin, it's okay. I'm not going to hurt you, I want to talk with you."

Erin notices that her screaming is silent, so she stops and glares at this man.

"Who are you and what do you want?"

"Thank you. I'm God and I wanted to talk to you about your son Johnny."

"You're God?" Erin says with a strong sense of being unimpressed.

"Yes. I mean, I am God , but God is Love which is a spirit. If I just woke you up and started to talk to you as a spirit, I'm sure you wouldn't hear a thing I said, so I made myself into this fine looking man, so you might be more comfortable." he says with a smile.

Erin looks him over, "Fine looking man?"

God stands up and looks at himself in the full length mirror on the wall, "You know, Erin, sometimes when I visit I wear real awful clothes with nothing that matches, just because I enjoy teaching earthlings not to judge a book by it's cover. But I just wanted to visit you and have a serious talk about Johnny, so I decided to come ... [he pauses as he studies the mirror before him] as a rather bland looking fellow I suppose."

He turns back and takes his seat again before continuing with Erin, "You know Sarah Johnson? She's Becky's friend."

"Yes." says Erin, still not sure about this man in her room.

God notices Erin's discomfort but decides to ignore and keep talking.

"Sarah asked Santa for a train set for Johnny. When Santa asked

Sarah for some more information, he decided that it would be a better project for me, given that I'm God and he's just Santa, so I'd be in a better position to take on this assignment and help Johnny out."

God pauses to see if he's totally lost Erin, or if she is still with him.

"You work with Santa? So you're saying that you are God and that Santa Clause is real?" says Erin with a large dose of sarcasm.

"Yes Erin. Santa is the spirit of Christmas, and just like I am Love, Santa also has no physical make up, so you earthlings made him an old man in a red suite flying around with a bunch of flying reindeer. It doesn't make a lot of sense, but if it promotes the spirit of Christmas, those of us in the spirit world are happy to indulge the earthlings."

Erin takes a moment to consider what God is saying. If it's real, she figures she won't get any rest until this God person leaves, so she may as well listen to him. If it's just a weird dream, she certainly hopes to wake up soon.

"So why do you want to help Johnny?"

"Because Sarah asked us to. Johnny is a great kid and after hearing what he's been going through, we agree with Sarah that it would be great to build a really cool train set in the barn."

Erin is now a bit troubled, "How did you know about the barn?"

"Erin, I am God. I know this is all really strange to you and I wish I could make you more comfortable. But I think if you just hear me out, you're going to see that I am offering you and your wonderful family a chance to have the best Christmas ever. I know how hard it must be losing your husband in a war like you did. I know he promised his son that he would build him a great train set in the barn when he returned from war – he even has most of the wood needed already in the barn. Erin, I want to build that train set for Johnny."

Erin, with tears in her eyes, considers what God has said.

"What do you want me to do?" she asks God.

"Erin, I just wanted to let you know that me and a couple of others will be working in the barn during the day when you are at work and the kids are at school. I just didn't want you to be alarmed if you saw anything out of place or anything."

"Well that shouldn't be a problem because me and the kids are off until the first of the year and we'll be at my parents home for Christmas. We won't be back until the 28th."

God perks up, "Really? That's perfect. So when are you leaving?"

"Tuesday the 22nd."

"Well, with your permission, I'd like to get a work crew in here on the 23rd and go all out for Johnny and your family."

"Why do this for us?" asks Erin.

"You know, Erin, I've been seeing a trend here on Earth of people becoming more and more selfish. So I decided to test out a new program here in Milford and see if it changes any hearts. I'm working with the Santa in the town square. If he has any child who makes an unselfish request, he sends it to me and I'll make it happen. Obviously, Sarah's request was perfect for me to take on. To be honest with you, I've always wanted to build a train set, so I jumped at the chance to do this assignment, instead of giving it to my angels." God says with a smile.

Erin smiles. She's still not certain, but she's getting more comfortable with God.

"Well I guess I can't say no to God, so if that's what you want to do, go ahead."

"You most certainly can say no to me, Erin. Honestly, if you don't want this to happen, I'm fine with it. I want you, Becky and Johnny to have a great Christmas. I also want to honor your husband by fulfilling his promise to his son. But I'm happy to consider your feelings for this. Are you really okay with us doing this?"

Erin smiles in thought, "It's been really hard for us since Eric died. I think we all have avoided that barn since, because it just reminded us of what we have lost. I wasn't sure what I wanted to do with that barn. I guess it would be a nice tribute to Eric and help our family to stop avoiding these things and begin to move on."

"I know it's been hard for you and the kids. You're a terrific mother Erin. I want you to go to your parents and have a wonderful Christmas. When you come back, I'll make sure that your family has everything you need to move forward – not to forget Eric, but to move forward with Eric in your hearts."

"That would be nice." says Erin with tears of gratitude.

"Well I'll let you get back to sleep. If you're close to your neighbors, you might want to let them know that there will be some activity in the barn while you're away. We don't want to cause any problems, you understand. And to convince you that I am God, I promise you that when you wake up in the morning you will stretch and feel like you've had the best sleep of your life. At that moment, I want you to remember our conversation and know that I truly am God and I'm here for you."

******

Would the Angel Train group please report to God immediately.

The angels gather around the campfire in their very comfortable seats as God gets started.

"Thanks for coming. I spoke with Erin and this is going to work out fine. Her and the kids are leaving on the 22nd to spend Christmas at her parents home. They'll be back on the 28th, so that gives us five working days to turn that barn into a magical train world for Johnny."

The angels all mumble comments of approval before God continues.

"So what's the situation with Billy and Brian's fathers?"

"It's going great, sir. You were right about their guardian angels – they were very excited about this assignment and are anxious to help us. They have been making weird things happen to their earthlings to kind of scare them. They're really having fun messing with them. They think that once we have a set plan, they will visit them the night before and without telling them too much, scare them enough to make sure they get to the barn at whatever time you want them there."

"Excellent. Just tell the angels that the less they tell them, the better. I have a pretty good indoctrination planned for them that should really make an impression on them."

God turns to Johnny's angel.

"How's Johnny doing?"

"Good. It's been a good few days for him. Just as you requested. He's looking forward to going to his grandparents for Christmas. He really loves Erin's parents, so he should be in good shape."

"Excellent. You just stay with him and make sure nothing goes wrong. And contact Becky's guardian angel and fill her in too. Make sure she has a nice present of my appreciation under the tree. I want this to be a good Christmas for the family and we don't need any hic-ups to gum stuff up." God says with a hint of pleasure, as he always loves to insert earthling slang whenever he is working at Earth Operations.

"And how is Sarah doing?"

"She's great sir. I had a nice visit with her and she is so excited that we are all doing this for Johnny. I even had the guardian angel of Sarah's mom talk to her – to let her know what we are doing and that it's because of her unselfish daughter. We asked her what we could get Sarah for Christmas as a special thank you, and she gave us some really good ideas. That's a great family, sir, and they are going to have a wonderful Christmas as well."

"Perfect" says God as he approves all the information this meeting has brought.

"So we're all set then. I'll be at the barn about 9am on the 23rd and I trust you will get the fathers there about that time as well. Any questions?"

All the angels shake their heads as they get up to leave.

"Thanks for your help. We'll get the Christmas spirit back on track with projects like this, that's for sure."

******

At exactly 9am, God appears inside the barn. He's already checked the place out before and has made sure that there is ample materials and tools to make the project work. As he walks out of the barn, he sees Billy and Brian's dads standing on the sidewalk looking rather lost.

"You boys must be Billy and Brian's dads" God says as he moves towards them with his hand extended.

"And you are?" God asks the first.

"Joe .... Joe Rockford." he says as he shakes Gods hand with a puzzled look on his face.

"So Brian is your son?' Joe gives an affirming nod with his puzzled look.

God turns to the other, "And you are?"

"Frank James.... What is this all about?" he says with a strong sense of annoyance.

"Billy's dad, Frank. Splendid. Follow me fellas."

God turns and heads to the barn.

Frank and Joe watch, then look at each other, neither moving an inch.

As God gets to the entrance, he turns and sees that the two have not moved.

"You both know how to walk, right? This project will not come to you, you have to come to the project. Let's go – we have a limited time to get things done."

The two slowly move towards the entrance with a combination of curiosity and resolve in understanding what their guardian angel told them regarding the lack of choice in the matter.

As they get inside, they look around the big room. The floor is cemented [God felt it'd be good to have a level, solid floor instead of the dirt, so he made that happen], there is a lot of various sizes of wood in one corner with saws, drills, nail guns, a tool chest as well as various other items that may come in handy.

"Either one of you any good with construction work?" Gods asks.

The two look at each other, then at God.

"I have a workshop in my garage. I'm not a professional, but I know how to use tools." says Joe.

"Excellent Joe. I'll let you be the main man on the saw." says God who turns to Frank.

"Don't look at me, I'm a banker." says Frank a bit boastful.

"Well then this will be a wonderful opportunity for you to learn something new. And if we run out of anything, I'll let you go buy it since you're obviously a good finance guy."

"I'm not spending any of my own money here! Besides, we don't even know what we are building or why." Frank protests.

"Good point, Frank. Please let's sit down." God shows them to chairs along the wall that were not there moments ago, which raises some eyebrows.

As they take their seats, God continues, "Have either of you heard of a Johnny Ellis? He goes to Brian and Billy's school, and I believe they are in the same class."

They both shake their head 'no' with one mumbling 'Never heard of him'

"I'm not surprised. Anyway, this is where Johnny lives and we are going to build Johnny a train set that is going to be the most awesomeness train set ever!" Says God with a tad too much enthusiasm.

"Why do you want us to build it?" asks Frank who is clearly not in his element at a construction site.

"Well it turns out that Billy and Brian – that's your sons – they have been pretty rough on Johnny. They tease him a lot. He stutters a bit and those two boys go out of their way to make fun of him."

Frank interrupts, "That's not our fault."

God quickly responds, "Yes Frank, it most certainly is. When I heard about Johnny's situation, I knew right away where it came from. I talked to Billy and Brian's guardian angels. They told me they both have good, loving mothers, but when I asked them about their dads – that would be you two – they both said you were pretty much worthless. BINGO! I was not surprised. And that is why you two are going to help me build a train set for Johnny."

"But why do we have to build it? Why can't Johnny's dad do it? Is he worthless, too?" asks Frank in a defensive tone.

"Well Frank that's the problem., you see Johnny's dad Eric,

promised to build the train set for his son. He even got a lot of the wood over there to do so. But duty called and Eric had to go to war. He wasn't there very long before he was shot and killed. Johnny's dad is never coming home. He will never be able to build this train set. That's why Johnny is such a sad little boy who stutters. And your two sons have taken a bad situation and made it worse for Johnny. That's why you two are going to help me build this train set. My hope is that this experience will help you two understand what being a good Dad is all about. Maybe your two sons will learn – from you – that it is much better to help those in need than it is to hurt them and make them feel worse."

God pauses as the two fathers seem a bit more settled into their chairs.

"So let's get started and see if I can get you two to grow a dad's heart." says God as he gets up and looks over his plans.

******

As God, Frank and Joe are busy building tables that will hold a massive landscape of mountains, valleys, farmlands and towns for the train set to explore, people keep dropping in. Mostly neighbors who Erin talked to before she left. Some come to help, while many others come to drop off many of the wonderful accessories that an awesome train set needs – miniature houses, businesses, animals, people, cars, tractors, you name it – neighbors who were aware of Eric's passing were happy to contribute to the Ellis project. Many brought gifts for Becky and Erin as well and many brought food for the workers and some for the Ellis family.

The snow bird, who had a bit of a problem finding God, but realized once she did, that flying to the barn was a lot easier than going into the forest, was still bringing God requests from the Santa in the town square. God was always happy to take a break and go out away from the crowd of workers with snow bird to fulfill every request.

All the volunteers took the 25th off to celebrate Christmas in their own way, so God took advantage of the free time to call a meeting at Earth Operations Headquarters for all the angels involved with earthlings in the Milford Massachusetts area to let them know that he was putting a postcard on every Christmas tree that read:

> *Love is always best*
> *When it comes from*
> *An unselfish Heart*

On the 26th, with three days until Erin and the kids came home, things quickly went into high gear.

There almost seemed to be too many volunteers as the word got out about the train set being built for Johnny. Sarah and her parents were there to help. The local chapter of Wounded Warriors Project were there to do whatever needed to be done.

God put Frank in charge of getting jobs for all the volunteers. God made it clear to Joe and Frank that he did not want people to know that he was God. He took on the name Bubba (he was quite humored with it too) and made sure everyone knew he was just helping out.

Frank and Joe went from being worthless dads put out about having to do this project, to two men totally embracing being a part of a great outpouring of love that the community had for this family.

There were people everywhere. Many in the barn helping to create a world of adventure for the train set, some people in the house with various jobs like fixing dripping faucets cleaning windows and carpets or doing light repairs where needed, and still others dropping off gifts and food. Frank even went out and bought a big freezer for the family with some of the donations that was quickly filling up with meats, ice cream and vegetables.

On the afternoon of the 27th, with the Ellis family returning in the morning, there was a lot of cleaning up and last minute items to finish up with.

After most of the volunteers made their way home, God turned to Joe and Frank.

"I hope you boys learned something this Christmas."

They both smiled in appreciation.

"It would have been easier to just punish your sons for their behavior, but I don't work that way. That's putting a negative on a negative. I like to take a negative and build an even stronger positive from it. Your sons have good hearts and I'm hoping that this experience got your hearts back to being a dad's heart."

They both nod in agreement.

"Thanks for your help. Be good dads." says God as the two men walk away.

God stops them, "Hey fellas. If I get an opportunity to build another train set, you want me to contact you?"

The two men look at each other, then at God with much enthusiasm.

"You bet!"

With God alone in the barn, playing one last time with the wonderful train set and looking at all the gifts and food donated by so many volunteers, snow bird flies in and lands on the train as it makes it's way down a mountain side.

"Chirp chirp chirpchirp chirp chirp chirp chirpchirp chirpchirp?"

"It is great fun, but no, I'm not sticking around. We had a good Christmas though. Made a lot of people happy. I think you and I got the Christmas spirit back on track around here. Earthlings have good hearts and sometimes it just takes something like a simple train set for a little boy to remind them of what they can do if they just open their hearts. Thanks for helping me out, little one."

"Chirp chirpchirp."

With that, God is off to create other worlds.

******

The next day around noon, the Ellis family pulls into their driveway. It's been a long drive and they are happy to be home.

As they walk into their home, they notice how clean and orderly their house looks. There are no presents under the tree which kind of disappoints Becky and Johnny who were hopeful that Santa would have dropped something off. Erin is quick to remind them how Santa dropped off plenty of presents at grandmas and grandpas.

But on the dinning room table was a gift.

To Johnny, from Santa.

Johnny opens the gift as Erin and Becky look on. It's an engine car for a train set with a note on it.

Johnny;
Take this, your mom and sister out to the barn
Merry Christmas
Santa

Johnny looks over at his mom and sister who shrug their shoulders [Erin of course knows what's going on and tries desperately to keep her composure in check].

They go out to the barn and hesitate before Johnny reluctantly pulls the big barn door open.

The three stand there in disbelief as they look at the beautiful train set – only missing the engine car in Johnny's hands – with tracks that wind through farms, up and around a mountain and down into a beautiful town.

In the corner is a Christmas tree with several presents underneath. Next to it is a table with plates of cookies, candies and snacks. And next to it is a large freezer that they will find full of food for the family.

As they stand in shock, the many volunteers – who had been waiting for them in the house across the street – slowly and quietly make their way across to the Ellis sidewalk. They all stand and give the Ellis family a moment to take in the Christmas miracle before they break out in, "We wish you a merry Christmas…."

The three turn around and see what seems to be the entire town standing before them singing.

Sarah Johnson is in the middle holding a big sign.

Merry Christmes
Ellis Family

Snow bird, perched on the top of the barn reflects;

"Chirp chirp chirp chirp chirpchirp chirpchirp chirpchirp"

[Now that's how you create Christmas spirit!]

Bonus Story

When I was writing my collection of Christmas stories, I wrote Nora and the EGAC Committee. I loved the story and how it developed, but when I was done, I decided to put it aside. It just didn't fit the magical spirit of Christmas theme I was looking for. It's not a Christmas story just because it has elves in it after all. This story could happen in July.... April .... any time, so I put it away.

But when I finished my twelve Christmas stories, I thought what the heck – it's Christmas for crying out loud. Give them a gift!

So here's a bonus story for you. It's not a Christmas story, but I think you'll like it.

13

Nora and the EGAC Committee

"Yes Nora, come in" says Santa.

Nora is a fairly new elf in the female toys division of the North Pole. There is a lot of buzz around the North Pole that Nora is one Elf to keep an eye on. She has a ton of ideas.

"Thanks Santa, for seeing me." she says as she takes a seat.

"Not a problem, Nora. I've heard a lot of good things about you, so I'm happy to have this opportunity to get to talk with you personally. Hope you are enjoying your work here at the North Pole."

"Yes sir, I just love it here. The elves are great and everyone works hard, so I couldn't be happier."

"Good to hear. So what brings you here today?"

"I was just thinking that it might be a good idea to create a committee composed of Elves from both male and female divisions and Guardian Angels from Earth Operations to work together for the benefit of the children we represent."

Santa rubs his beard in thought.

"I like it. The Elves and Guardian Angels working together."

"Yes sir. I know you and God are very busy, and I thought this committee would free up more time for you." says Nora.

"We could play more golf!" Santa says with a chuckle.

"Well I wasn't really thinking that so much."

Santa laughs and interrupts, "I'm just kidding, Nora. I've been golfing with God a couple of times, and it's really not much fun playing with someone who's perfect all the time."

"I can only imagine, sir."

"So how do you see this committee working together?" asks Santa.

"I was thinking that the Guardian Angels are assigned individual children, where the Elves work for all children, so if we got together, say once a month or so, we could share a lot of ideas from two different perspectives. We could even team up on some special assignments as needed with our combined priority being the good of the children."

"I do like it, Nora, and I have to say that you certainly live up to your billing. I've heard a lot of people saying to watch out for Nora, that girl has a lot of good ideas. I'm happy to see that you don't disappoint. Having the angels and elves working together has a lot of possibilities. I'm getting together with God soon, so let me talk it over with him. I'm pretty sure he's going to love it. Anything that benefits the children is always a good idea for God."

"Thanks Santa. Doing things to help the children have a good experience should always be our top priority." says Nora as she gets up to leave.

"I appreciate you coming by Nora. I love it when my elves have new ideas they want to share, so please feel free to drop by any time. I'll schedule a meeting with you after I talk with God."

******

"Thanks for coming, God." says Santa as God walks in and takes a seat.

"Not a problem. I love visiting Earth and seeing how the earthlings are doing. I brought my snow board. Thought maybe if you had some free time, we might hit a few of those mountains around here."

"Sounds good to me. Glad you're taking a liking to the snow boarding. It's a lot more fun than walking around a golf course watching you make perfect shots all day."

God laughs, "Oh come on. I put a couple of shots into the rough to give it a little adventure."

Santa laughs too, "Sure, and then you hole out the next shot .... from the rough! Playing golf with you is no fun at all."

They both laugh.

"I do love how the earthlings have created so many fun games. I tried Sumo Wrestling once and decided then to stay with non-contact sports. Snow boarding is much more my style. I want to have fun, not get killed after all."

They both laugh again.

"Listen, one of my elves came to me with an idea I wanted to run by you." says Santa to get the conversation going in the proper direction.

"Great. What do you have?"

"She was thinking it might be a good idea to form a committee composed of guardian angels and elves to work together for the benefit of the children. The guardian angels are all assigned an individual child, where the elves are involved with all children, so she was thinking it would be good if the two groups got together once a month or so to discuss any issues or ideas that would create a better experience for the children of earth."

"Wow. Who is the elf who suggested that?" asks God

"She's fairly new. Her name is Nora."

"Better keep an eye on Nora. She is one sharp cookie. I love that idea."

"No joke. She's a keeper for sure. I was thinking we'd only need guardian angels of children that live in areas that have Santa and flying reindeer as part of their Christmas traditions. They can work with a group of elves and work out all the details from there."

"Sounds good. I think we don't need to overkill the rules for this committee – that's an earthling thing to do. Certainly, the elves can work out whatever they feel best serves their agenda for the committee, and the angels can be more flexible depending on the season and the issues that come up." God says as he gets up to leave.

"I appreciate you coming over God. I'll meet with Nora right away and as the snooty earthlings like to say, I'll have my people contact your people." Santa says with a smile.

"Good grief, no snootyness on this committee, you hear? We're working with the children. You want to go conquer a few mountains with me?" says God who produces his snow board.

"I'll take a pass this time. I want to talk with Nora and have a few other items to get to first."

"Okay, my friend. If you need me, you know where to find me." says God as he heads for the door.

"I never know where to find you God. But I do know how to find you." Santa says with a smile.

"Good point my good man. Merry Christmas to all." says God as he heads out the door to conquer a few hills he's been dying to try out.

******

"Come in Nora. Thanks for coming."

"I was anxious to hear what God had to say." Nora says as she comes into Santa's office and takes a seat.

"Oh Nora, he loved the idea of the Elves and Guardian Angels working together. He's going to talk to the angels at Earth Operations Headquarters. As soon as he stops snow boarding, I assume."

"Excuse me?" says a confused Nora.

"God loves to play you know. He brought his snow board when he came to talk to me, so I assume whenever he's done, he'll head off to Earth Operations Headquarters to talk to the angels. That's why he makes so many planets. He's got lots of playgrounds to choose from."

Nora smiles and shakes her head. That's a side of God she was unaware of.

"So I thought I'd let you be in charge here on our end. Figure out how many elves from each department, and I think your best bet is to talk it over and choose elves that really want to be on the committee. You may need to have the first meeting with just a few elves and angels to toss around ideas before you get too set with building a committee."

"I already have about four elves that really like the idea. Do we have a place to meet somewhere?" Nora asks

"No. God said he'll talk to the angels and put one angel in charge of the EGAC [Elves and Guardian Angels Connection] committee and have them contact you to set everything up. You both are spirits, so you can pretty much meet wherever you want to."

"Okay. This is exciting. I really appreciate the opportunity to connect with the angels." Nora says as she gets up to leave.

"It's a great idea, Nora. Any time we can open up the possibilities for the children is a good time. They should be contacting you soon – if they can get God off the mountains."

"Thanks Santa. I'll let you know how it goes."

******

"Good to see you God, come in." says the angel at Earth Operations Headquarters.

"Good to be here. I was just doing some snow boarding up by the North Pole and thought I'd drop in and check on my earth operation angels."

"Snow boarding, sir?"

"Yes. Santa taught me some time ago, and I rather enjoy it. But between you and me, it really helps to be God when you're snow boarding, that's for sure."

"How so?"

"Well you get going so fast down the hill that it's really important when you see a tree in your path to remember that the tree is not going to move, you have to. Of course, being God, I just blink and the tree gets out of my way. I did a lot of blinking out there. I can only imagine how the earthlings must get a little banged up if they don't pay attention."

"Yes sir. There is a lot of sports that are fun, but you really have to pay attention for sure. So you wanted to talk to me about something?" says the angel, who wants to change directions.

"Oh yes, listen, I was talking to Santa and one of his elves suggested it might be a good idea to form a committee that has both Elves and Guardian Angels in an effort to work together and provide a better experience for the earthlings at Christmas."

"Are the angels doing something wrong, sir?"

"No! Your angels do wonderful work. It just seems like a good idea to have the elves and guardian angels working together at Christmas to get the best outcomes for the children, that's all."

"If there is a training issue, I'd be happy to work on it, sir."

God just stares at the angel in a rather uncomfortable length of time before responding.

"You're taking it a little too personal, you know. There are no issues here. It just seems like it's a good idea when you have two groups working for the good of one population, it wouldn't hurt to get the two entities together and compare notes. That's all I'm saying."

"Who would be in charge, sir?"

"Well sense you're a bit too sensitive about this idea, I would hope Nora would be in charge. She's an elf who is very well thought of at the North Pole, and I think she would be excellent in keeping both sides focused on the children."

"What do you want me to do?"

"I don't want to take too many guardian angels away from their assignments, so I think you should choose two or three supervisors and a couple GAs to participate. Maybe one that specializes in children issues, one that specializes in parents and a couple guardian angels with very creative ideas and positive attributes. Reassure them that there is nothing wrong, and that this is truly a positive idea to work with the elves, okay?"

"Understood. I just wanted to be clear, sir. When is the first meeting?"

"Pick your angels, then contact Santa. I'm sure Nora will have her elves chosen and maybe it would be best for you and Nora to get together first to work out the basics, then pull the whole group in from there."

"Got it. I'll start right away, sir."

"Well try to control your enthusiasm. This is a good thing. Have fun with it. The elves do a lot of wonderful things for the children every Christmas. The guardian angels do a lot of wonderful things for the children as well. There is a lot you can learn from each other that's going to make you both even better at helping out the children. How can that be a bad thing?"

"I'll make sure the children are taken care of sir. Do you want me to follow up with you?"

"No. I trust my angels. You'll do great. But if anything comes up and you need me, I'm happy to help." says God as he gets up to leave, "Have fun with it. It's a great idea."

With that God leaves Earth Operations Headquarters, and the Elves and Guardian Angels Connection – or better known as EGAC – is born.

******

"Thanks for coming, Nora. Please have a seat." says the supervisor of Earth Operations Headquarters as Nora comes and takes a seat.

Nora goes to shake his hand, "And you are?" she asks.

"Oh, well we don't really have names here at Earth Operations. The angels are simply the guardian angel of so-and-so, and those of us in management just go by our titles." says the supervisor.

"Oh, well we'll have to have names for the committee so we can talk freely. I'm comfortable with the guardian angels just going by the first name of their assignment, so how many do you have?" asks Nora with her pad and pencil ready to take notes.

"Well I thought I'd have two GAs – that's guardian angels, of course – myself and another supervisor who is in charge of current events. I plan to switch up the GAs every meeting so as not to interfere with their assignments. Every time we call a meeting, I'm sure there will be two GAs who don't have much going on that could join us."

"Great. So the GAs can take the first name of their earthling assignment, that would be fine. You ..." she studies the supervisor,,, "You can be Joe, if that's okay with you?"

"Joe?"

"Sure. It's an easy name, so let's just go with it. And the other supervisor. Male or female?"

Joe looks a bit confused, "Angels are spirits and don't have any gender. We deal with the earthlings heart, their emotional state, so we don't have any gender."

"Oh. Interesting. Since I gave you a male name, let's balance it with calling the other supervisor Mary, if that's okay?"

"Clever. Just like the Christmas story." says Joe.

"Excuse me?" ask Nora who doesn't understand.

"Joseph and Mary .... and baby Jesus .... you know – that's kind of what Christmas is all about," explains Joe.

"Oh, right. I'm sorry, the elves stay pretty focused on their jobs and don't really think much beyond making the best toys possible. But at least their names will be easy to remember, right?" says Nora a bit proud of herself.

"Sure. So when and where do you want to meet?"

"Well I was thinking for our first meeting, it might be best if we gave each other a tour of our work spaces so each group can get a feel for what the other group does." says Nora.

"Good idea. Let's start at the North Pole. You can show us around and give us an idea of how the Elf program works. Then we can come back to Earth Operations and show you how the Guardian Angel program works."

"Sounds great! I'm really excited to get started." says Nora as she gets up to leave.

******

"Welcome to the North Pole." says Santa as the angels appear.

The angels are spirits, of course, so Joe said they could take on any physical form they wanted, with only a height limit in place – being that the elves are rather small, Joe said nothing over three feet tall.

Joe and Mary were dressed rather casually in sweaters and jeans, while the two GAs, Harry and Lucy, were obviously unaware of conditions at the North Pole.

Harry is wearing a straw hat, Hawaiian shirt, shorts and flip flops, which he quickly regrets when they land at the North Pole, and Lucy wears a fancy gala gown with fancy, sparkling high heels, which she too quickly regrets.

Meanwhile, the elves are neatly dressed in unison with their green outfits, pointy hats and stripped socks, and seem a bit uncertain about their guests.

Nora chose two elves from the male toy department and two from the female department, as well as one engineer and one QA. She was careful to chose elves in alphabetical order, so they were named Avery, Butch, Cathy, Doris, Earl and Frieda.

"I hope you enjoy your tour. Nora will be your host. I just wanted to greet you, so I'll leave you in her capable hands." says Santa as he walks up to his log cabin home to get out of the cold.

Nora steps up and notices that the two GAs are turning blue and shivering with teeth chattering.

"We have extra coats, if you'd like, but once we get inside, I think you'll find it nice and warm."

"Great!" says one.

"Let's go!" says the other.

They move quickly to the huge building behind them.

As they get inside and take a minute to thaw out, the angels look out over a huge, open floor with rows of tables with elves sitting tightly together busily working on toys.

"This is the assembly floor. The toys start at the left, back corner over there," she points to the distant corner of the room, "The toy is passed down from elf to elf who all have specific tasks to perform until it reaches up here in the right hand corner where they move on to the wrapping department next door. Every other elf is a quality assurance elf who checks to make sure the previous task was performed correctly. "

"How cool is that?" says an excited Harry, who has thawed out completely.

"Totally cool!" says Lucy who picks up one of the toys to look it over.

"Please don't touch the toys" Nora says in almost panic mode. "We must not disturb the work going on here. Our elves must stay focused on their work with little distractions."

"Where's the Christmas music? You'd think being the North Pole, you all would be rocking out to some loud Christmas music, right" asks Harry.

"Oh no, we have a lot of work to do, so we can't have any distractions here." says Nora.

"I'd work way better if the music was cranked up, but that's just me." says Lucy.

"We work hard to insure that the toys are perfect for every child. We take a lot of pride in knowing that we have very few complaints at Christmas. That's what we celebrate." informs Nora proudly.

They move up the stairs to a floor with lots of elves busy working on their computers.

"This is the engineering department where our elves can go over every toy the children request and re-purpose a lot of the engineering to make it a better toy. You'd be surprised how many toys have a lot of unnecessary steps added to them. Since we deliver the toys already assembled, we are able to streamline the instructions and remove a lot of the marketing gunk that earthlings always add on."

"So do the engineers have freedom to create any special features for the toys?" asks Joe.

"Oh no," says Nora, "Our elves are very logical in their approach. They understand the toys requested by the children and are very methodical in making sure that's what the children get. We can never expand beyond that."

Nora takes them through the engineering room and out onto a

balcony, handing the angels heavy coats as she holds the door open for them.

"This building to your left is the cafeteria where the elves eat."

"Can they have whatever they want?" asks Mary

"No, the elves have a very specific diet of berries, nuts and of course, their main entre of red licorice."

"Red Licorice? That's crazy!" says Harry.

"Oh yes. They keep asking Santa to tell the children to leave out some red licorice. They get pretty upset when he returns with lots of cookies, apples and carrots for the reindeer, when we are the ones who build the toys. In fact, that might be something our committee could discuss later?"

"Who knew." says Lucy, "Guess if you eat too much red licorice, it will stunt your growth."

Harry and Lucy laugh, while Nora is not impressed.

"On the other side of the cafeteria is the sleeping quarters for the elves. Every elf works a 24/7 shift and then is allowed a 6.32 hour rest before they start another shift."

"What?! A 6.32 hour rest after a 24/7 shift? Who came up with that? Besides, I thought you all were spirits like us?" asks Harry.

"Not completely. You angels are 100% spirit so you don't need to eat or sleep in your world and can take on any physical presence you choose when you need to. Elves on the other hand, have some of the attributes of the spirit world – we can relocate from place to place without any trouble like you all – but we need our physical presence specifically set for making toys, so we do need to eat and sleep some. We found the 24/7 work and 6.32 rest to be the perfect formula for maximizing our output for Santa and the children."

"Well that's about it for the North Pole. We can head to Earth

Headquarters unless anyone has any questions." says Nora as they make their way back to the first floor.

"We don't have a cafeteria, so you might want to bring your own red licorice." says Harry as he and Lucy burst into laughter.

"Okay, knock it off." says Joe to his angels before turning to Nora, "Sorry. The GAs have fun, but they really mean no harm."

"Understood." says Nora as they all head for Earth Operations Headquarters to check out the guardian angel program.

They all enter the observation booth which sits above the big, massive floor below with cubicles full of angels monitoring their earthlings. The atmosphere is a lot more relaxed than the assembly room of the North Pole. There is a variety of activity going on, as well as movement. It seems a bit of organized chaos to the elves, who seem a bit uncomfortable watching the activity below.

"It's not the well oiled machine like your assembly room, but our angels work on an emotional platform. Our angels are connected to the hearts of our earthlings, so while you elves are meticulous in making perfect toys, we are busy working through the emotional roller coaster events of life." says Joe.

Nora is impressed, yet a bit hesitant in all the activity going on below them. "These angels are here all the time?" she asks.

"Yes. We are, of course, complete spirits, so we don't have any need for breaks of any kind. A guardian angel is assigned a child every time a child is born. They stay with that one earthling until they pass over to the spirit world. When their earthling passes over, the guardian angel can immediately take on another child, or they can sign up for another program." Joe explains.

"What other programs are there?" Nora asks.

"We have many programs at Earth Operations." says Mary, "We have angels who take on a physical presence of an earthling and can do any number of assignments on the planet. We have some who just like to wander from town to town helping those in trouble. We have angels on the planet in specific areas of need carrying out assignments. We have many angels working with our animal programs. An angel at Earth Operations has a variety of assignments available to them. We have angels who switch up often and we have some who just stay at one program. God wants it to be whatever the angels want."

"That is so fascinating." says Nora. "I'm so glad we got together. Just having the tours has shown me – and I hope you all – how important we are to the children we serve."

After their tours, the angels and elves agree to start meeting on the first Monday of every month at 6:30. Since neither group is a slave to time like the earthlings are, they set the meeting up for the first Monday at 6:30, but they really have no idea what month, day or time it really is, except when it's Christmas season and the elves are in panic mode. So in reality, the EGAC meets every now and then as they can.

******

"Come in God. Thanks for coming." says Santa as God walks in.

"Always a pleasure to visit with the hard working group of the North Pole." God says as he takes a seat.

"I asked you here to talk to you about the EGAC committee."

"Ah yes, the one Nora started? How's it going?"

"Well it's not really going as smoothly as I had hoped. They get along okay, but from what Nora says, it seems like we're trying to get squares and circles together and it's just not working." says Santa.

"Ah yes, why am I not surprised. Been a problem since the

beginning of time here on Earth. The elves are very mechanical as they need to be to create the toys for the children. The angels are very emotional, as they need to be, because they are connected to the hearts of the children. The key is balance. That's why I sent my son down to earth. Everyone was living a mechanical life, following rules, doing everything by the book. Jesus went to show them they needed to live emotionally as well. Love one another. Care about each other. Life needs to be both mechanical and emotional to be full…. and then they crucified him…. what can you do?" God says shaking his head.

"Well I don't think anyone in the committee is talking about crucifying anyone else, but Nora seems a bit frustrated and questioning if the committee even needs to meet."

"Oh it's not that bad. I'll go to their next meeting and talk to them. Have Nora let me know, and I'll be there."

That'd be great if you can. I think Nora just needs a little assurance that there is a point to all this."

As God gets up to leave, "Oh there is a point indeed. If we can get the elves and angels working together, then we can all have hope that the earthlings will eventually get it too. Let Nora know she's doing great and I'm happy to help her out."

"Thanks God. You going to hit the mountains while you're here?"

"Not this time around. I've got a new solar system in the works that I want to try out a few ideas for planets to get to. But I'll be at that meeting, so have Nora contact me."

******

"Thanks for coming everyone. I was told that we would have a guest today, but he hasn't showed up yet…."

Just then, God walks into the meeting.

"Sorry if I'm late. Got caught up working out a few kinks in a new solar system I'm creating. Did I miss anything?"

"No sir. We just started actually." says Nora.

"Great. Let's move on then." says God as he sits at the table on the far end and looks around at all the elves and guardian angels staring at him.

"You said you wanted to talk to the committee, so I left the agenda open for you." says Nora.

"Okay great. So how are things going for the elves and angels working together?"

There is an uncomfortable hush as even angels and elves are hesitant to speak up when God is in the room.

Finally, Nora breaks the ice, "We have a good appreciation for the work each of us do for the children, but working together has proven to be more difficult because we are so different in our approach. It's difficult for us to get on the same page. We thought maybe you could help us out a little."

"Absolutely. But let me start by telling you that the issue that is troubling you is exactly what brings value to this committee. Let me explain.

"Every living creature I create has two very important ingredients. I give every creature a brain to problem solve. To develop logical processes for survival and finding food. Every living creature has a brain. I also gave every living creature a heart to feel and understand consequences, to care, to have compassion. I call these two ingredients the mechanical and the emotional. Every living creature has the capacity for both, but most creatures are very heavy on the mechanical side. They need to be to survive."

"You elves are a good example. You need to be very heavy on the mechanical side in order to produce all those great toys that helps

Santa every year. Being mechanical is really a huge benefit for the elves North Pole program, to be sure."

"Now when I created the earthlings, I created them to have a good balance of mechanical and emotional ingredients. I put them in charge of planet earth because they had the capacity to understand both the mechanical and emotional parts of life."

"The Guardian Angel program needs to be heavy on the emotional side because each angel is connected to the heart of an earthling. The earthlings are in charge of all living things, so they really need to be strong on the emotional side. Earthlings not only need to be mechanical in problem solving, but they need to understand the consequences of how their problem solving affects all the living creatures."

"The problems you are having are the problems I have been dealing with since I created the earthlings. Earthlings are constantly struggling between the mechanical and emotional side."

The answer for this committee is not a matter of changing anything, but appreciating each other for what they bring to the discussion and using each others strengths to the benefit of every problem you face. Being mechanical and being emotional has to be a fifty-fifty mix, or it will always create problems. Having a mutual respect for one another is vital to the success of the work this committee can do, so you really are off to a good start. Every situation you come to with the children will require a response from both sides, and both sides need to understand when a situation needs a little more response from the mechanical and when the response needs to be more emotional. It's not a competition. You get no rewards for dominating the other, you only get rewards when you see happy results with the children."

God takes a break to let it all sink in and smiles as he looks around the tables at the terrified faces looking at him.

"You're doing nice work here. Neither group needs to change anything. Just appreciate each other and if you both commit to the fifty-fifty balance in everything you do, you're going to achieve great things for the children."

Once again, God looks around at many terrified faces as he laughs.

"You all look so terrified. Nora, this is a good time for you to tell these angels to scream at the elves to lighten up. Tell a joke, say something completely crazy … the air is way too thick in here."

"Anyone got any red licorice?" says one of the angels and the other angels burst into laughter. The elves hesitate, but start laughing as well.

"There you go. They're all yours, Nora. Keep up the good work everyone." as God leaves the meeting with everyone consumed with laughter.

******

After the visit from God, the EGAC committee started to come together much better. They truly began to appreciate each others input and actually started working together to develop strategies that would clearly benefit the children.

For instance, the emotional angels started to understand the parents objections to toys because the elves were able to explain the many hazards the toy could create. The angels really appreciated this because they were only focused on the children having fun before.

On the other hand, the elves agreed to incorporate Christmas music in their work place as the angels encouraged them to. They learned that the music puts the elves in a happy mood and that created a fun environment that did not take away from their focused work, but made it better.

Sometimes, an elf or angel would bring a specific need to the meeting and Nora found it refreshing how both sides would look at the need from their perspectives and discuss possible solutions without it becoming a competition.

The EGAC was becoming the group Nora had envisioned and both Santa Clause and God were completely satisfied with the work they were doing.

******

"Nora…. Nora…. wake up, Nora!" says Joe shaking Nora, who is on a 6.32 break.

Nora surfaces and looks at her watch, "Hey, I still have 37 minutes…." then looks and sees that it's Joe the angel supervisor. "Joe? What are you doing here?"

"Nora, there is an emergency and I need you to get me an elf to help us out."

"You need one of our elves?" she says, still suffering from the cobwebs in her head after being wakened 37 minutes too soon.

"Just one. I need one that is really good at staying focused and mechanical in any situation."

"Well most of our elves are good with that. That's why playing the Christmas music in the work shop wasn't that big a deal." she says.

"Nora, we don't have time so just pick someone and let's go." says Joe in a very anxious tone.

"Is it a boy or girl?" she says as she sits up, still a bit drowsy.

"Girl, just get someone and let's go!"

Nora looks around the elves sleeping quarters and notices one elf that appears to be getting up from her 6.32 nap. The elf is stretching and yawning as she gets herself ready for another shift.

"Excuse me – what department do you work in?" asks Nora.

The elf looks over to Nora , "Female …. why?"

"You have a new assignment, so hurry up and come with us."

The elf comes over to Nora uncertain of what she is getting into.

"This is Joe, he's and angel. Take his other hand and let's go." says Nora.

The elf looks at Joe with a very confused look, "Nice to meet you Joe the angel."

Joe glares at her, "My hand…. take my hand!"

The elf looks down at his hand, then back at Joe, "A bit bossy" as she grabs his hand.

At that very moment, they find themselves in Conference Room D at Earth Operations Headquarters. There are two other angels already sitting at the table.

"Oh good. Are these the elves that are going to help?" says one of the angels at the table.

"Yes," says Joe, "This is Nora. She'll stay with me and supervise the situation here at the headquarters. And this is…." he looks at the other elf, then at Nora, who quickly fills in.

"What's your name?" she says to the other elf as the angels raise their eyebrows.

"Dori." says the elf.

"She'll be working with you two at the scene." says Joe.

One of the angels looks at her, "Do you have experience working in extremely stressful situations?"

Dori looks at Nora, then back at the angels, "I make toys for Santa." she says calmly as Nora jumps in.

"She'll be great. You haven't seen stress until you're making toys for Santa on Christmas Eve. Let's move on. You two are?"

"I'm Elizabeth's guardian angel, so for now, you can call me Bo." says the first angel.

Everyone looks around with expressions that clearly indicate no one has a clue, so Bo clarifies.

"Her name is Elizabeth Bogart Harriet, after a rather distinguished grandfather, so to avoid any confusion, you can all call me Bo." he says with a smile.

They all look to the other who seems to be scrambling in thought.

"Well I guess my name should be Winnie, then." He says with confidence.

They all look at him with a pained expression as he explains.

"I'm Elizabeth's father's guardian angel and his name is Franklin Winchester Harriet, so I'll go with Winnie to make it easy as well."

"Okay, in the interest of time, let's go over our situation. Bo?" Joe moves on.

"Elizabeth is the only child of Franklin and Meredith Harriet. They are very wealthy people. They split up about five years ago and have been in court ever sense. Meredith wants full custody of the child – Franklin is known as quite a womanizer and Meredith, understandably, doesn't want Elizabeth being exposed to that world – so she wants full custody of half the fortune. I'll let Winnie take it from here."

"Yes. As Bo was saying, Franklin not only cheats on his wife, but he's known to get his way regardless of what it takes to do so. He hired two underground slugs – one named Harry and one named Frank – to kidnap Elizabeth and go into hiding. Franklin has an elaborate scheme set up to create the illusion that Elizabeth was kidnaped for ransom and was killed after the ransom is paid. Frank and Harry take the ransom as their payment and head out to their life of luxury in an Italian village, while Franklin takes Elizabeth to his private estate on a south Pacific island and everyone lives happily ever after."

Dori looks horrified, "Can they do that?"

"No," says Bo, "But you'd be surprised how many wealthy people think they can. Our assignment is to work with Elizabeth, Harry and Frank at their hideaway and get her back with her mom before anyone gets hurt."

"What do you need me for?" asks Dori.

"We need you to stand on Elizabeth's shoulder and help her to stay calm and focused while Winnie and I work on the two slugs standing on their shoulders. It should be fun!" says Bo with enthusiasm.

"I'm three foot, two... won't that be a bit awkward standing on her shoulder?" asks Dori.

"Oh, for this assignment we will each be two and one quarter inches tall. Elizabeth has beautiful long hair, so it should be no problem for you. I'll be working on Harry, who has long greasy, nasty hair – but I've got some awesome gloves to wear, and Bo will be with Frank, who is bald, but usually wears a hat." Winnie looks to Bo, "Good luck with that one."

"So what are you guys going to tell them?" asks Dori.

"Anything we want to. The key for us is to mess with Frank and Harry until they reach a point where they will gladly surrender and go to jail for the rest of their lives as long as those voices in their head stop talking. Which of course, we will stop once we get Elizabeth back with her mom.'" says Winnie.

"Oh I'm not so sure about that. If Frank gives me much grief, I can totally see myself visiting him from time to time when he's feeling a little smug and giving him another ear full." says Bo as they both high-five in laughter.

"Now Dori, you have the most important job. Elizabeth is only seven years old, and being an only child in a wealthy family, she can be a bit touchy in a conflict situation. It's really important to keep her steady and calm while Bo and I do our thing. Which reminds me. Dori, you will have this wristband on, " Dori looks at her arm and sees a wristband that was not there before as Winnie continues, "It has a button on it. You will always be able to hear what we are saying, as we will with you. Elizabeth will be able to hear you, but not us. You'll be able to hear everything Bo and I are saying to Harry and Frank, which you can use as you wish when comforting Elizabeth. If at any time you need to talk with us in private, just push that button and talk. Elizabeth won't hear what you are saying to us, so as not to be confused, got it?"

"Wow. That's a lot to take in." says Dori.

Nora looks to Dori, "Dori, I had no idea what we were getting into when I chose you. If you're not comfortable doing this, I'll go in your place. I didn't realize it was this kind of assignment."

Dori sits up with a hint of confidence, "No. This is an awesome opportunity and I appreciate the chance to do this for Elizabeth. This is a great chance for the elves and angels to work together for a child and I am SO up to the task!"

Nora smiles. This is exactly what she envisioned for the EGAC. She is so proud that she was able to randomly pick an elf and find her willingness to step up for the benefit of a child.

"So where does it stand right now?" asks Joe.

"Harry and Frank have Elizabeth and are currently driving to their hideaway." says Bo.

"Where's Elizabeth in the car?" asks Joe.

"They stopped and put her in the trunk because she was screaming so loud and they thought they were going to kill her if she didn't shut up."

"Perfect. Now is a good time to go. You all will change to your two and one quarter inch persona and be in the trunk with Elizabeth. Dori, you'll have time to calm her down and get her to a point of accepting you before they get to the hideout."

"What do I tell her?" asks Dori.

Bo and Winnie look at each other before Bo turns to Dori, "Dori. You work for Santa Clause and God. You don't make toys for the naughty list. You tell the truth. She won't believe you at first, but you keep telling the truth and she will come around."

"Nora and I will be monitoring the whole thing in the control booth. We'll only interfere if we have to, but we trust you three will do a great job."

With everyone in agreement, operation saving Elizabeth begins.

******

"Hi Elizabeth!" says Dori jumping and waving as she stands on the golf bag in the trunk. She is right in front of Elizabeth's face, so there is no way Elizabeth doesn't see her. But still, Dori is jumping and waving at her as if she doesn't see her.

Elizabeth's eyes are huge of course, as she has no idea who this little creature is jumping and waving at her.

"Dori, I think she sees you, so it might be good to start talking to her." says Bo who, like Winnie, is sitting to the side casually, as their work won't begin until they get to the hideout.

"Oh yea, right…. Elizabeth, can you hear me okay? Nod yes or no." says Dori who is actually thankful that they have her mouth stuffed with a hand towel and taped.

Reluctantly, Elizabeth nods yes.

"Great! My name is Dori and I'm going to help you get free. I'm an elf at the North Pole, but was asked to help these two angels get you free. That's Bo on the left – he's actually your guardian angel, isn't that cool? And to the right is Winnie. He's your dad's guardian angel who hasn't done a very good job as your dad and has been on the naughty list for a long time."

Winnie stands up in protest, "Hey now, that's not fair. Just tell her what we're going to do and leave the past out of it."

"Sorry," says Dori as she leans in towards Elizabeth's ear, "The angels tend to be a bit touchy too, that's why they wanted me to work with you."

Elizabeth continues to have raised eyebrows and confusion all over her face as Dori continues.

"Now I'm going to be on your shoulder throughout this ordeal. I want you to listen to me very carefully. I will help you stay calm and focused, okay? Bo and Winnie will be on the boogeymen's shoulders. They will be smack talking those creeps so bad, they're going to be happy to surrender in no time. The key for you is to stay calm and unemotional. It will really spook them if you just sat there still and unfazed by what is going on. Can you do that Elizabeth?"

Elizabeth looks over to the two angels, who smile and wave, then over to her shoulder where Dori stands with a big smile.

Elizabeth shakes her head positively.

Dori jumps up and down on Elizabeth's shoulder clapping her hands, "This is going to be so much fun, Elizabeth, so don't be afraid. Bo, Winnie and I are going to make sure you come to no harm, so it's really important for you to stay calm, okay?"

Elizabeth nods positively again.

******

God enters the observation booth at Earth Operations Headquarters where Nora and Joe are intently following the situation on the monitor.

"How are things going?" asks God as he takes a seat behind the two.

"So far, so good. They just pulled into the hideout cabin, so it's likely to get a lot more interesting." says Nora.

"Excellent. And the angels and elf are getting along well?" asks God

Joe jumps in, "Well the elf made one uncalled for comment about Winnie, but otherwise, it's been going well."

"Uncalled for comment? The guy's been on the Naughty list for forty three years! You can't tell me a guardian angel is going to be proud of that record." says Nora in defense of Dori.

"Oh stop," says God, "Here they come." referring to the bad guys getting out of the car and heading towards the trunk.

After a moment of thought, God backtracks, "Who's Winnie?"

Joe explains, "The two guardian angels took on names from the middle name of their earthlings, so Bo is Elizabeth's guardian angel because her middle name is Bogart, and Winnie, who is Franklins' guardian angel who has Winchester as a middle name."

"Sorry I asked." says God shaking his head.

******

Frank pulls out his gun and aims it at the trunk before he opens it. Bo immediately sees the gun and jumps to Frank's shoulder.

"Hey Pal, put the gun away! Are you afraid a seven year old girl with her hands tied behind her back is going to jump out and beat you up?! Oh that is soooo weak, my friend! Sooo weak!" says Bo as Frank jumps back and spins around.

"Who said that?" asks Frank who is holding his gun with both hands and looking around nervously as Harry stares at him.

"Good grief, Frank, relax! Put the gun away. She's a seven year old bratty rich kid for crying out loud. She ain't gonna do nothin'" says Harry.

"Disregard that comment, Elizabeth and stay calm. Slowly get out of the car and just stare at Frank like he's an idiot – which he is." says Dori clinging to Elizabeth's ear.

Elizabeth climbs out of the trunk on her own and straightens herself up before looking at Frank with a very unfriendly glare, which makes Frank squeamish.

"Okay, bratty girl, get moving before I pump you full of lead." says Frank in his tough-guy tone.

"Roll your eyes at him and walk calmly." says Dori.

"You idiot. You think you're going to get a million bucks if you deliver the old man a daughter full of lead?!" says Bo.

"Is this the best partner you could find? I know frogs who are smarter than this guy." says Winnie in Harry's ear.

Frank spins around again, looking for the source of the voice, as Harry also looks around in a confused posture, while Elizabeth calmly walks to the front door.

"Do you hear somebody talking?" whispers Frank as the two head for the front door.

"Get yourself together, man." replies Harry who nervously looks around as they all go inside.

As Harry sets his stuff down and opens up the curtains, looking out the window for any signs of being followed, Frank pushes Elizabeth over to a wooden chair and sits her down in it roughly.

"Hey Harry, you want me to tape her legs to the chair so she can't run away?" he says as he gets right in her face.

"No, you idiot. That's our payday. In fact, you should take the tape off her mouth. We don't want to give the old man any damaged goods. She's got nowhere to run and if she screams, no one will hear her." says Harry who makes his way to the kitchen and gets a few beers.

"Did you hear that, little girl?. Nowhere to run and no one will hear you if you scream, so be a good little girl and be quiet." says Frank who is trying to remove the tape from her mouth, but finds it pretty well stuck."

"Harry, I can't get this tape off." says Frank.

Harry comes over and grabs the tape, ripping it off Elizabeth's face [God in the control booth immediately claps his hands, removing all pain from Elizabeth's face.]

"Don't scream! It's okay, Elizabeth, don't …." Dori, surprised, realizes that Elizabeth is calmly sitting there unfazed, "Okay, good. Now smile at the men and say thank you."

"Thank you" says Elizabeth in a very sweet tone.

The two men stop and stare at her, then each other, before staring at her again.

"That didn't hurt?" says Frank, as they both look bewildered.

"I'd like to see you do that, pal. You'd be running around this cabin whining so loud like a little wimpy-poo that you are." says Bo.

"This girl is spooky . You better not mess with her, buddy." says Winnie into Harry's ear.

Both Harry and Frank take a few steps back from Elizabeth, as

Harry hands Frank the other beer in his hand and they both take a long swig.

"You be a nice girl and we'll leave you alone, okay little girly?" says Frank nervously.

"Okay, calmly smile and say yes sir… and bat your eyebrows real cute like." says Dori.

"Yes sir." says Elizabeth in a very precious manner.

"I'm calling her dad. The sooner we get this wrapped up the better." says Harry as he grabs his phone.

"Hey boss, this is Harry. We have the girl and the sooner you can get over here and take her, the better."

Click. The phone is disconnected.

Winnie laughs hysterically before yelling in Harry's ear, "You fool! That's not the phone call you were suppose to make, you idiot. Remember, the police are there and probably taping the phone calls and you just called Elizabeth's dad BOSS! Oh my God, you're even dumber than your partner!"

Harry drops the phone to the floor, as he stares off in disbelief.

"What'd he say?" asks Frank.

"Your partner really blew it this time, pal. He called him BOSS with police all around. Say goodbye to that Italian life of luxury, buddy boy" says Bo.

"What are we going to do now?" Frank says to Harry who is still numb with angst.

"Well we still have the girl, so maybe we still have a chance." says Harry unconvincingly.

"Tell them if you don't get home by seven, you'll be grounded, and if you're grounded, you will not be very happy with them." says Dori into Elizabeth's ear.

"Sorry, sir? I have to be home by six or my mom will be really upset with me. And if my mom gets really upset with me, I'm going to be really, really upset with you." says Elizabeth with an innocent smile.

The two thugs look at Elizabeth, then at each other.

"You got us into this, so now what?" says Frank to Harry.

"I did no such thing! Her dad called us. He bought us the homes in Italy and promised us a million bucks each to bring her to him. We're not the bad guys here!" says Harry.

"Stay calm Elizabeth. I know it's hard to hear this about your dad, but you must not get emotional." says Dori.

"He didn't have to buy you anything. I would have gladly gone to live with him if he only asked." says Elizabeth in a very sweet tone.

The two look at her as Winnie starts laughing in Harry's ear," That's rich! You guys are going to spend the rest of your life in jail because you worked for a rich man who could have just asked his daughter to live with him and she would have gone! Oh, that is rich!!!" says Winnie in Harry's ear.

Dori pushes the button on her wristband, "Bo is that true?"

"Dori, no. Elizabeth can't stand her father. This is awesome!!"

"Oh my child, you are brilliant!" says Dori into Elizabeth's ear, "Stay calm. Just smile. Girl, that is one lie that will not get you on the Naughty list!"

"Frank, we did this for nothing? What are we going to do now?"

"You did something good.' says Elizabeth as the two look at her, "I'm pretty sure mommy should have no trouble winning the divorce case now. Maybe you and father can share a cell together." Says Elizabeth as she laughs, and the rumble of trucks and cars can be heard outside.

The two look at each other in disbelief.

"You guys are rich! Gotta give it to you. RICH!" says Winnie into Harry's ear.

"You better hurry up and polish off that beer in the fridge. They don't serve beer where you guys are going." says Bo as he laughs.

Dori speaks up, "Elizabeth, we need to go now. We'll come back and visit you after things settle down. You were great Elizabeth! Absolutely great! You are totally on the Nice list this year, girl!"

Elizabeth turns her head towards Dori, "Thanks. I couldn't have done it without you three here. Thanks for your help."

As the door is busted open and SWAT team personnel come running in, Frank can see his gun that he left over on the counter when he was removing the tape from Elizabeth's mouth , as the kidnaping of Elizabeth Harriet comes to a happy conclusion.

******

As Dori, Bo and Winnie walk into Earth Operations Headquarters, they walk into an explosion of celebration as all the guardian angels are cheering them on.

They are warmly greeted by Joe, Nora and God with hugs.

The door opens again and in marches Santa Clause and all the elves, who are also greeted with a grand celebration unlike anyone has ever seen before.

Elves and angels are high-fiving, hugging and singing as Santa makes his way to Joe, Nora and God to congratulate Dori, Bo and Winnie.

God is in no hurry to stop the celebration, but being two days before Christmas, he assumes Santa and the elves have some work to do, so he gets everyone's attention.

"This is a prime example of when we work together for the benefit of children, LOVE will always win the day."

The building explodes with more celebration, and once again,

God is in no hurry to rush things. But soon things settle down as God continues.

"Now I realize we only have two days until Christmas, so ......"

There is a sudden, shrieking scream as the elves immediately disappear, leaving all the angels dumbfounded as they look around bewildered at the elves sudden exit.

"I'm guessing you have never told your elves about your ability to pause time on earth at times like this?" God asks Santa.

Santa smiles, "I've always approached those issues as a 'need to know' basis. I'm thinking if my elves start doing more projects with the angels, it might be a need to know moment."

"Good call, my friend." says God as he turns back to the angels, "Good job everyone. Make sure your children have a great Christmas!"

As the angels break into another celebration, God says goodbye to Santa, Nora, Joe, Dori, Bo and Winnie and encourages them all to keep up the good work, as he leaves the building and heads back to his new solar system.

Other Stories by Andy Smith

Available Through Most Online Book Stores

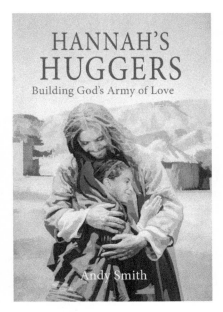